Quantum Justice

Quantum Justice

Global Girls Cultivating Disruption through Spoken Word Poetry

Crystal Leigh Endsley

UNIVERSITY OF TEXAS PRESS
Austin

All photographs were taken by the author unless otherwise noted.

Copyright © 2023 by the University of Texas Press
All rights reserved
Printed in the United States of America
First edition, 2023

Requests for permission to reproduce material from this work should be sent to:
Permissions
University of Texas Press
P.O. Box 7819
Austin, TX 78713-7819
utpress.utexas.edu

∞ The paper used in this book meets the minimum requirements of
ANSI/NISO Z39.48-1992 (R1997) (Permanence of Paper).

LIBRARY OF CONGRESS CATALOGING-IN-PUBLICATION DATA

Names: Endsley, Crystal Leigh, author.
Title: Quantum justice : global girls cultivating disruption through spoken word poetry / Crystal Leigh Endsley.
Description: First edition. | Austin : University of Texas Press, 2023. | Includes bibliographical references and index.
Identifiers: LCCN 2022062222 (print)
LCCN 2022062223 (ebook)
ISBN 978-1-4773-2805-7 (hardcover)
ISBN 978-1-4773-2806-4 (paperback)
ISBN 978-1-4773-2807-1 (pdf)
ISBN 978-1-4773-2808-8 (epub)
Subjects: LCSH: Girls—Social conditions—International cooperation. | Spoken word poetry—International cooperation. | Writers' workshops—International cooperation. | Girls—Political aspects—International cooperation. | Girls—Political activity—International cooperation. | Performance poets—International cooperation. | Child authors—International cooperation. | Teenagers' writings. | Children's writings. | Intercultural communication in literature. | Intercultural communication in the performing arts.
Classification: LCC HQ1229 .E54 2023 (print) | LCC HQ1229 (ebook) | DDC 305.23082—dc23/eng/20230111
LC record available at https://lccn.loc.gov/2022062222
LC ebook record available at https://lccn.loc.gov/2022062223

doi:10.7560/328057

To the girls

Contents

Preface ix

INTRODUCTION
Putting a Mic in the Margins 1

CHAPTER 1
Quantum Justice Leaps and Poetic Echoes 31

CHAPTER 2
"Understand This, and Be Happy in Life":
Contradicting Conditions, Complicating Community 65

CHAPTER 3
"Always Giving Something Up":
Decision Making and Subjectivity 103

CHAPTER 4
What Girls Want:
Dreams and Desires 131

CHAPTER 5
"My Shining Makes You Glow":
Motherhood and Girls from the Future 147

CHAPTER 6
Too Close for Comfort:
Motherhood and Girls Revising the Past 169

CONTENTS

CHAPTER 7
Girls Making a Way 203

AFTERWORD
Looking Back to Look Ahead 233

Acknowledgments 241

References 243

Index 265

Preface

One hundred girls sit on the floor, forming a lopsided circle. I'm seated with them, and we are watching the girl in the center—Nondumiso, a girl from Soweto, South Africa—who is using her small hands to gesture for emphasis as she shares her poem for the group. Her poem remains one of my favorites. Her poetics echo within my soul.

> I am a great learner
> I was born to heal, not to impress
> I heal people with my healing drawings
> I'm an early age artist
> I draw pictures that when you look at them you feel your past but when
>   you think about your future you must think bright—
> I draw and paint photos that are impressing but not born to impress.
> I heal people with my photos
> I inspire people to put more effort on their work like self-image.
> when you look at yourself what do you see?
> do you see a beautiful girl?
> Do you see an intelligent young lad?
> do you see a hero?
> do you see a future healer?
> or do you see a stupid young lady?
> I want you to look carefully and tell me what kind of girl are you?

Dramatic pauses and direct eye contact made it clear that this was not the first time Nondumiso has performed. She lengthened the questions in her final stanza, singling out specific girls in the circle for each one, shifting the tone of her voice for emphasis. Nondumiso had been turning slowly in a complete circle as she read her poem, so that she finished with her final question, "what kind of girl are you?" and looked directly in my eyes. *That's a good question*, I thought. The rest of the circle erupted with applause and loud cheers, and the sound startled me back to the present moment. Her slow stroll back to her place in the circle was peppered with kisses she blew at us playfully. The obvious pleasure she took at being in the center and holding our focus for those few moments keeps my memory hovering back to this performance. The questions embedded in Nondumiso's poetry were intended for girls living in the Bronx, New York, where I was headed next, but they continue ringing in my ears even now.

The objectives of this entire project are without a doubt imbued with my own life's purpose, which can be summed up in a single line from Nondumiso's poem: "I was born to heal, not to impress." Each memory I have as a cultural practitioner recalls a particular time, space, and place that spoken word poetry (SWP) has allowed me to enter intimate fellowship within communities around the world and to connect girls to one another through performance. As a spoken word artist and a scholar, I have been called to this work and am able to perform it because I am also called into being *through* this process. Relationships let me know who I am and who I am not. Our collective liberation is directly linked with the deep accountability that genuine relationships require. Each community of girls represented in this body of work has expanded my understanding of embodied identity as a politicized process. For global girls, that process is shaped by localized contexts. In different ways they have shown one another, and me, how they experience life, how they understand what it means to be a girl where they live, and how they express their desires for the futures of girls like them.

During each gig leading up to my official founding of the project, I knew the girls' creative work was sharing critical information, and I was sick of the empty political rhetoric that promises sweeping social change on behalf of girls without consulting them. Often legislation passes that claims to protect girls and yet refuses to engage them as contributors or consultants on the development of that policy. Their political sovereignty is not acknowledged at all, and their desires are disregarded. I took inventory and thought through the resources at my disposal and how they might deepen and make consistent the impact of SWP in the day-to-day lives of girls. I began to shift my workshops to deliberately put girls in contact with one another. The eventual outcome was my development of Girl Gone Global. Since 2013 Girl Gone Global (GGG) has operated as an international project aimed at positioning global girls in transnational dialogue, using their own narratives to explore the localized policy and social issues that affect them. *Quantum Justice* explores the gaps and overlaps between the lived realities of girls, popular representations of global girlhoods, and well-meaning policy, expressed through the critical tools of SWP, artworks, and performances by girls around the globe in their pursuit of meaningful connection with each other and access to social justice.

I invited girls from all over to work with me—from New Jersey, Illinois, South Carolina, New York, and Louisiana to Zanzibar, South Africa, Ethiopia, and more—to connect through GGG and participate in creative writing and performance workshops that make use of the arts as tools of social change. I spent time in each location to facilitate workshops that developed SWP, performances, and photovoice projects with girls. We used the creative arts to discuss and examine a variety of social issues collectively within each location, and together we explored other options for sharing their work. Sometimes those options included an incorporation of elements of virtual or online activism that showcased their SWP and multimedia work. Sometimes we rehearsed and put on a live performance followed by a discussion for their local community. Sometimes the girls' work stayed within their group if to host a discussion that was open to the public would endanger the girls or draw unwanted attention to the local organization. (All names are changed for girls under age eighteen, as are those of some adults at their request.) Ultimately, their SWP and other artworks were made with the intention of being exchanged with another community of girls participating in GGG in a different geographic location. In other words, they were writing with and performing specifically for an audience of global girls. From 2014 to 2019, the girls' artworks from various participating communities were also incorporated into the Girls Speak Out program hosted at the United Nations Headquarters in New York City, because I was codirector. In short, we put a mic in the margins and amplified it (Taborda, personal communication 2019). (View all Girls Speak Out programs here: https://media.un.org/en/webtv. For 2018, see https://media.un.org/en/asset/k1x/k1xmttkbn6. For 2019, see https://media.un.org/en/asset/k1j/k1jotdfoup.)

Marginalized girls are historically, and often deliberately, under-resourced and either completely neglected or grotesquely misrepresented by mainstream discourses about girlhood. Girls in the margins make their living beyond the center of social hierarchies and norms and are therefore beyond society's consideration. SWP is an effective tool for revising the narratives that maintain the status quo and govern our relationships with girls; it invites imaginative problem solving staged in dialogue with community audiences and stakeholders. Accountability is at the core of this creative exchange: when global girls compose and perform within their communities and with other groups of girls living in different places, they grapple with the inconsistencies of power and the nuances of privilege across local contexts while inviting collaboration. In each community SWP provides important insight into how girls understand and share about their lives with each other. GGG is unique because girls are performing and writing for a primary audience of other girls. Working for social change requires that we disrupt the status quo and implement a revision of mainstream narratives, and to do so we must consider and consult with girls in the margins. These insights, when shared through SWP, create moments of transformative opportunity for the local and transnational community to offer support by centralizing the girls' desires and goals. Global girls have a lot to say to each other, and they want to be heard, too.

INTRODUCTION

Putting a Mic in the Margins

Amanda Gorman, the first National Youth Poet Laureate, captivated the world with her spoken word poetry performance at the January 2021 presidential inauguration in Washington, DC. Gorman found energy and hope in our nation's ongoing conflict. Her example, while beautiful and powerful, is not singular. Around the world, girls know how to perform.

The world was amazed by Amanda Gorman. I want to show that she is one of many powerful young voices. As Dr. Brit Williams (2021) famously tweeted, "There's an Amanda Gorman at every HS you call underperforming, inner city, and/or the G word. Honor. Black. Students. Art." Williams succinctly points out the hypocrisy of exceptionalism: Black girls, students, young folks, girls in the Global South are brilliantly and consistently shining through SWP and performance. Gorman's live performance on national television brought me satisfaction because she deserves upliftment and praise for her mastery of poetry, but I have had a front row seat to the poetic genius of girls like her for years. So, while many folks registered surprise at her captivating performance, I did not. Rather, I remain hopeful that the same sort of recognition and acknowledgment of Gorman's skill and brilliance can be translated into the everyday lives of Black girls, Indigenous girls, and girls of color, especially, and all girls broadly, who will never be acknowledged on television yet who shine in their homes, neighborhoods, and schools. This hope propels me onward. After the GGG work is done in each location, I act as a liaison, a carrier, a medium in between groups of girls across time and space by coordinating the exchange of their artwork and performances so they might connect and share their work with other communities of global girls. Indeed, the poetry workshops, advocacy trainings, and art exchanges I coordinate with girls are more urgent now than ever. Global girlhoods are taking the stage. But these representations are often scripted by journalists, marketers, politicians, educators, or any number of other gatekeepers of the status quo that shove global girls of color to the margins in the first place. By contrast, *Quantum Justice* highlights global girls telling their *own* stories through SWP, Hip-hop culture, and photovoice rooted in the historic legacies of creativity and resistance embedded in these traditions. Most importantly, through this creative informal network, girls are speaking with one another as their primary audience. Adult stakeholders and their wishes are not relevant to the girls' desire for connection with other girls who live in different places.

To facilitate a girl-to-girl SWP connection, I designed Cultivating Disruption: a research framework that translates the stages of constructing a spoken word poem into a qualitative analytic procedure. The four stages of Cultivating Disruption include: *Mic Checking, Connecting with the Community, Call-and-Response,* and *Showcase and Remix.* Creative function and knowledge production are embedded in this new outline for an analysis that centers a cypher of the mind, body, and spirit for the girls who participate as well as for the poet researcher who works with them. This research method is meant to be engaged with as a Hip-hop cypher: a circular communal cultural arts practice where everyone has equal value and takes turns to share (usually lyrics or dance moves) and both gives and receives affirmation and mutual support (Levy et. al 2017, 4). A cypher incorporates self-reflexivity, accountability, and creativity into an exploration of the fifth element of Hip-hop—the knowledge of self. I did not want to replicate a hierarchical power structure within the analysis, and the cypher is one way to unsettle the patterns of patriarchy and the individualism of White supremacy that years of schooling ingrains in us. Hip-hop cyphers are performance-based systems that destabilize power because the mic passes from one community member to another, and everyone in a cypher has a chance to participate both as a speaker and as an active listener. Cultivating disruption channels the same fluidity of embodying multiple roles throughout the entire process of a research project like the one modeled here. In this cypher the poet researcher is guided by values and embodied practices that are intentionally designed to center deep listening, an ethic of love, care for community, attention to relationships, having fun, and the productive enrichment of the imagination.

When SWP is positioned as a research method framework, the praxis offers new theoretical contributions to the field of transnational girlhood studies and performance studies through the amplification of girls' unapologetic poetic expressions about their lived experiences. Performance and literary analyses of

INTRODUCTION

SWP composed by global girls for a primary audience of global girls defies the mainstream narratives that pit girls against each other as apolitical victims in competition for survival and limited resources. Cultivating disruption mirrors the process of writing and performing SWP and thus is already rooted in the interactions of daily life and inherently includes an autobiographical project as a point of reflection. How else except through such a model might I hope to begin an examination of the intangible joy and energy that are in play during girls' SWP performances? A poetic method functions to accommodate the thick performance work created by and for global girls and structures a way to trace the poetic echoes that resound in their SWP responses to each other and the events of their lives. Yet cultivating disruption raises the need for a new theoretical intervention that can accommodate the small, specifically localized daily moments that matter to girls and that are embedded in their creative work while simultaneously encompassing broader universal themes that they address. Out of this necessity, I developed *quantum justice theory* to name the links, movements, and momentum that occur when global girls are networked and connected to one another through creativity. Quantum justice suggests that global girls write and perform SWP within and against mainstream discourses to create social change. SWP and performance is difficult to trace, measure, and translate through different modalities such as a live performance to concrete semipermanent text. Therefore, the theory of quantum justice is useful for understanding how small, everyday relationship-building interactions can puncture oppressive systems and mobilize transformative relationships between girls.

The action of quantum justice occurs at a cellular level—at an energetic, spiritual level. Quantum justice theory provides a way to more clearly understand what occurs within the disruptions that global girls are cultivating, and how to recreate or sustain the relationships and conditions that make them possible. Therefore, it is necessary to approach SWP at an equally granular scope. Although quantum justice offers a highly magnified examination, it is impossible and undesirable to parse every detail of the SWP performances included in this project. Writing and rehearsing are key spiritual stages of the creative process too and often don't receive as much careful attention for the part they play in the culminating public performance event. Yet writing and rehearsing are critical components that are brought to the forefront through quantum justice theory because of its reliance on the belief that poets have agency, and that process matters as much as product. Thus, quantum justice provides a potent localized analysis of the issues girls address and when they choose SWP to do so. It was important for me to write and theoretically engage with the girls' spiritual creative works because they deserve analysis, and there is so much nuance that can be gleaned only from creating space to examine the links between writing, rehearsing, and performing SWP. The method of cultivating disruption honors those aspects of the work and the generation of data through poetry and images. Quantum justice theory shapes how this text reads and remixes those analyses.

The crossroads that global girls navigate are treacherous, and SWP holds space for them to write, revise, and rehearse how they make decisions about the critical issues impacting their lives. Yet their links to each other are almost never considered by the academy or the political world unless they develop into large-scale events or garner the attention of the mainstream media. Every day non-celebrity girls who become poets are overlooked in social justice considerations, yet their networks and informal workshops that disrupt routines, like the ones held by GGG, are exactly what make possible the large-scale public impactful moments. Quantum justice theory performs the function of tracing global girls' intangible momentum within the spaces they occupy, across margins and Time, and crystallizes the small-scale connections they have with each other through an analysis of their SWP and performance pieces. Quantum justice theory magnifies the engagements and interactions between girls that go unnoticed and amplifies what they have to say about them. My friend and colleague Dr. Caty Taborda used the phrase "putting a mic in the margins" to describe my project when I asked her to read my first draft (personal communication 2019). Even in the draft stages, this work is collaborative and relational. Amplification was precisely what I was trying to get at, and Caty generously let me use this concept. When the microphone is in the margins—of society, of power, of gender, race, and age—what do girls have to say to each other? Cultivating disruption offers a critical and contextualized analysis of the desires and strategies designed by global girls who are relegated by the mainstream to the social and political margins, whose lives are projected upon and then ignored.

When a shift takes place because girls are exchanging ideas and information about a particular topic through their creative works, that energetic movement is best understood as a quantum justice leap. This leap leverages the momentum of girls' performances in two ways. First, to reposition their perspectives about an issue in a new way because of the information they gather from their counterparts' knowledge systems as shared in SWP performances. Second, the leap accounts for the agency and energy girls maintain to move again in a different direction or to stay still. The connections and divergences of their movement are the quantum justice leaps that shape the thematic chapters of this book. SWP provides a way to manifest the richness of girls' relationships so that ultimately a pathway toward justice and liberation might be found and followed. Everything I know about creating spoken word involves continuous evolution and rejects the notion of a "finished" poem. If each live performance produces a different set of meanings and new information, then research which is built from SWP and performance can never be solidified beyond usefulness; rather, it remains fluid with a politicized objective grafted through collaborative work and rooted in unpacking power relations.

In a time when girls of color continue to experience racial and political violence, the international crises of a pandemic, climate disasters, and global protests for Black lives, they are already making use of creative activism and resilience learned from each other. Adults and authority figures such as educators, community workers, and politicians who work with global girls are desperate for new approaches for supporting and elevating girls. The powerful insights everyday global girls share through SWP and performances provide sophisticated analyses of their lives and offer sage advice to other global girls about how to navigate, prevent, produce, and imagine a different version of the world they inherited.

What It Means to Put a Mic in the Margins

Girls' cultural production is never simply art for art's sake. According to the girls' SWP, they are exercising the ability to reconfigure contradiction during moments of struggle and demonstrating agency through their creative production and relationships. Among and across each group of girls, their performances reinforce and disrupt complex relationships with each other. Global girlhoods are constructed and imbued with meaning within the forces of colonial history, economics, and power relationships and must be engaged through the context of these systems but not constricted to them; it is their relationships with each other that provide clarity, joy, and the energy necessary to move beyond and between them. Jen Katshunga (2019) recenters Black African girls in her scholarship and calls out the ways in which Black girls from the Global South within the field of girlhood studies must not be positioned any longer as "perpetual victims, lacking agency and autonomy, and consumed with poverty, hunger and violence" (56). While GGG remains a work in progress with plenty of room to improve, one especially helpful and unique feature of GGG is that it deliberately connects girls of color from the Global North and the Global South to each other and thus further interrupts easy binaries that position girls from the North as saviors and those from the South as victims. Girls from a variety of communities across the globe have been grappling with variations of similar issues while simultaneously embodying subversive disruptions to them and operating around them. This struggle ain't nothing new.

Since some of the communities that invited GGG are based in different continents, their creative exchange must be taken seriously as a transnational project. In a globalized context, historically underserved girls are positioned to compete for limited opportunities, recognition, and survival. The systems enforced by White supremacy and patriarchy normalize the perception of global girls of color existing in isolation, separated, singular, and responsible not only for the deficits projected onto them through these systems but for the uplift and economic successes of their families and communities. The experiences conveyed through their artistic performances directly contradict and challenge the static representations of global girls that erode their political legibility (Switzer et al. 2016). I am particularly concerned with how the commonly employed "successful girl discourse" that assesses success through "individual academic performance which is then used as evidence that the success is achievable, and the current educational policies are working," demeans girls who do not meet these expectations (Ringrose 2007, 471). Successful girl discourse ignores the racialized and gendered inequities that remain entrenched and embodied among global girls (Koffman and Gill 2013, 85). They must navigate myriad social issues, including sexual harassment, identity and subjectivity, interpersonal relationships, and inequity in their specific geospatial locations. Quantum justice theory shows how girls are using SWP to navigate and link up at the crossroads between their lived realities, representations of global girlhoods, and well-meaning policy by employing performance as a tool for social justice. One example of such a policy was approved in December 2011, when the United Nations General Assembly adopted Resolution 66/170 declaring the International Day of the Girl. This resolution aims to recognize the rights, needs, and challenges of girls around the globe. That same year a small nongovernmental organization, the Working Group on Girls, under the direction of Adwoa Aidoo, Beth Adamson, and Emily Bent, developed the first iteration of the Girls Speak Out event in partnership with the United Nations to mark the occasion. Some of the work in this book was produced as a part of my collaboration with these powerful women in my role as codirector of Girls Speak Out and cochair of the Girls Advocacy committee. This momentous annual event is a triumphant cause for worldwide celebration of girls every October, yet for the rest of the year the disconnection between political ideology and their everyday life remains unbridged. For this reason, most girls remain unaware of and untouched by such well-intentioned legislation and well-meaning adult advocates. Yet SWP and performance provide entry points into a transnational network that connects girls from communities at a smaller scale through GGG, which offers new ways to understand how girls enact political agency and sovereignty with specificity in their home communities.

Traditions

Critical pedagogy, in tandem with Black girlhood studies and feminist and intersectional theories, has taught us a great deal about how race, gender, and sociohistorical context shape girls' understandings of social change. Influenced by Natalie Clark's (2016) work on Indigenous intersectional theories, I understand that Kimberlé Crenshaw's contemporary theoretical approach is an iteration of a feminist history with roots that are attached to gender and the land and concepts of possession. Geography, resources, and ownership can be read from specific cultural perspectives and have been engaged as a means of resistance by feminist scholars (Agarwal 1994; Jackson 2003; Kieran et al. 2015; Löw 2020; Walker 2003). I cast my poetic analysis back to such a history and throw it forward to include spiritual and artistic practices like prophetic forecasting as part of my research method and, ultimately, this text. I diverge from these theoretical traditions: my research method is structured to mirror the stages of composing a spoken word poem and seeks to graft an overlay of quantum physics for a scientific analysis of cultural production by global girls of color. For a poet researcher examining how girls engage with identity and how they see themselves in relation to other girls and embedded within local or national policies, I required a flexible, justice-oriented theory. I name with intention the scientific, spiritual, and artistic in every step when I work with girls. The structure of the GGG workshops, my methods of gathering and recording the data, the analysis of the poetry, and the connections global girls make in real time through performance are full of tensions and in-between such practices.

The pressure of in-between spaces is where valuable gems of knowledge are produced. I focus on SWP and performance firstly because I am a spoken word artist. Performing SWP is a temporal, imaginative implementation of a powerful method for uncovering the ways girls are experiencing and confronting gendered practices (Durham 2014; Pough et al. 2007). I invite girls to perform and to experience the productions of their global peers as a means of framing their identity through their life experiences and critical thinking about local and national issues (Fisher 2003, 371). My research reveals how girls on the margins use creative performance to challenge their objectification as "at-risk" and to demonstrate that acknowledging their vulnerabilities need not equate to a lack of agency. In her important research about creative Black girlhoods, artist and scholar Ruth Nicole Brown (2013) calls for critical engagement with "the direct and necessary interrelatedness of representation and lived experience . . . for the purpose of articulating new and different paths of justice" (102). Bridgett Krieg (2016) establishes the critical need for a "holistic approach" that recognizes how young people are already engaging with "an inclusive understanding of historic, systemic, and cultural analysis" of their lives to address and confront issues they face. Krieg's work focuses on Indigenous girls and centers the agency that girls on the margins exercise through their cultural practices and identities. Through SWP, performance, and a research process designed to reflect what happens when global girls connect, my project does precisely this, contributing to an important and ongoing conversation about girlhoods of color, transnational networks, and creativity and performance as modes of intervention and extension. Further, critiques of existing transnational girlhood scholarship and nonprofit work, especially when focused on African girls, insist on an analysis that situates global girls in dialogue with one another, facilitating connections and communication among girls and not just about them (Katshunga 2019). To this end, quantum justice works to disturb the traditions of top-down power dynamics of Western research and transnational scholarship, and my multisite research project reconfigures the ways girls have access to each other across time and place. Girls living in eight different global communities have contributed to this book, and their poetry is traced in these pages, providing a uniquely complex approach to global girlhoods.

Thus, this project enters an important and ongoing conversation about culture, justice, and transnational girlhoods and puts to work the ways creativity and performance offer modes of intervention for a more strategic and less linear engagement with global girlhoods. In the US and globally, everyday acts of political engagement undergird all aspects of girlhoods of color and respond to the echoes of Brown's call to action to articulate new paths exposed in the poetry unpacked here (Cox 2015). I have taken this calling in seriously, especially given the historied oppression and suppression that systems of White academia continue to wreak on communities of color worldwide. Hip-hop and SWP share nuances that are specially performed, embodied, and uniquely resistant and reenergizing when they are understood as unraveling the globalized narratives about what it means to be a girl (Endsley 2016). Through SWP and performance, girls' everyday encounters with each other and with society at large are magnified and made particularly impactful when they take on artistic forms of representation to directly address the social issues they must navigate within their specific geospatial locations. This research methodology responds to the demands for radical imagination and extends this call globally to girls by working with and for them. Through SWP and performance, I invite researchers, girls, and policy makers to "envision new ways of conceptualizing Black [and global] girlhood" and to emphasize the relationships between them (Toliver 2019, 21). The origins and parallels of SWP practice and its connection to Hip-hop across cultures requires us to honor and account for the evolution, critique, and reaffirmation of the cultural contexts that continue to produce them. GGG seeks to honor such legacies from Africana feminisms, Indigenous histories, and Hip-hop culture, by loving and serving the girls hailing from the communities that produce them. Because this is a scholarly project, the very system that financially supported GGG and collaborated with these communities was also designed to function as their erasure. One way I have endeavored to navigate this power dynamic is to "try to connect with the humanity of others . . . as an act of resistance" (Hsieh 2021). The GGG workshops, performances, and scholarship rely on connection to others' humanity to activate critique through the research cypher as one means of resistance and transparency. Another way to disrupt the ideology of Western educational systems is to "rethink how and for what purpose Black girls experience programming, organizations and activist collectives" (Brown 2013, 228). Adults working with girls are called to reconsider how we approach working with girls, and ultimately, *why* we do so. The echo of this inquiry crescendos throughout the transnational collaborations represented here, and SWP is one effective tool that responds to that request.

In this project most girl participants self-identify as Black, Brown, of color, or mixed race. GGG did not limit participation to only these groups of girls—my workshops are always open to anyone who shows up. However, the girls and adult advocates represented here were eager and available to collaborate and issued GGG invitations to do so. For this research framework to avoid perpetrating the pattern of Global North as Western savior that replicates the project of White supremacy within and beyond US borders, GGG must be grounded in a constant praxis of critique and reflection on the function of power in every aspect of its implementation. While cultivating disruption is not an infallible framework, because it is patterned after SWP its development insists that right relationship is a core value, and that power is continuously interrogated.

Knowing the self through spoken word performance provides a critical embodied avenue to pursue these questions while working toward social justice through pedagogy (Endsley 2016, 2020). I define SWP as "poetry written for public performance through which meaning is negotiated" (4). This definition is useful because it explicitly foregrounds the interactions that shape how language maintains power and privilege and has the potential to disrupt discourses (Weedon 1997). The relationship between a spoken word artist and their audience uses performance to render visible how their bodies are scribed with this power and privilege and refracts their ability to revise new outcomes with each performance iteration. *Quantum Justice* situates SWP and performance as both an artistic Hip-hop practice and a praxis—the combination of activism with academic theory—which is a clear tenet of Black feminism. For context, SWP is linked with Hip-hop in two ways: as an epistemological, cultural, and historic act of literacy, and conceptually, as the "emcee" in the five elements of Hip-hop, coconstructed with audiences in multimodal and multidimensional ways (Belle 2016; Fisher 2003; Jocson 2006; Potter 1995; Price-Styles 2015; Walker and Kuykendall 2005). Here, SWP is applied as a participatory arts-based research method and embedded as a praxis that assumes the audience are knowledge producers and thus motivated by pedagogies rooted in Hip-hop culture and values, such as knowledge of self; SWP performance hearkens to the fields of critical Hip-hop pedagogy and critical Hip-hop literacies (Emdin 2017; Keith and Endsley, 2020; Kim and Pulido 2015; Love 2016; Rose 1994). SWP is versatile simply as a performance art, but it is also and always a form of pedagogy. Specifically, the analysis advanced by Elaine Richardson (2009) anchors Hip-hop feminism in the pursuit of social change through cultural production via her framework of "critical Hip-Hop literacies" in which girls might manipulate Hip-hop's rhetorical moves "to position themselves against or within discourse to advance and protect themselves" (2009, 333). Girls are cultivating disruption to such discourses through SWP performance, and this confrontation of "the politics of knowledge and power as part of reading, writing, listening, and speaking holistically about ourselves in society" is where my project begins (339). Hip-hop feminism scholarship anchors GGG for girls and scholars who are artists, intellectuals, and lovers of the culture, but who do not all identify as Black and/or American, yet who desire to change and resist the social conditions they must operate within. Making these academic connections clear is crucial to link the evolution of SWP as a vehicle for the messages and meanings constructed by global girls in the quantum justice and cultivating disruption iteration, an evolutionary stage made possible by Hip-hop feminism.

"Hip-hop feminism" was named thus by Joan Morgan (1999), when Black women scholars like Shani Jamila and Gwendolyn Pough solidified the connections between the power and complexities of Hip-hop and the state of feminism. Whitney Peoples (2008) provides clear context for what these scholars argued: namely, the spheres of Hip-hop culture and feminism had potential, *and* both were rife with contradiction and gaps, especially for young Black women and women of color. Peoples defines Hip-hop feminists as those who are "influenced by . . . the feminist movement and hip-hop culture, and [who] use both for the development of their own identity" (26). The meaning that is made by global girls who negotiate their identities through SWP marks this project as a descendant of such interdisciplinary traditions. The praxis of SWP is an effective tool for global girls interested in forming new understandings of solidarity while maintaining sovereignty and remaining distinct. Distinguishing differences enriches community collaboration and clarifies communication. As a methodological entry point for tracing the transnational relationships between girls and their networks, SWP uplifts the experiences of global girls of color and therefore the knowledge they produce as told and performed by them, for them, and simultaneously implies accountability on behalf of their audience. Katshunga (2019) expressly calls for an elevation of just such stories from girls in the Global South in order to forge meaningful connections *between* Black African girls and girls in the Global North and to ensure those links are sustained (46). Cultivating disruption employs performance to create opportunities and platforms for those words to be heard by girls. Performance has the unique flexibility to adapt to theoretical and lived-in spaces, the real and the imagined, in both the community and the academy, playing in the in-between, and rendering these seemingly dichotomous spaces as its stages. Performing on those stages also implicates the audiences who are watching.

Photovoice

While SWP anchors this research, it was produced in conjunction with photovoice. Photovoice is a critical reflexive arts-based methodology that lends unique possibilities for conducting feminist research with girls. It was created and implemented as a concept, theory, and participatory action research method (Wang 1999; Wang et al. 1998). According to Wang (2006), the main goals of photovoice include representation of people's realities and provoking critical dialogue to ultimately reach policy makers (148). This practice invites participants to visually recreate their experiences and desires through the selection of words and images, concretizing power dynamics between the artist, their image, and the viewer during the research process (Wang and Burris 1994; Wang et al. 1998). Photovoice is effective in catalyzing marginalized youth; it was initially designed to engage policy makers around public health issues and is often used to explore other social issues faced by underrepresented groups (Garrett and Matthews 2014; Moletsane et al. 2008; Wang and Burris 1994). Because it incorporates the girls' analysis into the creative process, photovoice is a critical technique; the process situates them as knowledge producers and inserts their reflections explicitly into the research (Mitchell 2008, 374). Like poetic transcription, photovoice positions girls as researchers rather than only subjects of research and focuses intently on mobilizing communities across geopolitical landscapes.

Photovoice also provides an effective tool for unpacking power dynamics that arise around language in the development of transnational girlhood networks. English is my first language; for many of the communities I partnered with, it was not, although most of the girls were fluent. Visual techniques offer an additional means for clearer connection between girls from various topographies. I do not mean to imply that it is more possible to entirely comprehend the girls; rather, that the signals they send to one another can be heard differently. On a quantum level, the girls can use photovoice to detect the poetic echoes even if they could not communicate verbally. Complete comprehension, like perfection, like authoritative truth, is not the goal. Since GGG combines SWP, performance, and photovoice, we have more opportunities available to engage with what the girls want to say. Further, photographs either posed by girls or taken by girls (oftentimes both) for an audience of girls take up different meanings across cultures and create opportunities to dialogue about cultural and contextual differences in a way that presentations on history, politics, and facts during a workshop might not. The viewer engages differently because people who can relate to the issue presented in the photo share their own stories (Knowles and Cole 2007). This method improves cross-cultural communication and produces insightful firsthand accounts by girls about their own experiences. The method provides an autonomy that most research does not allow for; it uses photos and sometimes words selected and composed by the girls themselves to share what they deem most critical and important first (Mitchell and Sommer 2016). However, ethical implications for participatory visual research with girls in rural communities, particularly when conducted by a Western researcher, can mean a chance to publicize important issues as well as the possibility of increased vulnerability for already marginalized girls (Treffry-Goatley et al. 2017, 45). Although active participation becomes increasingly accessible, the girls also become more exposed to a broader public that cannot always be trusted with caring for them. In my efforts not only to do no harm but, as Moletsane et al. (2008) urge, to consciously "do most good," photovoice became a critical part of cultivating disruption, because it invites a combination of language and girls' own visual perspectives to amplify and emphasize what they find most important (114). By employing both photovoice and poetry performance analysis as methodology, cultivating disruption counters the invisibility that research with minors

INTRODUCTION

or marginalized communities often requires in the name of safety. Safeguards are necessary to produce ethical research. Therefore, I engage cultivating disruption, and I trust spoken word poetry—because these methods require me to develop relationships with communities as one defense against reifying hierarchy and White supremacy. Cultivating disruption provides a structure that is multimodal: self-reflexivity is built into the process of creating, data collection, and analysis so that these tensions are continuously engaged rather than avoided by the poet researcher and the girls who participate throughout the experience. Re-presenting the girls' photovoice projects, along with their poetry and interviews, is wrought with potential that is empowering, dangerous, and unpredictable. At best, and perhaps at the most useful, this book is a remix of the original source, and the stories here gesture toward the quantum justice leaps that are yet to be fully felt or measured.

Girls and Agency

Taken together, discourse and literary analysis along with poetic transcription and visual analysis of photovoice projects unpack a robust range of possible meanings from the stories that global girls of color want to tell each other. Right relationship must exist for energy to flow, gain momentum, and initiate shifts—cultivating disruption requires working together. Girls' accounts of their lives emphasize "relationality [and] offer a framework for analyzing girls' lived experiences as differentially embodied, varied and disparate" (Bent and Switzer 2016, 3). It is the expression of these lived experiences as articulated by the girls that offers clarity of the specificities of their struggles and the nuances of their joys. We don't often hear or pay attention to those narratives of laughter, of peace, of moments in contentment and happiness. *How* the girls perform their knowledge of self is as significant as the words they say in those poems. I turn many times to LaKisha Michelle Simmons's (2015) archival work on girls in Jim Crow era New Orleans, Louisiana, for historic context on the awareness girls have of their bodies in spaces. Simmons writes about "Black Girl Mapping" as a navigational tool that considers the physical landscape, as well as the "virtue and vice" of that place, and its racial histories to inform girls how to move through and within an area (41). Risk assessment governs movement and the body and is ever-present in girls' performances.

The act of live performance insists on the fleeting temporality of any sense of community while also implementing that same sacred sense of space that establishes community through the event of performance. I position this work at the nexus of current critiques around girls in development (GID) discourses by Africana feminisms, which address the incongruencies of development theories because they ignore the colonial histories that created a need for them to begin with (McFadden 2010). Africana feminist scholars have consistently demonstrated the limits and shortcomings of White Western feminism as it pertains to the needs, experiences, and concerns of African women and girls. Africana feminist scholarship has roots in African women's participation in struggles for democratization and national and economic liberation (Ampofo et al. 2004; Mama 1996; Nnaemeka 2003). Meanwhile, narratives positioning African women and girls as constant victims have since been vigorously denounced and the studies of women in development (WID) have been roundly critiqued for this construction of women in the broader scope of the Global South. There is a long legacy of political action and solidarity led by women and taught to girls and Africana feminists have developed theories rooted in nationalist activism and in their analyses of African women's agency and voice. Amina Mama (2011) advocates persistently for a gendered lens via African feminism as "a call to end patriarchy and to expose, deconstruct and eradicate all the myriad personal, social, economic and political practices, habits and assumptions that sustain gender inequality and injustice" (2). Other African scholars, for instance, Oyeronke Oyěwùmí (1997), insist that gender is a Western colonial invention that should not be given primacy over other factors, such as age or social station, when theorizing African women's lives. She writes that "universal concepts of biological gender" imposed by Western colonialists are of little use in the "local milieu" that grounds the lives and experiences of African women (16). Girls' lives are further scripted by competing discourses, and powerful social consequences shape their identities and how they enact political engagement in their home communities. The localized context shaping girls' decisions is complex, and my project uses SWP to unpack how girls operationalize age, gender, and additional categories of social literacies to subvert or approximate how they are scripted. Girls are imaginative, flexing their agency through language and performance of SWP to ensure that girls who live in other places can perhaps connect or relate to their personal experiences. The SWP presented here should be understood as a creative exploration of the roles global girls are assigned and how they choose to maneuver, negotiate, and experiment with those positions.

Despite this history and body of scholarship, girls of color, especially throughout the Global South, remain largely ignored or are constituted as hypervisible in GID discourse. These scripted binaries are false, binding, and suffocating. More importantly, such narratives are deceitful, obscuring adults' complicity in their maintenance. An application of theoretical "relational politics" in practice means centering focus on culture produced by global girls of color, especially when authored for other global girls (Bent and Switzer 2016; Fisher 2007; Richardson 2007). Focus on their uses of cultural production pays homage to the genius of the adolescent global girls who author them and demonstrates the everyday subversiveness girls apply, always pointing us back and forth at once toward the legacies of Black feminist theory shaped profoundly by Patricia Hill Collins (1990). Yet such interventions employed by girls are routinely ignored in scholarly and mainstream discourse. Instead, disenfranchised Black and Brown girls' bodies are manipulated throughout popular public consciousness via the media with negative stereotypes, insofar as these girls' bodies are silenced and not asked for their input. Their silence is ensured by the story sellers, supplying them fame without agency. Black girls in the Global North and the Global South who go "off script" by talking back to this narrative or defying the people dictating to them are swiftly muted, ignored, punished, or otherwise silenced. Caricatures about global girls that are circulated through the media benefit White supremacist ideologies and those who stand to profit from such stories. The adage "children are to be seen and not heard" remains a dangerous tradition perpetuated within GID (McLaughlin et al. 2012). African girls are especially targeted by GID programs established in the Global North that claim education is the key to economic viability for girls in the Global South and cloak these capitalist aims in the language of empowerment. But Tanzanian feminist Elinami Swai (2010) confronts empowerment discourses and argues that "to restore their power and agency, society needs to acknowledge women's activities and knowledge and look for ways through which they can be applied in school and development policies" (14). Swai's work draws out the ways that agency is embedded in the everyday practices and rituals of Tanzanian girls and women, and her scholarship centers their knowledge and cultural production as emancipatory. This project follows a similarly motivated trajectory by demonstrating how global girls are using SWP to access the resources of their counterparts' knowledge systems and then auditioning subjectivities in response to those knowledges. Although the girls involved in GGG represent the geography of the Global North/South, they disrupt how those positionalities are understood. Examining their relationships through the occurrence of that disruption is perhaps the most important aspect of this project. Transnational feminism is a critical perspective for considering how girls resist GID discourses in "oppositional" dyads of Global North and Global South (Bent 2013a). Situating girls from the Global South as producers of knowledge about their own existences requires engaging them as political subjects rather than objects or victims in need of saving. Cultivating disruption means establishing the principle of knowledge production and knowledge of self, the fifth element, through SWP. The fifth element relies upon a coconstructed relationship with the self and with the world. Quantum justice theory builds on the fifth element to clarify how girls are forecasting their futures even as they recognize and work within their present restraints of local political systems, and the inherited pasts of gendered oppression. The global echoes of those futures as prophesied in their SWP converge and differ in unexpected ways.

Cultivating disruption to institutions, relationships, and existing anecdotes about girls' lives and experiences must be done strategically. Global girls use creative arts to talk back to the deficit-based narratives about them because there is not always a safe or beneficial way to directly address the root causes of social issues that they confront. When SWP is performed by girls about their lives, and for each other, the emphasis shifts from the individual girl to her relationship with others. Relationships and collaboration become more obvious through the dynamic of the performing poet and the audience member: girls learn how to perform as artists and how to play the role as an audience, rehearsing the duties of both just as in a cypher. Reconsidering the power of the audience and the responsibility girls have to each other, no matter where they live, is at the heart of quantum justice.

Cultivating Disruption: The Concept

Disrupting the globalized systems that benefit from divisiveness among transnational feminist solidarity work is no small task, nor should it fall to the women of color scholars to only and always be the ones actively working to dismantle those practices. Constant vigilance is exhausting, and I am reminded of Toni Morrison's (1975) immortal words about the primary function of racism: "The function, the very serious function of racism is distraction. It keeps you from doing your work. It keeps you explaining, over and over again, your reason for being." I refuse to position the project of GGG and the girl poets as only mobilized around anger or in reaction to oppression; no, this is light work, energetic, spiritually affirming light work that acknowledges fear without succumbing to it. Rather, the girls are already charting paths toward liberation in their everyday creativity. GGG elevates that creativity by linking these girls with one another to introduce them to the possibility and practice of solidarity at a younger age. We know the power of SWP performance when it functions as a counter to divisiveness. When I sat down to write this book, I imagined what might happen if girls were writing and performing their wildest dreams with and for each other across their communities.

INTRODUCTION

GGG emerges from such a community. Recently, interdisciplinary scholars joined together to document some of the critical genealogy of the burgeoning field of Black girlhood studies (Owens et al. 2017). Their work situates an important legacy of critical attention that has been given to Black girls in the Global North, which is much needed, and simultaneously points to existing gaps in the scholarship. Aria Halliday's (2019) powerful edited volume presents a transformative collection of Black girlhood studies and pioneers deeply thoughtful diasporic scholarship in its pages. Her critical attention to Black girlhoods across nations is necessary, as there is a continued dearth of scholarship that centers transnational girlhoods and is intentionally focused on girls' connections with each other (Chesney-Lind and Merlo 2015). I turn to a strong model of dialogic collaborative work where Nash presents the question that serves as a major catalyst for GGG, a question first posed by the great June Jordan: "What in your feminist practice, theory, and politics is working to 'end tyranny,' violence, and inequity; to forge intimacies and affiliations where they weren't before?" (Falcón and Nash 2015, 8). GGG is uniquely poised to contribute one possible response to that question: as an interdisciplinary and transnationally focused project, it presents a juxtaposition of the girls' SWP as a means of forming intimacy and relationship, to best critique the ongoing dominant discourses about their lives. Because GGG centers transnational girlhoods in relationship to one another, it offers useful connections and identifies similarities while disrupting the "stable, homogeneous narratives" that situate global girls as safe economic investments (Khoja-Moolji 2018, 14). My interruption of these constrictive narratives about girlhoods occurs through a practice of participatory action and feminist arts-based research that engages what Soyini Madison (2007) describes as "co-performative witnessing" (829), which asks that we do "what others do *with* them inside the politics of their locations, the economies of their desires and their constraints, and most importantly inside the materiality of their struggles and consequences" (as cited in Cox 2015, 32). Although the workshops varied across the different locations, the output always focused on poetry, performance, and photovoice. While often overlooked, localized contexts and intersectional analysis are critically important when girls, specifically girls of color, are constructing and sharing self-representations across transnational boundaries. Knowledge of self inevitably leads to knowledge of others.

From this orientation, cultivating disruption serves as a call-and-response from the perspective of girls in various locations in North America and Africa. I have not evenly distributed the attention or space in this book to each community of girls. Rather, I zoom into the crossroads based on where the girls' SWP deepens and turn up the volume on the poetic echoes that resound most loudly with one another. I found it more transparent and useful to conduct my analysis in that way, rather than to performatively organize chapters based on geography alone. In each chapter the utility of performance and SWP for girls who dialogue with each other from disparate geopolitical sites grounds solutions for engaging with disconnected government policy and elevates what occurs when girls speak and perform with each other, for each other. Cultivating disruption is a way to name a praxis that is not new but has not been identified. Calling something by its name is powerful.

Preparing with girls for a SWP performance is not a fast, gratifying experience, with the reward of large funding and applause. Instead, the conscious daily decisions to commit to microphoning the voices of girls from the margins is what Carmen Kynard (2015) reminds cannot be merely a hope for applause after "an academic performance [of the work] and not a way of engaging the world and the oppression in it" (2). Interactive anti-oppression work with global girls requires that girlhood scholars, nonprofits, and White women who benefit from traditional Western academic practices disrupt the systems that funnel these benefits back to the privileged, thus maintaining stasis. How can well-meaning scholars who are adults and outsiders and who simultaneously benefit from systemic privilege hope to undertake this work? Although no single method or framework is substantial enough to achieve this goal to completion, cultivating disruption offers another avenue to approach the internal and external work of the self that must take place to ethically center girls of color and contribute to right relationship with community. Relationships across difference and research methods that support those relationships are sorely needed.

An integral part of this work is internal, a reframing of the minds and approaches of Western feminist academics, particularly from North America, and requires a deliberate centering of Ruth Nicole Brown's (2013) call-and-response: "The Act of Recognition" to acknowledge "who walks with us" (64). In this work, Recognizing has a twofold purpose: the first is an expression of gratitude to those who came before and a commitment to the responsibility of our roles, and the second is a recognition that those who walk with us defy myths that promote isolation and individualism—we honor our position in community. I would not be able to do what I do without the foundational work and friendship of Black and Brown women, Indigenous women, artists, and scholars who, although suspicious of my embodied privilege, mentored and taught me. I read their works and engage in or imagine community with them: I have always identified as the ambiguous "Other," racially, experientially; and to survive and to thrive I have grown adept at seeking and creating connections and overlaps in the middle of spaces and identities that seem gray

INTRODUCTION

to most, which is why Hip-hop feminism is so important to me. I am deliberate about Recognizing because I cannot take for granted any assumed solidarity based on race, gender, or life experience, as these categories are constantly shifting for me. I experience nuanced embodied privilege within the US, which is often read differently when I travel in other locations. I have never had the luxury of fitting in or enjoying representation, and so I learned to stop expecting to find connection through easy identity categories. This exclusion is precisely why I prize the spirit first in my work. The rejection and awkwardness I experience because of my positionality as Other shifts according to my immediate context, and that context alters how I am read through my race, social class, and gender. This instability has directly informed my development of a research project and method that incorporates performance and focuses most keenly on creating genuine and authentic connections where at first they may not appear to exist. I know quantum justice offers answers for working in both specificity and broad generality because I have used it to navigate through my own life. Transformation can occur only through destabilization and disruption, which is why I invest in cultivating those conditions and rehearsing them. My graduate school advisor, although she does not relate to me through lived experience, nor is she an artist, unfailingly provides support and correction to me. My momma, who raised me, although she is White and is not an academic, prays for me, my community partners, and the girls I work with during all my travels. My mentors within and outside of the academy and the spiritual giants who cover me have equipped me across and through the boundaries and borders: our relationships occur in the in-between (Ellsworth 2005). Every word I write that is good or powerful is infused with the spirit of these folks and combined with the defiance of the girls who have worked with me to overcome pain and reconstitute pleasure. Gloria Anzaldúa (1987) especially influences my perspectives on what it means to abide in ambiguity, in the "mestiza consciousness" of a third space that borders conflicting zones and feeds on the "lifeblood" of both (25). They have taught me that SWP performance thrives across the boundaries of the in-between space where we are both destabilized and transformed (Ellsworth 2005). Therefore, I acknowledge those who walk ahead, with, and behind me whispering warnings, giggling at my missteps; this is my gratitude for the great cloud of witnesses hovering, provoking, and protecting. I initialize this work with the ritual of an Act of Recognition, and gratitude in my heart to enter this space with you, reader. We have been brought together through the fifth element accessed via SWP, and performance creates this community and this communion. Writing and performing poetry is how I maneuver the ever-shifting middle of my subjectivities and the volatility of social justice work and artistry—the transformation I know is possible is why I keep coming back to this spiritual work (Cox 2015; Richardson and St. Pierre 2005). The stage is how I began working with girls, through performance, and it was my introduction to advocacy with them, and what I have learned keeps me returning here, too.

SWP and Hip-hop offer tools that can provide fresh insight on girls' perspectives on the social issues, cultural norms, and political policies impacting their daily lives. More importantly, these cultural forms and contexts contribute to an ongoing critique within the field of girlhood studies, which is to say that scholarship on "global girlhoods" must move beyond the socially constituted binaries of the Global North and Global South to consider how girls' lives coalesce in powerfully informative ways. This is not to say that identification with the girls by the audience is needed, or that response requires relatability to the girls' subjectivity or their social issues. This imagined link is not necessary to propel a social-justice-oriented response to the experiences of girls; rather, the girls' stories ultimately resist and talk back to those narratives that operate with a goal of "homogenizing girls of color in many different geographic and historical locations as subjects lacking agency" (Gilmore and Marshall 2010, 684–685). The historical practice of SWP operates to counteract the dominant narratives that form discursive snares, capturing us and limiting our ability to listen back to girls and actively coconstruct the discourses that shape us. Dominant narratives lull us into complacency, so we assume that each girl in the Global South is poor, victimized, and lacking agency. To this end, Gilmore and Marshall also assert that the disidentification with racialized girlhoods can provoke more-complicated forms of "witness[ing] and respond[ing]" (685) for audiences, because autobiographical poetry might challenge the supposed familiarity assumed "via the shared experience of the fiction of global girlhood" (689). What I've learned is that SWP acts in a multitude of unpredictable ways, to connect and simultaneously discern the fissures between girls, stages of girlhood, and locations. That makes the work thick and heavy but also worthwhile.

By honoring the generational inheritances of everyday knowledge production already occurring in girlhoods of color and their communities, I "acknowledge the[ir] significance" (Smith 1999, 5) and simultaneously recognize the impact of my subjectivities as outsider within (Collins 1990; Lorde 1984). I am guided by Linda Tuhiwai Smith's (1999) instructive work on decolonizing methodology; thus, I "approach cultural protocols, values and behaviours as an integral part of methodology . . . built in to research explicitly, thought about reflexively, to be declared openly as part of the research design, to be discussed as part of the final results . . . and to be disseminated back to the people in culturally appropriate ways" (15). Working with girls of color living in communities in which I am not a member intensifies the necessity of paying close attention to the workings and management of such cultural values and declaring them as priority in the spaces where the girls are participating and where I am writing about their work.

The framework for cultivating disruption was created out of my personal need and search for a theory that is evenly rooted in the body, spirit, and mind; one that incorporates race and ethnicity but does not rely solely upon it. I needed a framework and theory that could envelop the social justice and advocacy work as well as the spiritual praxis that guides everything I do in addition to providing an embodied racial analysis that would hold privilege and access accountable and manage the fluctuation of how we negotiate those categories. I honor with deep gratitude the foremothers of these academic theories, and I am intentional about pointing others toward them because those theories have profoundly shaped my academic knowledge of self. Cultivating disruption departs from this starting point in its foregrounding and integration of spirituality, artistic praxis, and more, one that was specifically designed for the body, mind, and spirit the way SWP requires. My personal philosophy and purpose are shaped by the fifth element of Hip-hop culture; the "knowledge of self" (Endsley 2016, 2017, 2020). Perhaps most importantly, I understand the absolute importance of relationship with others because of Hip-hop culture and, relatedly, SWP. I needed a framework that was based on the fifth element.

Hip-hop Feminism and Knowledge of Self: Spoken Word Poetry

Knowledge of self insists that the more we know who we are internally, the more we can connect with others externally and lead the life we are called to on this earth. KRS-One (2002) said it best: "Know thyself, and you will know the universe, and God." For me, the fifth element is accessed and shared most readily through SWP, and knowing God means that my relationship with the divine holds me in grace and accountability as a compass that calibrates my decisions. This means I draw constantly on the spiritual to do the embodied work of creative performance on the stage and with my students. The *internal* relationship between my own body, mind, and spirit allows me to recognize the *external* ways these components work in others. If I am an emcee, then I'm an MC—I "master the conditions" to "move the crowd" (Keith 2019). To activate these functions, I intentionally bring mindfulness to the development of the fifth element. Knowing myself allows me to identify issues and skills in service to others and requires that I continue to evolve and monitor

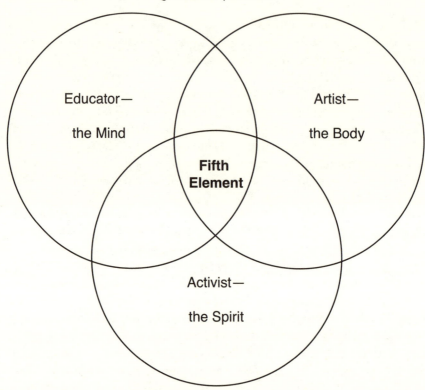

Dimensions of the fifth element

my spirit. The more I know myself, the more quickly I can access and surrender to learning and then show up authentically in social justice work in my collaborations with others. The more I invest in my own praxis of SWP performance, the more comfortable I become with being uncomfortable. The three main sources of knowing myself include my mind, body, and spirit. Each source provides information, and SWP requires that I access all three simultaneously to produce creative work. The more information I can gather and analyze through SWP and performance, the more I know myself, others, and God. In this way, my artistic academic praxis is also a spiritual praxis. I use the chart on this page as a reminder.

Knowledge of self provides a method of accountability, encouragement, and creativity—three key ingredients found in Hip-hop. Hip-hop is an art form that originated in the United States, with clear roots in the African Diaspora (George 1998; Potter 1995; Rose 1994). Birthed by Black and Brown youth in the 1970s Bronx, New York, Hip-hop music, fashion, and language continue to shape and influence popular culture worldwide. The five elements of Hip-hop are typically acknowledged as the DJ, the MC, graffiti, B-boy/B-girl or break dance, and knowledge of self. Peace, love, unity, and having fun are core Hip-hop values that should be identifiable in anything claiming to be Hip-hop—if these values are not evident, then it ain't Hip-hop (Chang and Watkins 2007). This is not to say that the presence of such values is all it takes to engage Hip-hop culture. Fifty years later, the culture has evolved and boomeranged around the globe, which makes the use of SWP not only accessible but generally familiar to the girls who participate in GGG. At the same time, Hip-hop culture—creative work that originated as a form of resistance to the social and political climate in the seventies and eighties—quickly becomes a commodity that is easily marketable to promote mainstream narratives (Kellner 1983; Peoples 2008). Global girls' bodies are commodified and represented in similar discursive ways. What began as resistance has been co-opted in ways made visible through the political economy of Hip-hop (Peoples 2008, 24). To refuse commodification, Hip-hop continues to evolve and present new opportunities, like SWP, for agentic representation. Artistically, through the fifth element and academically, through Hip-hop feminism, girls advance political agendas and agency through the culture. Political power is wielded to produce and regulate social and economic capital, so girls leverage SWP as critique that does not remain within the bounds established by the ivory tower as a stale, if familiar, debate; rather, it moves the dialogue as a form of resistance between the community and the academy to build and grow (Durham et al. 2013; Peoples 2008; Pough 2003). The values that guide GGG—collaborative creative work rooted in disrupting power—are aligned with Hip-hop feminism.

SWP provides an effective and accessible avenue for producing critical counternarratives and imaginative possibilities for the future, and ultimately the objective of Hip-hop feminism is to localize activism and to adapt knowledge and practice to ever-changing social conditions and thus effect systemic change (Peoples 2008, 45). Quantum justice theory provides one approach to such an adaptation, because it frames girls' SWP as an intelligible translation of broader societal issues specific to their lives. Indeed, Treva Lindsey (2015) reminds that Hip-hop feminism engages the "both/and" approach to advocacy for marginalized girls and women, and Elaine Richardson (2013) argues that it is complex enough to function as "a feminism for the gray areas of life" (331). As a research method, Cultivating Disruption holds space for revising and rehearsing the "both/and" contradictions and experiences of our lives in "gray" spaces through collaborative coconstruction. Girls' SWP can support an exploration of their identities, engage with political policy, work to enact social change, and function as counterstories, fostering critical dialogue between institutions of power and girls themselves.

On both ends of this project and from multiple perspectives, there is a critique that requires deep engagement, and an opportunity to share and respond to feedback. For a project endeavoring to avoid replicating colonial research practices, and as a transnational girlhood studies framework, a mode of critique provides useful moments of reflection. Active participation bathes the critique in love; a demonstration of this ethic of love insists on a remix, a chance to correct and reposition with urgency so that new models for social change that do not cause harm in the form of racist, sexist, colonial ideologies can be put to use (Durham 2014; Peoples 2008; Pough 2003). When SWP is the mode of remix, then the critique also insists that an audience member is as responsible as the artist for what meanings are coconstructed during a performance event (Endsley 2017). Therefore, the fifth element acknowledges the community and its contributions and promotes self-awareness with a feminist attention to power and a Hip-hop insistence on creativity and freshness. In this case accountability is key for the methodology and the method. Cultivating disruption pulls the cypher together through the revision and reexamination of the motivations, outcomes, and procedures of research and scholarship.

Research Framework

The four stages of Cultivating Disruption are Mic Checking, Connecting with the Community, Call-and-Response, and Showcase and Remix. Detailed steps for each stage of cultivating disruption are included in the afterword in case any poet researchers are interested in experimenting. Absolutely critical to its application is implementing a *cyclical* approach to the stages. Remember, this is a cypher—a linear one-and-done approach to this rich nuanced material would not suffice. Although I number the stages in chronological order, this is for organizational purposes and does not denote a linear movement through the steps. There should be a return to previous stages, adjustments, and revisions through this process. One key area in the Cultivating Disruption framework that must be brought forward here for clarity is how I identified the "poetic echoes" that sounded between the girls' work.

Identifying and tracing poetic echoes is at the core of this analysis. The first part of call-and-response analysis requires intense listening to each of the poems. Deep listening is a critical skill that cannot be overemphasized. The themes are designated based on this portion of the process. First, I identified a theme by marking a word, phrase, or sentiment and then reviewed each

INTRODUCTION

poem to see if the theme was viable and could be tracked across more than two of the poems. I began with the geographic locations of the communities as an organizational starting point. Next, I compared all the poems containing the theme, regardless of the location of the workshop where the poem was written, to consider who, how, and why that theme surfaces in those poems for those girls. I analyzed the poems and then considered the girls who created them: do the girls have similarities? Do they engage with the theme or enact the theme in different ways depending on their age or location? How do they write about it? How does the poetic data itself call out across the project, and who responds via poetry? During a deep listening, the poems must be read aloud, they must be linked and then disconnected. Deep listening requires a focus on each group of girls, and then a larger tracing of the themes *across* the groups of girls. How do the girls' poetry performances respond to the prompts, and then how do the other groups of girls respond to the poems after they are exchanged? How are the girls' SWP performances responded to by each other and their community audiences? I used Nvivo, a qualitative research software, to organize and code the large quantity of poetry. The final list of themes used to code the poetry is as follows: making decisions, what girls want, making a way, contradicting conditions, dreams and desires, culture, identifying race/nation, backtalk, motherhood, advice to other girls, feeling afraid, chains that bind, haters gonna hate, and feeling myself.

Where the themes resonate is best understood as poetic echoes. Echoes are never identical to the original callout; instead they resemble it and yet feature clear nuances that reflect the localized environment of the girls who either created or responded to the performed poetry. The expansiveness of echoes refuses any suggestion of an absolute and singular truth, revealing the multiple refractions of singular experiences of girlhood. The poetic echoes are composed of what is returned to the poet researcher in the analysis of call-and-response between the poems. Holding space for these echoes and exploring what they reveal even when they don't consistently harmonize is critical for cultivating disruption. After designing cultivating disruption as a framework and method, I developed quantum justice theory to reveal and trace the unknowable possibilities, the multiple entry points for transformation that were made available through the processes of remixing and reflection. Beams of light are key to the quantum observation process, and light redirects and bends the image that our eyes can see. Much like quantum justice, sometimes the shifts in energy or focus are granular, but they matter, nonetheless. For this book's scholarly iteration of the girls' work, I attempt to infuse academic traditions with artistic inclinations to enhance and rebalance the distribution of focus that the academy gives to the mind as a component of the fifth element. Only when each aspect of the mind, body, and spirit is accounted for and honored can scholarly theorization and knowledge production about girls be made relevant to the very girls who make it possible. This text is itself also an example of cultivating disruption. To this end, some chapters take on a traditional format for scholarly writing. Poetic transcription and photovoice analysis make up others. Finally, the closing chapter is designed as a strategic foresight projection and as such features creative auto-ethnographic and prophetic writing. This work is dialectical, it is living memory, it is ripe with meaning and hope for our futures. The nature and properties of creative work are unwieldy, and they alter meaning even as they transform.

Chapter Outline

Quantum justice theory is helpful for it invites us to return again and again to the origin stories to shine our light. One such origin story for GGG centers the NYC girls. Below I introduce an excerpt from a poem written by the group of girl performers who cowrote, edited, revised, and rehearsed the 2019 Girls Speak Out performance with me. The "Crossroads" poem is their collective response to our poetry writing prompts, and the final version of the poem eventually became the opening number for the show that year. Girls Speak Out is a performance event sponsored by the Working Group on Girls, a nonprofit coalition that partners over fifty organizations committed to advocating for girls' rights. Girls Speak Out features girl activists, advocates, and performers who share stories and artwork sent in by girls all over the world. The girl performers work with me and other creative directors to develop the artistic submissions into a cohesive script and performance that takes a different genre each year—sometimes we stage a full-blown theatrical play, sometimes a collection of vignettes, or SWP and song. Performance is interwoven with more traditional formal statements researched and read by girl advocates who work with us year-round. Global girl activists are also invited to speak about their community work and to articulate concrete demands on the high-level policy makers attending Girls Speak Out. Selected officials are invited to offer a brief response to the girls' statements, and they usually include a representative from each of the sponsoring missions (Canada, Turkey, and Peru), UNICEF, UNFPA, and UN Women. Girls Speak Out is so impactful because it is the only event of its kind that incorporates creative performance, is completely run by girls, and overwhelmingly attended by girls, that centers global girls' voices and politicizes their experiences and demands. The girl performers who make up the cast are local to the NYC

INTRODUCTION

area because that is where the organization is based and is also the location of UN Headquarters. We rehearse for about six weeks for the live performance, which is livestreamed globally to an audience in the tens of thousands every October 11. This culminating celebration serves an important purpose for girls to physically take over the symbolic space of globalized political power by gathering en masse, performing each other's stories, and speaking truth to power in a literal way. Yet the widely recognized Girls Speak Out is powerful and possible only because of the much smaller and less acknowledged work that takes place year-round with girls based in their home communities, nurturing and supporting their ideas, practices, and realities.

Because I'm based in New York City, and given that we spent three months together in preparations for Girls Speak Out, I enjoyed a familiar relationship with the mostly Bronx-based girls. Their accessibility made it possible for me to consult them about my ideas and to learn how they understood themselves and the world for girls like them. All the girl performers except for one were seniors in high school and infused me with such hope during our time together. This is not to say they enjoy an easy life, but they did enjoy one another. This group became a point of reference, a Point A for quantum justice leaps by helping me to identify the themes from the creative works of the girls in some of the other locations, which developed into the poetic echoes that shape each chapter. During our first week of rehearsal, the Bronx girls were still learning about themselves in the context of the stage, performing, and what it meant to read and perform the work of a girl whom they would never meet. Each rehearsal began with a physical warm-up, a vocal stretch, and a poetry prompt. One afternoon, individually, they composed their "Crossroads" poem and then corporately revised and delivered this piece as a community poem, each girl sharing her selected lyrics until there was a cohesive poem.

> LUNA: It's like we each have good and bad—
> IVY: Yeah, the lines we kept really, you know, they really show both sides.
> SIERRA: I mean, we have to make up our mind—
> AMY (nodding): Yeah, I'm just, I'm so tired of that. Sometimes it gets to be a lot.
> CRYSTAL: It's like that old Bone-Thugs song (singing) "meet me at the crossroads."
> *(Girls eye each other but don't make a sound, clearly letting me know I sound like trash when I sing and that they have no context for a Hip-hop song that made it possible for grief to become public, masculine, and to express a belief in the afterlife.)*

Oh, so y'all are too young for that? Or are you just wanting me to sing more?
ATHENA (laughing): Yes, sing more!
LUNA (laughing): No, we don't know that song.
AMY: That's good, though, it's like make up your mind, make all these decisions and do it right now.
CRYSTAL: So you won't be lonely? No, I'm kidding, I'm kidding.
IVY: What? (shaking head) No, so you won't get the decisions made for you!
LUNA: Or worse! You won't have any say-so, and then something bad will happen.

Even though our discussion was informal, the girls were clearly feeling the pressure to make decisions that seem to permeate their lives. How can girls understand such decisions, and is there always a choice available at these intersections of girlhood? Chapter 1 opens with the girls' "Crossroads" poem as a gateway for the quantum justice leaps to pass through in each following chapter. The detailed groundwork for quantum justice theory draws connections between Indigenous Futurity praxis and Afrofuturism, which are important techniques applied by global girls through SWP. The poetic echo of Backtalk synthesizes their SWP examples.

Chapter 2 presents Contradicting Conditions to describe the specific circumstances each girl poet faces, interrogates the construction and function of race and nation through SWP and performance, and explores how those understandings impact girls' decision-making processes. The key elements used to assess GID include the following: (access to) education, control over resources, decision-making authority, and physical safety. To complicate and localize these elements that represent a "one-size-fits-all" approach, I problematize what counts as "decision making authority" through an examination of the SWP that centralized education in the girls' lives. Notions of community are troubled through the girls' poetry. Anchored by two poems written by refugee girls living in the US, chapter 3 interweaves them with research about the ways education, race, and the category of "girl" contribute to the false construction of cohesive global Black girl subjectivities. To do this, I examine their SWP as a lens for understanding Making Decisions and incorporate poems that were also significantly coded with the corresponding poetic echoes.

In chapter 4, I trace the quantum justice leap of What Girls Want to investigate how the development discourse categories of physical safety and resources are understood and employed by global girls. Chapter 4 begins with an introduction to Anthony Keith's (2019) Blackout Poetic Transcription (BPT) method and disrupts this text with a poetic intervention. BPT provides a process to engage with multiple pieces of data and the creation of "data

Quantum Justice Leaps (artwork by Bentrice Jusu)

poems" that cover a broad swath of themes and groups of girls. Following Keith's innovative method, this chapter combines the data collected across all locations and links the girls' experiences and strategies from a macro perspective that is then presented in chapter 4 as data poems organized by theme rather than geography, age, or any other category. Girls' dreams and desires are foregrounded through their prophetic poetry.

Girls in the present and girls in the future consider themselves in unique ways through the theme of mother-and-daughter relationships. Girls' perceptions about motherhood are highlighted in chapter 5 and again in chapter 6. The poetic echo of Motherhood splays into two distinct and important quantum justice leaps. Chapter 5 centers girls from the future as mothers, while chapter 6 redirects girls' gaze to the pasts of their own mothers, rather than positioning the girls as mothers themselves. Finally, chapter 7 situates photovoice projects by global girls in dialogue about Making A Way. Their images and SWP manifest a final example of how girls navigate mainstream discourses that structure their lives through the decisions they make and the advice they give to other girls who are figuring out how to make a way. Chapter 7 also recognizes the ways love and liberation are used to fortify those of us who do the work. Forged together, these concepts fuel the practice of cultivating disruption to analyze the girls' written and performed work and the political constraints that position them across a global network linked through SWP. The quantum justice leaps that emerge guide us from one chapter to the next and offer one of a multitude of possible readings. Quantum justice follows a tradition of critical feminist works that foreground embodiment and spirituality, responding to the call for a reconceptualization of what it means to work globally with girls.

CHAPTER 1

Quantum Justice Leaps and Poetic Echoes

SIERRA
I am a girl at a crossroads. On the one side I could live a life of silence and the possibility of contentment.
And on the other is a life of fighting, hardship, adventure, excitement, and new experiences.

AMY
I am a girl at a crossroads. Sometimes confused and scared of what I see happening around me
I am always thinking of my happy place.

LUNA
I am a girl at a crossroads. If I cut my hair too short my family will look down on me.
Am I happy being confined by my own culture? The answer is NO.

IVY
I am a girl at a crossroads. Scared to take either path
Nervous of what is to come
Haters will only stand there, look at me and laugh.

ATHENA
I am a girl at a crossroads. I do not know where to go, but I will figure it out one way or another.
I am the girl at a crossroads. I can go either way. I have nothing but time and patience.
I am the girl at a crossroads. It is time to find my way.

EXCERPTS FROM "CROSSROADS," PERFORMED BY THE GIRL PERFORMERS
AND AUTHORS AT IDG GIRLS SPEAK OUT, OCTOBER 11, 2019

There are two ways that most of us learn; either through a mentor or through personal experience. The tensions girls maneuver as they make decisions are magnified through the advice they offer to other girls. The girl poet sharing her advice is one who is drawing from her well of experience and either teaching a lesson she had to learn on her own or sharing wisdom that has benefited her or kept her safe. The words of advice incorporated into the girls' SWP contain enough broad value to be applied by another girl in a unique set of specific circumstances. Their advice models backtalk and is applicable across transnational planes because, even without my suggestion that it is true, they understand their futures are conjoined with other girls. The girl poets foresee their futures unfolding only with and in relation to girls from disparate locations. Their ability to fuse a network across oceans and various planes of space and time should be understood as prophetic work. They express this work through SWP. If cultivating disruption is the research method, then quantum justice is the theoretical understanding that has emerged for me to make sense of the synapses between the girls' work.

Quantum justice theory resembles what Black Spatial Imaginary artist Kitso Synn Lelliott describes as the "productive arena to engage with the ideas of narratives moving in and out of settled form, where the elided might emerge" (as in Bates et al. 2018, 255). The temporality that Lelliott acknowledges occurs at a crossroads, which is why I open this chapter with the 2019 Girls Speak Out girl performers' poem of the same title. The intersection of the crossroads is busy and ever changing, and quantum justice theory is a concept that is not interested in claims of knowing truth with any certainty or finality about girls and creative cultural production and social justice, because that is impossible and, frankly, uninteresting. However, quantum justice traces the pathways that emerge, shift, and converge, that link and overlap and then disappear again like a palimpsest re-membered, rewritten, and re-visioned as needed. Quantum justice provides a conceptualization of what occurs during the Act of Recognition (Brown 2013) and the performance of SWP by, with, and for global girls. It does not permit claims that assume to quantify or measure the impact of social justice work with global girls, but it does allow us to trace and perhaps follow the trails, causes, and effects of small acts of relational social justice work through the arts across, within, and through transnational relationships. Quantum justice translates acts of transformation.

Quantum Justice: A Transnational Feminist Theory for Cultivating Disruption

Based on this theory, there is energy that always exists and must be accounted for yet goes unacknowledged, mostly because we live in a world that is unconcerned with the subatomic, yet the minute becomes critical in a world where the small goes unnoticed or overlooked. My work with global girls and SWP is cellular, underground, and mostly rendered invisible within the larger systems that control the resources of the academy and politics. Work with girls is easy to overlook. I was growing concerned about accounting for girls and how their connections formed powerful networks across Time, space, and place. Their networks do not appear to move mountains or explode dictatorships; girls mostly go unnoticed, but there is energy being absorbed and released, coursing through these informal connections, and since quantum mechanics only begins to make sense within a scale of the very large or the very tiny, there seemed to be a helpful way to forge the two concepts together.

Quantum justice is a theory I developed to better highlight how social justice work with girls occurs through SWP and performance and provides a way to analyze the poetic echoes and relationships that are illuminated through that methodology. My research indicates that we can observe the tiny movements incurred during performances and engage them as quantum leaps that take place when an electron is mobilized. Accordingly, I call these quantum justice leaps, and I have organized the analysis within the chapters based on the leaps indicated within the girls' SWP. I needed to combine the intense focus of quantum mechanics on the small, resilient, and unpredictable social justice possibilities that occur only through performance praxis. I am not a trained scientist, but I am an avid Marvel comics fan, and I started my quest to understand more about quantum physics in service of justice, much like the superheroes and villains whose stories I follow. I am always interested in the ways that the supernatural and the scientific are merged in the plots of comics, and I imagine the work of the spoken word artist as both spiritual and dependent upon science to explain how the intangible becomes tangible. The comics bring these spheres together seamlessly. Although comics are presented as fantasy, I started digging to see if I could understand or better explain why my very small, very specialized poetic work with girls produces social change and, more importantly, actually works for girls. Quantum justice leaps help to translate the transformation that transpires when girls link up through SWP.

There are basic fundamentals about quantum justice mechanics that are important to understand. This term encompasses micromovements of social justice that are catalyzed by girls and occur at a minuscule scale, which has made it difficult for traditional instruments that researchers commonly use to assess or analyze social change to trace them. Micromovements that are unorganized and organic remain unacknowledged or ignored, and the profound contributions being made by networked girls of color are neglected. Yet these movements form critical disruptions and thus required a new research method and analysis. Quantum justice reminds us that although we can use the research tool of cultivating disruption to measure where the girls *were* when we observed and interacted with them, we can never presume to know where they *are* or where they *are going* as a result of our outsider observation

(Ford 2004). The energy of atoms, specifically the electron, is the heart of quantum mechanics (Ferrie 2018; Ford 2004). Electrons typically move around an atom, sometimes in an orbit, sometimes in other shapes. Electrons always have energy, and they can absorb energy to move up, and they must release that same energy to shift down. The amount of energy that causes an electron to change places is measured and named a "quantum." Every electron, even at rest, contains at least a minimal amount of energy.

In the past decade, the intimate casual gatherings and workshops and the large-scale global exchange programs coordinated and implemented through GGG have been possible only because of the participation and energy of many, many girls, and the persistent support of women who function as advocates for them. These contributions, when taken singularly, would be measured as minuscule. Marginalized further via a multitude of historic racial, economic, and cultural forces, girls are often the least counted or listened to among us. There is a growing sect of scholars whose work I consistently cite and reference and among whom I have found academic refuge, and who have dedicated tremendous time and energy centered on Black, Brown, and Indigenous girls, girls of color and mixed-race girls, global girls, White girls, and dismantling the systems that enact violence toward them. I honor these scholars and rely on their incredible work. While these academic readings offer a sort of intellectual haven, I was also looking for hands-on support, a real investment to make my off-campus work more sustainable. It is lifegiving and exhausting all at once. There was not as much practical guidance or infrastructure for the cultural service that gave meaning to that very same intellectual work with girls and made it possible. I was struggling with institutions that are eager to showcase girls while refusing to support them, or their adult advocates, in real ways. There is still a deep chasm between the campus and the community. The creative processes girls undertake and the ways they manage to build connection provided a new framework for me to reflect on my own work as a cultural practitioner and to engage with the girls' artwork. I encountered real resistance to that work and challenges that demanded that I constantly prove that arts-based work with global girls of color is rigorous, valuable, and valid. I am used to not fitting in, and I was not looking for acceptance—I was looking for cooperation. I know that you can love someone and not understand them. Not being understood did not hinder me or the work of GGG. As junior faculty, I needed the words to encapsulate an ethic of love that acknowledged and counted the difficult work I was undertaking off campus.

I also needed a methodology that could account for and explore each end of the spectrum of these informal and creative interactions between global girls and their adult advocates, because they exist and create impact only in relationship to each other. Girls Speak Out at the United Nations, with its thousands of worldwide viewers, is meaningful as an annual celebration only because of the intimate gatherings, rehearsals, workshops, planning meetings, trainings, and developments that occur on a microscale throughout the rest of the year. While contributing performance pieces or visual art to Girls Speak Out is not a targeted outcome for all the other interventions or occasions for GGG, the relationships between each of the programs still exist, and tracing their overlaps can offer important insights into the type of energy and work that contributes to the "cultivating" aspect of cultivating disruption. Large-scale events like Girls Speak Out are easy to identify as disruptive, because they are celebrated at a macroscale. There is prestige and massive attention attached to being associated with the United Nations that translates into social and political capital in every other geographic location around the world. But it is only when taken together that the micro and the macro offer the richest and most-complex readings. The large disruption could not exist and have the same impact without the small one. One would not matter without the other. Each event and its effects are felt and shaped by the other.

The clash of the micro and macro is how I found quantum physics, because it is only at the extremes of the very tiny or the very large that this science begins to make sense. For this reason I make a connection between quantum physics and poetic performance social justice work with global girls. My experiences using SWP begin at a particle level, an idea forms in my own brain. Most of the workshops I conduct take place under the radar of mainstream media and with groups of fewer than thirty girls at a time. I am not famous; I don't get high numbers of social media "likes" when I post about these workshops (which is not always or consistently). Yet I understand the power and momentum that transforms us within these intimate spaces. Like those electrons that absorb or release energy and shift upward or downward, the girls' work and networks literally move those of us involved. Vibrations are shifted within poetry and performance workshops that won't typically register on a massive or largely public scale, especially when, to remain safe for the girls and nimble, such programs are often intentionally executed on the fringes of the mass media or capitalist machine that would catapult them to the social center. Yet according to quantum mechanics, just like those electrons, the energy that accumulates within them does not simply dissipate when the workshop session concludes. Instead, according to the principles of quantum mechanics, energy must always be accounted for, although it can be converted. Just like the fifth element and SWP, accountability is already a part of this concept. The conversion of energy also assumes that continuous (r)evolution or change is an inherent characteristic of energy. Poetically, this means that what the girls write and then send through their networks locally and transnationally is a release of the energy they absorb when they receive and witness other girls' poetic creations. Incremental moves toward justice occur first and most critically at the smallest points of daily life through a practice of cultivated disruption before gaining momentum and shifting heavier objects or obstacles by thrusting to a new orbit.

Momentum building is critical to sustainable social justice work among girls. Quantum justice theory accommodates this slow process and applies when this energy is carried by the girls through their SWP and performance, naming what occurs through the diffusion of energy in their communities as the girls leave the workshops and continue to move through their daily lives and routines. Quantum justice energy is amplified as the girls develop SWP and performances, and functions for global girls by making the abstract imagination do good in our everyday universe. Doing good work is a concept at the core of Africana, Black, and Indigenous feminist scholarship and research praxes—an academic paradigm that insists on using the academy as a tool for "doing good" in a material way through centering the people who participate in the research, usually those communities outside of the academy (Moletsane et al. 2008). For academic work, I think of the struggle that occurs between theory and praxis; while they are not binary, they are exceedingly different, with unique demands, and it is a difficult yet necessary task to synthesize the two. Translating abstract concepts that can be useful and important in their complexity is often fraught with friction because of the power struggle between knowledges produced within the academy and those produced in the communities we research and call home. The margins of the academy are the centers of the lived experience of people who are often historically deliberately disenfranchised. Gloria Anzaldúa (1987) activates spiritual work to be fruitful within these thresholds of liminal space, this in-between. She writes powerfully about hybridity, the "mestiza," that exists within borders and the promise that it holds for "overcom[ing] the tradition of silence" (250). Similarly, SWP and performance trigger spiritual effects. Poetry helps to archive, track, and trace small movements that reflect the spiritual work of doing good. Poetry stimulates quantum justice theory and readies us to tune into what is mostly undetectable spiritual work, because it relies on the movement of minute particles, in this case disregarded global girls who are silenced when they become inconvenient or no longer serve the interests of power and privilege. For me, for GGG, and for the delicate strands of transnational networks clinging to the girls, SWP is how we become aware of our inner workings and analyze our outer worlds, often in direct opposition to the institutions that purport to educate us.

Academic knowledge, scientific knowledge, and objectivity are assumed to be the only appropriate and rigorous ways of knowing in Western institutions, which privilege a White patriarchal mode of learning. Using creative methods of scholarship complicates the privileges of being an academic for me in two ways that I continually reckon with. First, I enjoy privileges associated with academia, yet I work in communities where I am not a member. Second, because I use arts-based and creative scholarly tools, I encounter deep suspicion within the academy. Decentering Western ways of knowing as the only legitimate source of knowledge production requires a simultaneous decentering of the hierarchy and exclusivity of academic disciplinary fields (Alexander 2007). Currently, theater, Hip-hop culture, and other forms of the arts remain regarded as fringe accessories to education. To counter this rhetoric, performance studies scholar Dwight Conquergood (2002) writes that performance enables us to "open the space between analysis and action, and to pull the pin on binary opposition between theory and practice," and that performance is revolutionary because it exposes how knowledge is organized in visceral ways (146). Elinami Swai (2010) reminds that when girls and women of the Diaspora tell their own stories, it becomes "a practice of freedom" that constitutes them as powerful before and beyond Western formal education, which is why SWP is critical to the success of GGG's narrative disruption (35; Ogola 1995; Oyěwùmí 1998). Ruth Nicole Brown (2013) further warns that "research that is creative, public, grounded in collaboration with marginalized communities, conducted by scholars of color, is always and already suspect" (31). Embodied and experiential learning and creativity produce knowledge of self through performance that cannot be substituted with traditional and conventional forms of schooling or learning. To contribute to this widening, I posit that when global girls' SWP is positioned as a valuable contribution that pushes scholarship and policy development forward, the hierarchical tensions in community and academic spaces are exposed, and change is possible because pressure produces transformation.

To disrupt normative academic spaces, and to forge connections, I turn to SWP and my background in theater for an embodied interpretation and a new perspective to engage with the struggle between abstract theory and daily lived experience or praxis. Although art and science are often positioned as dichotomous, just as the mind and the body or the spiritual and the scientific are, there exists an overlap of these disciplines and ways of knowing the world. Because of how and where I enter and understand the academy, my artistic praxis and embodied life, I make my living moving in ambiguity and use it regularly to make sense of the everyday, and to translate that everyday into the abstract. My experience connects to a concept like quantum mechanics and how it might be applied to make sense of creativity. Hybridity is at the core of quantum justice theory. Like the principles underpinning the field of STEAM (science, technology, engineering, art and design, and math) that center the role of the arts in fields of hard science, quantum justice offers a new way to think through the impact of creativity and creative practices when they are embedded in daily life. These concepts are useful for me personally to make sense of my experiences with ambiguity as a multiethnic woman from the US who self-identifies as "Other" but is often racially read as White, and how I might make peace with my attraction to academics as social mobility, my ministry to the community, and accountability to Hip-hop culture, poetry, church, working with girls, and the ways I am also, always, excluded and how my privilege is constantly exclusionary to others. Creative and artistic practices like SWP allow me to be nimble in the in-between, and to discover new ways of being in right relationship and to search for reconciliation. Quantum justice requires accountability for the energy that my life contains and also assumes that same energy will convert or transform to produce change or evolution beyond my life and in my orbit. Hybridity asserts that the tension we struggle through has always been inner, yet that turmoil is played out in the outer terrains, and for this reason "awareness of our situation must come before inner changes, which in turn come before changes in society" (1987, 109). Quantum justice assumes already that I exist as a contradiction, yet with the capacity to grow and change, and helps me to resist the socialization of dichotomous binaries. Instead, my contradictions are acknowledged and tasked with alchemy, the transformation that is only possible through creativity: I have no fidelity to any groups except those that I cocreate. My expansive identities are complex, but they are not crippling, and there is no easy ego to rest on, no coherent clique that I can blend into if the work gets hard and I want to change my mind. For my own sake, this research matters; I cannot afford to be frozen by fear or intimidated by tradition, and I rebuke the paralysis of anxiety through accountability and responsibility checks with my inner circle and the girls. Quantum justice invites rehearsal and this allows me to be fruitful and resist being seized by fear of making mistakes. Knowledge of self becomes a spiritual praxis of liberation as represented by the fifth element. The fifth element is foundational to the social responsibility poet researchers share when we use the tool of education as a commitment to freedom. SWP helps to trace this movement and identify this spiritual work. Quantum justice renders visible the dynamic and energetic power relationships that exist in small occurrences, making it possible to link the tiny to the massive systems of power girls contend with. Hip-hop feminism ensures that an analysis of power and equity further guides the work taking place between scientific principles and spiritual artistic praxis.

Recognizing Quantum Justice in Action

Quantum justice theory combines the principles underlying the science of quantum mechanics with the artistic praxis of SWP for social justice pedagogy. In physics, a very simplistic explanation of a relationship might read something like this:

There are two particles: Point A and Point B.

The only way for Point A to know about Point B is to bounce light off of it.

If we shoot a light beam at B, it will bounce back to us at Point A. Now we know where B was located when the beam of light hit. But the fact that we bounced something off of B changes the speed, direction, and pathway of B. This tells us two things. First, something must travel between two objects to locate them. Second, the mere fact of observation changes a particle's trajectory. Observation changes the nature of both A and B because observation requires interaction (Ford 2004). Interaction between particles is the genesis of change.

If we understand Point A to stand for one community of girls and another community of girls to be Point B, then the relationship and exchanges between the girls are the "echoes" from the poetry they create, which I have carried back and forth between them as represented by the beam of light in this example. The "poetic echoes" bounce off of girls in Point B, altering their pathway. Even as the poetic messages and artworks are delivered and interpreted by each new community of girls, the girls from Point A have also already changed as soon as they were introduced to me. I have momentarily located them through their SWP and performances, and I have made the points of girls aware of each other via their poetic echoes. Simply becoming aware that girls in Point B want to be involved by fusing into their network shifts Point A's trajectory. Quantum justice forms and strengthens these tenuous and flexible connections and occurs when enough energy is concentrated from within this network to make a social change impact on a microscale. In the same way that quantum energy gathers and moves a single electron to a new orbit—it is minute, but there is a shift—the girls' new awareness and connection to one another coupled with their poetic performances gather and expend enough energy to transfer or move them closer together, and closer to justice.

Only the very, very small movements make a difference, but small is all that counts (brown 2017). Small is accessible for what girls have. Quantum justice does not manifest on a "regular"-sized or macro-object. For example, according to the principles of quantum mechanics, when light shines on a chair, we don't see the chair physically move, although the beams of light are impacting its molecules and providing us with information. In the same way, quantum justice can be applied and understood only in terms of the micro, and that makes this theory suitable and applicable to those who are often socially minimized or disregarded, like global girls and a SWP project. Movement is happening whether we recognize it, acknowledge it, celebrate it, or remain oblivious. SWP instigates the movement, quantum justice theory helps to trace the spiritual impact, effect, and affect. There is always a lag, and just like any performance it's never predictable but change still occurs.

Additionally, quantum mechanics agrees that such an exercise requires observation and thus can tell us where Point B was, but not where it's headed next because of our observation interference. The more information and detail we gain about one aspect of Point B, the less we know about its other aspects. In terms of quantum justice, this means the poems and photos created by girls in Point B draw us down deep into certain aspects of their world and experiences, providing rich insight about their unique specificities, but this insight cannot be mistaken as a whole, singular, or stable truth or the entirety of context for girls in Point B. The extent to which we are invited to understand the nuances of one facet of girls in Point B is the same extent to which we lose balance. The macroscale becomes obscured and momentarily irrelevant during this observation. In quantum mechanics the more you observe about the aspects of speed and trajectory, for example, the less you understand about the characteristics of time for that particle. Because in quantum justice we are observing and interacting through SWP and performances, we are for a brief and intense moment chest-to-chest with the girls' experiences, but only one version of them. This observation should not be mistaken as the entirety of the girls' complexly shifting lives, and quantum justice theory accounts for these blind spots while also holding space for the deep dive into the experience we are invited to observe. In this way quantum justice is also a feminist theory, because the relations of power between the observer and the points are never presumed to be equal or balanced. We engage already understanding that inequity is at play, and with this awareness we might work to diffuse its power. Further, quantum mechanics does not claim that it can predict these quantum leaps; rather, the equations predict the *probability* of the jumps. Electrons do not "know" when or where to move; they only react to energy (Ford 2004, 112). In the instance of quantum justice, then, the researcher can never claim with any absolute certainty what the outcome or response of an audience will be to a performance of a poem; similarly a teacher cannot guarantee the impact of a lesson, only its likelihood. A more useful way to think of scholarship and performance is to understand and center relationship—the stronger the relationship, the more likely the quantum justice leap. Connections are key. Power and knowledge are produced relationally in quantum justice and are therefore always unequal, proffering necessary transparency between the researcher and the researched subject, and Points A and B, about their exchanges.

During the SWP performance event, or at the time we hear the poetic echo, we cannot comprehend or fully process all the stratified levels of the girls' lives. We are limited in this interaction and observation due to the multitude of always changing factors that shape girls' performances. To gain detail about one aspect of their lives, other types of data and information are obscured from our observation. Interaction is limited. What can be read and understood through one performance event may be scribed with an entirely new meaning at the next performance event because of the uncontrollable factors of audience, society, and other systems that are constantly influencing and determining knowledge production and interpretation. Therefore, total comprehension is not only impossible but also undesirable for a project shaped by quantum justice. For us, the instability of this poetic transaction provides our network with critical information and, most importantly, varied instances of *contact* with each other. The emphasis is on our relationship. Quantum justice theory furnishes a frame of reference rather than a singular all-encompassing truth about all girls' lives everywhere. Releasing all expectations for complete truth allows us to develop a deeper relationship with the girls themselves free from expectations, thus repeating the cycle of quantum justice. This theory supports spiritual work that quantum justice analysis can mark and archive, knowing the only guarantee is that change will only change again as we cultivate it. Molecular-level shifts toward social justice caused during SWP can be understood as the occurrence of quantum justice movements and position us to demand more from the macroscale systems that the girls' poetic network is buried within. Quantum justice never allows us to qualify or measure the social change for girls from another point, or community, because they may be experiencing the shift differently. However, if nothing—including data or information—can move faster than the poetic echoes of the girls, then the quantum justice they demand and enact will inform us all. The real question is, are we going to quiet and humble ourselves enough to listen?

Deep listening is critical to keen observation. Octavia Butler (1993) reminds us that all we touch, we change. All we change, changes us. This Afrofuturist concept is foundational to maximizing what a project like GGG can offer to girls. Cultivating disruption intervenes on behalf of the small change, which is realistically all that we can hope to contribute to the current or next wave of social evolution. Quantum justice sutures the hope of the educator (the eternal optimist), the spoken word artist (the embodied performance), and the Hip-hop head (the rebellious imagination). To create more possibilities, we must cross-pollinate, retry, restart, and remix. How do global girls use SWP to navigate the crossroads? How might their creative performances and poetic echoes be deciphered and traced to the decisions they make, their resources, and the messages of resistance they transmit? How can girls' SWP be understood as an expression of the future that is in motion and oriented toward justice for other girls? These questions propel us through an exploration of the SWP from GGG locations that specifically overlaps the poetic echo of backtalk through examples of the girls' work that literally talk back to master narratives. In this poetic echo, girls raise their voices from various geographies to prophesy a destiny for themselves that strays and pushes against the stories and systems that constrain their lives. Their backtalk is futuristic and manifests how global girls understand themselves in ways they have not yet become. These poems foretell who the girls might be together, how they decide to get there, and what they want other girls to wise up to if they are going to arrive in the future together. From Canada to the halls of the United Nations, to Tanzania to Ethiopia and Soweto, the poetic excerpts in this chapter foreground how SWP functions to support processes of futurity for global girls. My theoretical creation of quantum justice springs from the ways that feminist Afrofuturism and Indigenous futures have foundationally informed this pursuit to record the echoes of girls' poetic imaginations and desires loud and clear. Janell Hobson (2012) remains a guiding light for engaging feminism, mediating popular cultures, and grappling with the body. She explores the "relational feminism" that must necessarily confront the challenge of crossing borders and decentering Western feminism as such networks are engaged with (142). Hobson argues that the movement of feminisms during transnational work must be attended to in order to do work that builds coalition. Coalition does not necessitate unanimity or even consensus; rather, it implies a working relationship that can endure disagreement and growing pains. Hobson warns that the insidious "ideologies of domination, which elide our differences, also work to erase our geographic specificities and how these might impact our resistance strategies" (151). I open here with Hobson's firm guidance because I often had to remind myself during the actual work of facilitating that the ways that girls in global communities "talk back" to dominant discourse are not singular. The girls' collections of poems and recordings of performances refuse any shallow analysis of their messages; at its core, backtalk is resistant and specific. Backtalk is sometimes vocal and quite literal. Other times it is more subtle and does not require the use of a girl's voice at all but manifests itself in other embodied forms of cultural production and resistance. Backtalk is the first poetic echo I introduce, because it can be traced through each of the SWP pieces in the remaining sections of the book; it undergirds all the girls' creative work to dismantle and reconfigure power through their joint, conjured future, vital and unexpected against their lived realities. Girls are always resisting the pressures of hegemony and normative assumptions about their girlhoods. They are always working within and against. Backtalk requires deepening a praxis of SWP to better engage the critiques leveraged by the girls and to nourish their revision and enactment of the future they determine. To decipher this poetic echo, quantum justice theory reconstructs each example of SWP in this chapter and provides insight into what global girls consider self-determination, and sovereignty.

The existence of hope does not preclude feelings of fear even though backtalk appears bold when it occurs. On this journey sometimes we are afraid. Of course we have doubts, and we make mistakes. "We are creating a world we have never seen. We are whispering it to each other cuddled in the dark, and we are screaming it at people who are so scared of it that they dress themselves in war regalia to turn and face us" (brown 2017, 163). Girls, gathered together, somehow the most vulnerable, somehow the weakest, pose the greatest threat. One way to cultivate disruption is to confront this public fear of girls' autonomy through performance and SWP, and Girls Speak Out at the United Nations provides just such a venue for girls to take the stage.

Indigenous Futurity and Afrofuturist Leanings for Transnational Girlhood Work

At the 2019 Girls Speak Out, Indigenous girl activist Sophia was a featured speaker. Sophia is a member of Metepenagiag First Nation, New Brunswick, Canada, and she performed a song written by her uncle and shared part of her activist story. Canada forms an integral part of the triad that cosponsors Girls Speak Out at the UN, and the codirectors had endeavored to enlist and bring an Indigenous Canadian girl activist to speak, yet each previous year there was always a barrier that prevented our shoestring budget and the Canadian government from making it happen. In the seven-year history of Girls Speak Out, Sophia was our first in-person Indigenous Canadian girl activist and performer. It soon became a personal mission of mine to ensure a girl-performer and girl-activist cast that was the most diverse possible. The annual themes for IDG are determined by UNICEF, with input and revision by the IDG Summit, and a few other stakeholders, like mission representatives and non-profit directors. The Day of the Girl Summit key players shuffle depending on the personal and professional demands on the lives of the women who work on the team. At the forefront are the directors and founders, Adwoa Aidoo and Dr. Emily Bent, who are exemplary in numerous ways and whom I admire a great deal. Then there are creative/artistic codirectors, such as Dana Edell and myself. There are a number of other essential team members that make this program possible—in 2019 this included a technical/web guru, the thoughtful Caroline Christie, who also serves as stage manager; a logistics and volunteer coordinator, the talented Anne Canter; an intern, usually one of my students (in 2019 it was Frances Johnson) or a Girl Scouts intern, who does a slew of small jobs and covers social media footage; and a host of volunteers. The Day of the Girl Summit and Girls Speak Out falls under the auspices of the Working Group on Girls (WGG), a coalition of organizations advocating for girls' rights as human rights with ECOSOC status at the UN (for more on WGG, see www.girlsrights.org; see www.dayofthegirlsummit.org for more on the Summit). All the work and planning for the annual Girls Speak Out begins one year in advance. This planning is in addition to the other smaller-scale programs that WGG provides for high school girl advocates based in the tri-state area, which occur September through June.

By the time Sophia arrived with her mother to NYC, our excitement was buzzing. When Sophia met the girl performers, she was reserved at first, which is understandable given that the rest of us had spent weeks together in preparation. I was so honored to meet her mother, and I was in awe of the incredible activism Sophia had already coordinated for First Nations people against the pipeline in Canada as director of a grassroots youth-led movement, the Earth Guardians Crew in the Ottawa/Gatineau region of Canada. The girl activists arrived the day before Girls Speak Out to rehearse and run through the show in the physical location at UN Headquarters. Sophia's role was unusual in that she was not only serving as a girl activist who would read a statement of her work in the community that directly addresses the high-level mission representatives and policy makers in the audience but was also participating as a girl performer. Typically, the girl performers are a cast of local NYC girls who cocreate the script, and we rehearse several times a week beginning in September. Because girl activists don't arrive to the scene until the day before, we conduct most of the work coaching them, drafting, and working through revisions, and rehearsing with them over the phone and internet. Scheduling the time for each phase of this program is exceedingly difficult, and because we rehearse so intensely with the girl performers, we usually keep the girl activists in the role of reading their statements. Sophia, however, agreed to fill several roles during the event. She was the first girl activist to speak when she greeted the Indigenous people of the New York City land and thanked them and thanked her own ancestors. Sophia did not perform her song until the end of the program, and she was the final girl activist to share her statement. I consulted her about this placement and shared my artistic understanding of the climactic theatrical framing of the performance content. On the phone Sophia gave a wry chuckle and agreed that it was best if she were the last girl activist to speak, as she had strong words for the Canadian mission. The committee is required to submit a draft of the girls' statements to the missions for the high-levels to review prior to the live performance so that they are not caught by surprise. This requirement has been part of the standing agreement between the missions and the IDG Summit team so they have time to prepare a response to the girl activists. While we are rarely asked to submit the script in its entirety, the mission representatives ask for a synopsis at the minimum. When I informed Sophia about this, she laughed again and said she was not surprised. There are additional bureaucratic protocols that have adverse effects when we work to situate girls, as Bent (2016) reminds in her foundational work on girl activists in the UN space: "While we might applaud the UN for including girls in their advocacy efforts, we must also trouble the approach to girls' political engagement and empowerment" (111: also see Bent 2020 for a rigorous critique of this particular Girls Speak Out). I told her not to hold back but to send me what was really on her heart to share and that the worst that would happen is that we would have to revise her statement. She agreed and said she understood. I was really worried about what Sophia would think about me: that the level of clearance and the "approvals" and permissions we had to go through to be live at the UN would cast me and the girl performers as sell-outs in the eyes of someone like Sophia. She lived her life on the front lines protecting Indigenous lands and waters, taking risks in courageous ways that I never would, and I was asking her to be okay with choosing her words, not for fear that the other girls in the crowd at the show would somehow misinterpret her but because the UN and NGO partners literally held the keys to our access, and approval is always tenuous (Bent 2013b; Strzepek 2015). I sat on the floor in the building where girl performer rehearsal was held and leaned against a window looking out from the thirteenth floor onto the sidewalk below. This girl had never met me in real life, barely knew me beyond emails and this first phone call of many.

Pressing my forehead against the cool of the windowpane, I closed my eyes at the scene below of Forty-Second Street and strained to read Sophia's voice. Was she disappointed in me, in the project? I was in the hallway outside the room where the girl performers were rehearsing, and I was struggling to balance my duties and my emotions. I felt so proud of them for their great strides and dedication as they rehearsed. I also felt shame asking Sophia to be okay with a revision if we had to do it. I told her I realized how inappropriate the request sounded and that I was sorry to be in a position that reified the silencing or censoring of her truth, especially as an Indigenous girl. She listened quietly while I poured out about the girl performers, the other activists, and how everyone had the same protocol, but I knew it was especially insulting for her because of the long violences and then convenient forgetfulness of Canada's government and the Indigenous resistance that persists on those lands. When I ended my torrent of explanation, Sophia laughed once more. "I have to finish my statement draft, but I've been here before, and I will be here again. I know how to speak so they will hear me. If they send it back, then I will write it again, just in another way." "Thank you for understanding." I released a breath I didn't realize I was holding. "I can't wait to meet you—and the girls can't either." By this point girl performers Ivy and Athena had hooked themselves around the door to the rehearsal room, trying to get my attention. I was no-nonsense strict when it came to rehearsal time, jealous for the few minutes we had together to get mountains of work complete, but seeing the two girl performers made me drop my shoulders and smile. *That's why you walk the tightrope, Crys*, my heart said. *For them. May they never forget.* I held the phone out at arm's length in their direction, and said, "Ya'll, say hi to Sophia!" "HIIIII, Sophia!!" They shouted together. I brought the phone back to my ear and caught the tail end of Sophia's greeting "Hi, everyone!" She laughed, wholeheartedly this time. "I can't wait to meet them too." An excerpt from Sophia's statement at Girls Speak Out is below:

> We cannot talk about Indigenous girls as if we exist in isolation. We cannot talk about our families, our communities, our ancestors, the waters, the lands, and all who call them home without talking about ourselves. . . . But we also share that with this earth. That is why Indigenous peoples around the world refer to the land that I'm standing on right now as Mother Earth. Girls no matter what we come from or what language we speak we can relate and connect deeply to Mother Earth because we are our future mother's grandmothers and leaders, Earth's and water protectors. This world does not exclude our other important traditional rules

like medicine pickers, healers. . . . I think the destruction of Earth of the earth globally is devastating to Indigenous girls . . .

Our land is destroyed, and our water is poisoned. Leaders cannot pretend to be feminists to defend and respect girls rights while permitting our first mother, Mother Earth to be desecrated. We are also at risk of being viewed as a commodity and our traditional role of guardians cannot be fulfilled, we cannot be Warriors if there's nothing left to protect. We cannot lead in a world that has been destroyed by people and corporate entities that have refused to respect Mother Earth . . .

Because of our traditional roles and ways of life, for girls like me along with my brothers and sisters on the front lines all over the world protecting the land that we love . . . we are still suffering from deep trauma. Acknowledging the deep connection Indigenous people have to their land can show how past events have left devastating effects. Locations of reserved land families were separated as children were stolen from communities and sent to government-run residential schools and some communities were further separated from their traditional ways due to non-consensual resource extraction projects that have ruined their territories indefinitely . . .

There is sex trafficking and rape occurring at the man camp set up as pipeline workers come on to our territories . . . we are in a crisis.

Missing murdered indigenous women and girls was recently launched into what they're calling a national emergency and found that Indigenous girls are 12 times more likely to go murder go missing than any other demographic group in Canada. Canada is responsible for committing genocide against Indigenous peoples that is still continuing today. As Indigenous girls our health and our very existence is more at risk than ever as our communities have suffered and are suffering by acts of genocide.

Our connection to our lands and Waters in order to fulfill our traditional role as life givers but these are increasingly at risk as we stand on the front lines of climate change and genocide . . . talk to your elders. Talk to people from different backgrounds. Think of some simple solutions that you can take action on. Find others who want to take action with you. Use your gifts like your voice, your art, your music, whatever it may be to express your Truth at every chance you can get. Our voices are stronger together than apart. We will need to take a strong stand to change the way things are and shift over to renewable energies and this will make a lot of people uncomfortable. Regardless, we must do it to ensure the safety of

Indigenous girls and the Earth we protect. Above all else please take care of yourselves and take time to reconnect with the land . . .

Sophia's girl activist statement and performance of her song at Girls Speak Out embody the convergence of decision making and Backtalk for global girls. Her statement is rich with clear calls to action for Indigenous girls in Canada and beyond, and her broader audience of policy makers, global girls, and adult advocates. Sophia calls us to witness her experiences and demands. Natalie Clark (2016) describes an activist framework of "Red Intersectionality" that centers sovereignty, resistance, and activism of Indigenous people through a focus on stories like Sophia's and implicates listeners "as essential partners in their resistance" (54). Clark continues, "I believe that Indigenous girls' stories, writing, and poetry are medicines, and are also acts of resistance against the colonial and academic presentation of Indigenous girls." Sophia's medicine is intent on healing the girls listening, as well as her own spirit. The government perpetrator of her oppression must bear public witness, and Sophia is focused on not just sharing about the experiences but changing them (56). Her art is transformative medicine, personal and powerful. Sophia affirms past experiences of her Indigenous community and enacts a new future simultaneously.

For Indigenous Futurity scholar Danika Medak-Saltzman (2017), it is no coincidence that there is a convergent and reciprocal uptick of activism and scholarship occurring. She writes that "the creative arm of the Indigenous Futurist movement joins the more overtly political arm of the movement evident in the protest, legal and advocacy work . . . all vital to seeing our way toward, fighting for, and calling forth better futures" (144). The discipline and practice of futurity is innately as political as it is artistic, and addresses the conjunction of artistic practice, political action, and social justice on behalf of Indigenous communities in the face of Western genocide. The term "Indigenous Futurism" was first conceived by Anishinaabe scholar Grace Dillon (2016), who defines Indigenous Futurism as a means of renewal and recovery of the voices, traditions, images, and themes of Indigenous people to envision a future. Images and themes in science fiction are utilized distinctly in art and culture to manifest complex alternative strategies for Indigenous peoples' political and cultural futures (Lempert 2014; Lidchi and Fricke 2019). Forecasting these futures is a strategic form of political resistance to settler frameworks (Matters 2019). As such, stories that engage with concepts of the future and sovereignty catalyze the political and intellectual imaginings of Indigenous communities as having the power to cocreate future realities. Bookending the 2019 Speak Out with Sophia's musical performance and activist statement embodies this convergence and explicitly demands acknowledgment and immediate intervention to end the war being waged against the land, and her people. In Canada, specifically, "the history of trauma and violence" that Sophia refers to in her statement has already impacted the present. The future is yet to be made. From this perspective, Indigenous futures are necessarily generative and shaped through "creative mediation, temporal reimagination, and political urgency" (Lempert 2018, 178). Further, Indigenous girls who imagine and enact their future talk back to dominant settler discourses that work to erase them from the present and relegate them to the past. Through creatively performing the future, Sophia rejects the death sentence and invisibility that scripts her existence.

Talking Back, Moving Forward

Sophia makes a futurist argument that reveals the ways that "Indigenous girls in Canada suffer because the lands and waters that make up their lives are destroyed." Indigenous Futurism allows for a reconsideration of traumatic historical pasts through the narration of empowering counterstories of the future to be imagined and enacted. Cultivating disruption to these dystopian historical narratives is an ongoing survival practice for girls like Sophia. Anna Shah Hoque (2017) links future-making to identity and investigates the consequences of the dissonance between history as it is taught in schools and as it has been experienced by elders in the community. Hoque asks her audience:

> If the stories around you don't show you a version of reality that you can identify with . . . what does that do to your sense of "self"??? Some very real outcomes emerge in the Canadian landscape . . . including impacts to quality of life, health conditions, literacy, and community growth for Indigenous populations. (2)

The setting of dystopian futures that make up much of the landscape of the genre of science fiction has already occurred for Indigenous peoples. Bridgett Krieg (2016) points out that a damaged sense of self has catastrophic suicide rates for Indigenous Canadian youth, and the disconnect that many experience can be addressed through "cultural continuity" practices that conduct resistance work to their erasure. Krieg argues that the arts strategically pivot from erasure by affirming the value and vision that Indigenous girls have in the imminent future (30). Circling to rituals of the past reaffirms that a future is coming.

Time operates as a key element in the construction of what Hoque calls "Indigenous futurity," which she suggests can be used to "destabilize the colonial narrative of Indigeneity as being situated firmly in the distant past" (3). She disrupts Time as it is typically situated in the linear colonial sense, occurring in chronological fashion, and shifts Indigenous people to modern times, thus splintering colonial imaginations about Indigenous cultures. Refusing the scope and limitations of settler time is an important concept as girl activist Sophia reminded us in her statement.

> Leaders cannot pretend to be feminists to defend and respect girls' rights while permitting our first mother, Mother Earth, to be desecrated. . . .
> We cannot lead in a world that has been destroyed by people and corporate entities that have refused to respect Mother Earth.

Sophia recites the dystopian past and present her community experiences and by doing so challenges the Canadian government's feminist claims. She looks to the past when she references how "our land is destroyed," and the present, "we are also at risk of being viewed as a commodity," and uses those sites of Time to construct the future when she writes, "We cannot lead in a world that has been destroyed." Mark Rifkin (2017) examines the concept of temporality as experienced by and assigned to Native people as "consigned to the past, or inserted into a present" situated by colonial settler conceptualization (vii). Building on works by Paul Chaat Smith, he reconsiders Anna Lee Walters's (1992) critical question, "Was the future laid to rest with the ancestors?" (135). Sophia's statement responds to that question with a vibrant prophecy about the future for Indigenous girls like her.

Sophia's working of the future is predicated on what she knows from the oral histories of her community and her present, as well as what her own voice speaks out about her hopes and dreams of what is to come. She represents "Indigenous youth who have a vision for their future and understand what is needed for future success" (Krieg 2016, 30). Her activist statement echoes poetic Backtalk to the narrative set forth about Indigenous people by "leaders" and "corporate entities" that are eager to destroy natural resources for profit. Sophia employs the spiritual work that redefines Time and converges with her own re-vision of the past, present, and future. Through quantum justice theory, her work can be encapsulated as prophecy; Sophia's performance is powerful in the space of the UN only because she first experienced it in the past and then performs it in the present moment of the Girls Speak Out event. Her rehearsal of activism on the front lines of her community allows us to trace the cause of her quantum justice impact during her confrontation of governmental power at the UN. The transformative effect of Sophia's performance in that exact moment of Time was possible only because of her previous engagement in resistance. Quantum justice theory identifies Sophia's repeated acts of disruption in her activist experience as reenacting transformation during her performance—her activism was rehearsal for her future identities and impact. Her impact in a "big" space for an audience of thousands began long before and will ripple far into the future in unpredictable ways. Quantum justice theory dictates that we, her audience, must also mobilize to demand more for girls like Sophia because her words prophesy that it is so, and her declaration implicates the audience as witnesses of her performance; thus, we are charged with the cost of cocreating the new narrative she has written.

As a praxis of futurity, quantum justice theory asks us to reconsider how Sophia's prophecy incorporates the future and "emerges in response to everyday forms of relationship and struggle" (Rifkin 2017, xiii). Prophecy is a spiritual gift that foretells future events, edifies the hearers, advises strategy for current situations, and exhorts a shift in behavior. Prophecy is sometimes a warning and sometimes a calling to an individual or a group of people to a new personal focus, a new level in their profession or life course, or a different spiritual territory. This gift requires no special tool or instrument other than the body: this is special, too. Speaking out as a conduit and listening deeply to the Spirit are core skills for a prophet. However, prophecy is not to be taken lightly. If a false prophecy is given, there are consequences. Prophets take risks because they ultimately answer to the Spirit, and their messages are not always pleasing to hear. Sometimes they are charged with delivering an exhortation to someone or a group of people who reject the warning and thus reject the prophet herself. Prophecy is developed via the intangible and untraceable relationship between the Spirit and the prophet. To be received, prophecy depends upon the relationship between the community and the prophet. This gift is interwoven with and reliant upon everyday exercises. Rifkin's argument insists the prophetic—the spiritual—be acknowledged in the daily relationship and interactions between the physical and spiritual worlds. The in-between and crossroads of these landscapes is a prime space of cultivation, because the overlaps generate the fifth element; therefore, the body and spirit must work together for prophetic disruption. The mundane and repetitious rhythms of overlooked practices become ritual, infused with the spiritual, and yet remain disregarded and uncounted because they are considered inconsequential or too common. Why are we taught that accessibility equates to a lack of rigor or value? However, everyday forms of cultural production that colonizers and the academic West overlook and deem ordinary continues to surface as a theme of resistance to domination in each GGG community.

Indigenous Futurisms are not simply additive; there is overlap between critiques of the West and colonial futures from which Indigenous people and people of the African Diaspora have been erased. To this end Afrofuturism and Indigenous futures converge as generative paradigms and refuse erasure of their existence from the dystopian futures imagined by the colonial West. "Indigenous futurism explores this reality . . . through reconnection" (Matters 2019, 7; Tiger 2019). Africana feminisms offer another helpful lens to conceptualize what Sophia's experience means as an Indigenous girl undertaking transnational activism. The challenges Amina Mama (2004) raises in her confrontation of "developmental feminism" ring true in Sophia's experience at the halls of the UN Headquarters: Mama called out Western feminism and the UN for its lack of a transformational agenda, and her search for lasting change has only returned the realization that "unequal power and authority has ensured an unequal power dynamic of appropriation and incorporation," which is echoed in Sophia's statement to her government (121). Sophia's powerful call to accountability from a global platform was issued to "progressive" policy makers in Canada and is based on her connection to the land, which her government has "viewed as a commodity." The commodification of the land and water extends to how Canada's government continues to view Indigenous girls like her—as political economic property. Hip-hop feminism refuses this pursuit of profit via appropriation, and Sophia's backtalk magnifies the agentic resistance made visible when her cultural production is centered. Indeed, Mama (2014) asserts that girls and women at the "postcolonial periphery" like Sophia "have seen their prospects deteriorate further with each developmental era" despite her government's acknowledgments of social and racial inequities and claims of desire for reconciliation with Indigenous communities (121). In this context Sophia understands her own experience as a girl navigating her life on this margin, within this border. Her environmental activism embodies her beliefs about Indigenous futures—namely, they happen. Sophia continues

> As Indigenous girls our health and our very existence is more at risk than ever as our communities have suffered and are suffering by acts of genocide.

She overlaps the past and the future through her current "suffering" and the generational trauma inflicted by the Canadian government, specifically.

To shape the Indigenous future, Sophia shifts her attention from the guilty government to her counterparts and "the Earth we protect above all else." Sophia's assertion of her connection to the environment, sovereignty, and future of other Indigenous girls contradicts "centuries of explicit and implicit associations of Indigenous people with the past" (Lempert 2018, 174). By invoking her future as an Indigenous girl aloud, Sophia is backtalking the discourse positioning girls like her as existing only in the past and invites unknown and unexpected participation by her audience, who must then make a decision about how they will respond to her. As Aimee Cox (2015) reminds us, "It is easier to discursively erase real live human beings in the past and future than it is in the present" (62). Sophia reconstitutes her community's past struggles, and her own fierce advocacy and resistance to these scripts, through the reassertion of her humanity and her prophecy of her Indigenous future.

Calling Out and Calling In: Power Dynamics and Quantum Justice

For girl activists and artists like Sophia, transnational girlhood is an experience that they inhabit all day, every day. For Sophia's community, a dystopia "is not something set in the distant future but rather lived realities in the daily interactions with settler colonial spaces and regulations" (Hoque 2017, 3). Sophia's connection to the land, the conflict between her Indigenous community and her citizenship in Canada, and her traverse among her subjectivities place unique demands on conceptualizations of transnational girlhood that assume movements occur only across borders drawn and enforced by colonial settlers and between geographic locations. The complications that arise are indicative of the limitations of transnational girlhood studies as they are currently understood and point toward the assumptions that settler-scholars must examine before undertaking work with Indigenous girls. Eve Tuck and Rubén Gaztambide-Fernández (2013) define this encroachment as "settler colonialism," which situates the colonizer as "the sovereign, and the arbiter of citizenship, civility, and knowing" (73). Building on Patrick Wolfe (2006), they situate access to land as the primary motivation for settler colonialism, based on three actors: settlers, Indigenous people, and the enslaved—in the case of North America, Africans. Tuck and Gaztambide-Fernández (2013) address the temporality of settler colonialism in projects of curriculum and pedagogy, when it works to camouflage Whiteness and perpetuates itself as if it already occurred, while constantly erasing its perpetuity as "the curriculum project of replacement" (75). Their argument focuses on schooling that is different from Sophia's intervention; however, their contextualization of the aims and project of "settler colonialism" and their explication of "curricular replacement" align with her strategically offensive advance on the Canadian minister who was assigned to respond to her statement during the live performance of Girls Speak Out. Sophia embodied her right to "refusal" that "exact[s] expropriation; to speak without explication; to claim without settler colonial justification; to refuse any response or allegation" (Tuck and Gaztambide-Fernández 2013, 86). Girl activists and performers like Sophia cultivate disruption of easy, familiar patterns of settler futurity and challenge the power dynamics scripted in Western adult-to-girl relationships by insisting on her very present, young existence and her visceral construction of the present and future. Sophia tells a story that inserts her subjectivity as a present and future being, and as such creates a future against and within the settler discourses that would disavow her (77). She resists the settler narratives and their relegation of girls to the long-dead past, performing her version of "Indigenous stories and realities to juxtapose and override existing settler narratives . . . to destabilize the linearity of time and space as constructed in settler narratives" (Hoque 2017, 2). Stories that pose such challenges to Time are dangerous and continue to position their tellers at risk of being ostracized, endangered. Sophia's performance is an example of quantum justice resistance—she shifts Time, posing a threat to existing systems exerting their control. Her performance is disruptive backtalk to the stories commonly recited about girls, as medicine to revise those narratives employed to do them harm.

Through her statement Sophia uses her words, voice, and memory to activate the praxis of everyday prophecy by speaking things into existence while simultaneously calling other girls forward to step into their gifts and talents to cocreate the new world. She affirms "gifts like your voice, your art, your music, whatever it may be to express your Truth at every chance you can get." Centering everyday creative cultural production is central to the environmental justice activism that grounds Sophia's call to action for other global girls. In chorus the voices of girls instigate the "strong stand to change the way things are," and Sophia calls on her audience to join her, not as singular individuals but working together in community. Her strategy suggests not only that she acknowledges the strength available in collaboration with other girls from varying positions but that moving to instigate change causes severe discomfort and is not likely to be well received by those invested in the status quo. Yet Sophia's critique is valuable insight into the contentious relationship with so-called progressive politicians and their governments, for Sophia's call for accountability is "critique *as a participant* who is shaping the work" (brown

2017, 120, emphasis in original). She is on the front lines, literally, so her criticisms are rooted in what Jones and colleagues (Jones, Presler-Marshall, et al. 2018) describe as "participatory experiences which encourage them to identify their own goals and think through the barriers to achieving them" (78). Sophia's call reflects Hoque's (2017) question that asks what Indigenous stories like hers "do" to the self, subjectivity, and to the world—they cultivate disruption of linear Time and portend a multitude of futures that deepen the connection to the waters and the land for girls like her.

Imagining a future that allows for the ambivalent process of rehearsing identities, and Afrofuturism, much like Indigenous futurity, accounts for the always shifting energy and rehearsal that take place for girls who play with Time. The cultures that constitute the production of the future and the self "are embedded and nurtured" through Sophia's demonstration of backtalk as a form of resistance (Appadurai 2004, 59). In the examples below, the girls contradicted themselves and each other, all while presenting a mixture of critical realities and hopeful futures through their poems.

"Naughty, But Smart" Advice on How to Talk Back and Look Forward with Afrofuturism

I am a naughty girl but I am smart
I am a talented girl with many things to do
I'm not a better person but I'm perfect in what I do
I am talented
I'm confident of what I do
no one can let me down I know I can do it
I know I will achieve my goals
I know I will make my dream come true
I am a proud South African girl
I'm a grateful black child
I am who I am

my community is beautiful
my community is grateful lovely truthful
my community is most great example to me what kind and loving you
    see the best
what about yours?

THANDOLWETHU, SOWETO, SOUTH AFRICA

Thando's SWP exemplifies backtalk well. Backtalk is a thing that will get you in trouble. It means you mouthed off to authority with an attitude. Backtalk will make your momma mad and will get you in trouble with teachers. Backtalk is a literal talking back to power, in whatever form it manifests. Power doesn't take kindly to getting corrected—especially by girls. Toby Jenkins (2017) defines backtalk as something often perceived as disrespect, especially when children are speaking to adults. She writes, "When examining the conditions of the world, the ways that many populations are oppressed, and the social systems that sustain such oppression, talking back becomes a necessary form of oppositional thinking" (55). SWP invites transformation through the embodied action of performing oppositional thinking. Thandolwethu's SWP and performance rests at this intersection of "naughty, but smart" because she understands that her social position as a girl child in a culture that reveres old age means that any vocal opposition she poses to the normative discourse about who she is and how she is expected to behave is going to render her "naughty." Good girls in Soweto do not contradict any adult in a position of power. Yet she is proud of being "smart" too because that intellectual agility has likely excused her unconventional behavior or at the least lessened her punishment for acting out in ways not socially sanctioned. Backtalk is a critical tool for political resistance among those marginalized by mainstream society. SWP and performance offer girls like Thandolwethu the individual agency to underwrite the risk of publicly performing alternative narratives that operate in necessarily contrary waves, thrashing back at dominant discourse, which, by rule, ignores and minimizes their lives both real and imagined. Thandolwethu operationalizes the cypher of the emerging girl poet when she revises and rehearses her negotiated meanings and mediated subjectivity (Endsley 2017). She writes, "I'm not a better person but I'm perfect in what I do." This line alone encompasses worlds. The self-determination that Thandolwethu exudes throughout her SWP reflects a necessary characteristic for girls who backtalk. Thandolwethu's line shoots out tentacles that grasp onto her network, reaffirming them even as she reaffirms herself. She constitutes herself as a peer to her girl audience—"I'm not a better person"—and concurrently validates herself in her current state, not in the past and not in the future—"I'm perfect in what I do." She does not position herself as competing with other girls, nor does she compare herself with them to measure her own success or to mark herself as good or bad. Perfection, to her, is whatever she decides to do in any situation she finds herself in. She doesn't merit perfection based on moral judgement or some arbitrary assessment of proper girlhood. Instead, she models what Marnina Gonick (2003) explains as disruptive, "reveal[ing] the strands and tensions webbed in the intricate and shaky fabric with which identities are imagined, stabilized, and reinvented" (92). She doesn't have to earn it through performance. Her refusal of the socially competitive nature of becoming a girl is expected. For Thandowelthu, SWP cultivates disruption in its generality; no matter where her global girl audience hails from, Thandowelthu's poem is broad enough to reflect their experience, too. She relies on the instability of girls' subjectivity and assumes other girls are also working to contest the narratives forcibly constricting them and suppressing their "talents," "dreams," and "goals." Thandowelthu's SWP firmly connects her to specific geography as she states, "I am a proud South African girl," and racially in her line that reads "I'm a grateful black child." Yet her lyrical lasso grows wider and then narrower as she works her SWP to talk back to narratives about girls like her. Her knowledge about global girls and her connection to her audience relies on the normative tropes she assumes they struggle against within their own specific contexts of race and location. She calls those scripts up to render her global girl audience intelligible and to reveal their incompleteness. Thandowelthu's SWP disrupts as it constructs in order to instruct her girl audience about how she backtalks what is circulated about girls like her in broader discourse. Her current developmental stage seems to be focused on how she is viewed and scripted, and she seems to weigh and consider what others have spoken over her life, ultimately to determine whether to engage with others' assumptions about her. She declares, "I know who I am," and rather than read this as some finite statement of finished subjectivity, Thandolwethu seems to demonstrate a sense of self-possessed security that echoes for girls in other locations as well. Thandolwethu knows who she is becoming and aspiring to be and who she has been, and builds her present self rooted in the confidence that she will succeed on her own terms. Cultivating disruption through SWP is both a declaration and a prediction for Thandolwethu; if her words have power to create worlds that she wants to live in, she can also speak her selves into existence, becoming what she says even as she says it. She prophesies the future for girls like her. Her backtalk is positive affirmation for her girl audience across space, Time, and place.

Thandolwethu's SWP ends with a question that provokes the audience to respond when she asks, "What about yours?" Posing this question in closing demonstrates the didactic function of SWP and the expectations of the role and response-ability of the audience. Thando understands performing, like girlhood, isn't simple, and it isn't a one-way street. Even as quantum justice theory assists us in analyzing her performance, SWP is Thandolwethu's epistemology that "looks backward and forward in seeking to provide insights about identity, one that asks what was and what if" (Nelson 2002, 4). She uses poetry to respond to external perceptions and justifies herself and the qualities that make her feel strong. Her confidence is clear in each line, and its expansiveness applies to her community as well. The Act of Recognition is working for Thandolwethu, discursively positioning her as an agent making personal choices and as a part of a greater, externally facing body, artist to audience, and girl to community. She talks back and looks ahead through SWP and performance. Her poetry models another iteration of quantum justice theory in action at a microscale and makes it possible to understand how Afrofuturism might be used in connection with SWP to manifest social transformation.

Afrofuturist Connections

Crossroads again surface as an apt metaphor for the locus of activity that quantum justice theory illuminates. The inner workings of creative power and prophecy, of poems by girls like Thandolwethu and performances like Sophia's, open up another path that leads through the crossroads with Afrofuturism (Dery 1993; Nelson 2002). Afrofuturism functions as a broad term, and Alondra Nelson insists that the ideas shaping Afrofuturism have always been developed collaboratively (2010). The collectivity required for documenting, archiving, and engaging with Afrofuturism aligns with the feminist organizing principles at work in GGG, particularly because of the cultural influence and practice of Hip-hop, feminism, and the racial identities of many participating communities in the project (Eshun 2003; Womack 2013; see also Kali Tal at www.afrofuturism.net). Further, Afrofuturism is an adaptable lens for engaging with creative work that combines a centric focus on Blackness, culture, and critical theory (Womack 2013). From these beginnings, Susana Morris's (2016) work explicitly merges feminism with Afrofuturism and creates the threshold by which SWP ushers in the cultural production of global girls. Morris centers Black women as agents and subjects and "as fundamental to understanding futurity" and elaborates that envisioning a future for Black people resists erasure and relegation to a forgotten past (35). Cultural production is integral to an Afrofuturist exploration of re-membering the past, present, and future so Thandolwethu's confident poetry that declares, "I will make my dream come true," moves through the intersection of time, space, desire, with nonchalant ease that contradicts the White imperialism that shapes discourse about girls like her.

Quantum justice theoretically operates to center an opportunity for Black girls to thrive as they explore their futuristic subjectivities through SWP and performance. The girls' creativity extends their subjectivity "as an act of resistance and liberation" (Morris 35). So for Sophia and Thando, who are bound by the locality of their context and geography, their acknowledgement of the contradictions and pain in their "fundamental imaginings" of the past and present provides hope in their simultaneous imagination of a future they have never witnessed. Their networks function in ways similar to Nelson's digital community—they build worlds and ideas together but employ them according to their specific experiences. To cultivate the disruption that global girls are already engaging is to appreciate their creativity not solely as a means of backtalking oppression but as an integral characteristic of their relationships to each other. The girl poets have existed and produced culture in spite of the forces working to dominate and repress them, and they construct "the center," proving that global girls, and not just grown women, "remain fundamental" (35). The girls have always already been conducting this imagination-conjuring work; it did not begin when GGG and I arrived on the scene; the only difference is that now girls are speaking with each other through SWP, which sparks unexpected synapses traceable through quantum justice theory.

Afrofuturism plays with Hip-hop feminism's insistence on "keeping it real" by pushing our concepts of the future beyond what has already been experienced in the past and the present. Nelson (2000) provides a long list of artists, thinkers, and writers from the Diaspora who exist beyond the boundaries of mainstream discourse about Black experiences. She suggests that Afrofuturism is for "outliers," and I think it is important to expand on this definition to specifically address power and how it operates in the lives of girls. Outliers exist in the social mainstream margins; they are not decentralized in their own lives (Endsley 2017). Outliers are not just those who perform alternative versions of the present within the moment of the present, which puts them outside of Time and marks them as already unusual: they exude a sense of excellence as well, rather than just performative curiosities. Hip-hop spoken word Afrofuturists are already living and creating outside of the bounds of mainstream discourse and serve the global imagination as a propelling force for cultural work that has come forth and has yet to be conceived. Hip-hop and SWP as we know them presently were once formulations of Afrofuturist work. Afrofuturist ideas are formed and commonly acted out in creative spaces because these spaces make rehearsing imagination permissible, which suggests that global girls who produce backtalk about their lives are also playing in this realm. Morris (2013) describes the fruitful ways that Black feminism and Afrofuturist concepts can be combined:

> Coupling Afrofuturism with feminism expands the former's capacity to transgress normative boundaries of not only race, but of gender, sexuality,

ability, and other subject positions; this coupling also catalyzes the latter's capacity for reimagining the past, present, and future. (154)

The cypher between Afrofuturism and feminism is like a double Dutch rhythm made by ropes swinging a steady tempo. When the global girls from GGG flex their poetic skills in communication across communities, they are leaping into the rhythm, keeping Time, though not falling on either rope's count. However, feminist Afrofuturism is not meant to confine or restrict all jumpers to the same tempo. Rather, as Morris writes, it "expands" and "catalyzes capacity," which is the transgressive and transformative work of SWP. Morris continues to cite three important defining features of Afrofuturist feminism: "the creation of a parallel feminist universe; the remixing of dominant futurist discourse; and futurist scenarios in which black women are centered as agents, but not as martyrs" (35). Hip-hop feminism is evident in these features through the acts of creation, remixing, and recasting Black women as agentic girls. The girls' creative production bridges these two concepts effortlessly. On one hand, their artwork showcases the realness that marks Hip-hop feminist work as reliable, truth-telling, and firsthand speaking with those who are outcast and denigrated, and rigorously interrogating power. On the other, the girls' SWP reckons with the far out, the uncommon, the unexpected and uncomfortable new visions of what might be when girls determine their future on their own terms. Ruth Nicole Brown (2013) expounds on Michelle Alexander and Gloria Anzaldúa's work in her considerations of "making time" to "access the past as a way to change the future in the present moment" (51). Brown situates Time as a vehicle we build, one that carries us across and through. SWP functions as a necessary bridge, then, embodied by global girls and possible only in partnership with them. The futures they articulate and the histories they enact revise the current moments of time and space to be something better than what we can see or understand. Quantum justice holds space for this interpretation of Time because we cannot clearly observe all aspects of the lives re-presented in the girls' SWP, including Time. The specifics of geography, age, and more obscure how Time is employed by these girls. Interrogating Time makes our grasp on the other contexts of their lives and creative work loose at best. Remember, quantum justice allows the observer to interpret only a singular aspect at any given moment.

We desperately need both the acknowledgment of the rawness and powerful realness of Hip-hop feminism, and the remix possible only through Indigenous Futurity and Afrofuturist work. The ability to tap into the middle spaces occurs in the ambiguity of liminal space and Time. Sometimes, we can access the crossroads we abide in through SWP as a praxis that Toni Morrison

(2019) writes about: "Memory (the deliberate act of remembering) is a form of willed creation. It is not an effort to find out the way it really was—that is research. The point is to dwell on the way it appeared and *why* it appeared in that particular way" (327, emphasis added). The *why* of remembering becomes the *how* of quantum justice theory. SWP performance cultivates this critical disruption in the space between the realness and the imagined, where we exist. The girls create as "both, yet neither" and are capable of doing so through their SWP performances (Endsley 2020). Each stage of cultivating disruption invites us to rehearse how to sustain and create opportunities for global girls to identify and explore their own enactment of quantum justice at this deeply intimate microlevel within the archive of the self before sealing connections to the larger world beyond. Knowledge of self remains the force determining our orbit.

This conjunction of science, technology, and emphasis of the future is where SWP with and for global girls illuminates who they are and are becoming. I find S. R. Toliver's (2020) literary analysis of the carnival and Afrofuturism especially useful to understand how an intangible imagination of the future might be translated and interpreted through embodied experiences. As subversion of this ideal, the girls' poetics "situat[e] oppressive systems and individuals as the true monstrous bodies" (3). The girls' poetry calls up a monstrously disfigured historical and contemporary time through their rehearsal of the past and present and then performs "abstract concepts of systemic oppression to the sphere of earth and body by presenting intangible ideas.... They subvert oppressive ideologies by mapping the grotesque realities of oppression" (3). The subversion of such ideologies occurs explicitly throughout the SWP of the girls in each community in the GGG project. As Thandowelthu's SWP audaciously reminds us, "I am who I am." She asserts herself as a "grateful Black girl" who acknowledges her community as the "most great example to me what [is] kind and loving you see the best" and flips her SWP performance on the audience by asking "what about yours?" Thandowelthu's SWP puts feminist Afrofuturism to work, constructing her community in Soweto as "kind," "Loving," "the best," and promptly asking her audience "what about yours?" The audience will be interrogated as well, positioned as the subject, and required to activate this performance with their own self-examination. Thandowelthu has shared what she would like to, and now it is the audience who must acknowledge, Recognize, and perform their own perspectives and complicit role in her tale of history (Endsley 2016). Where does her audience belong in the future she foresees? How will they be allowed to participate and expected to perform within Thandolwethu's vision?

SWP creates the opportunity for audience and artist to "better understand the challenges and invitations that social responsibility might offer us," for it is "through our relationships with one another that we gained the courage to act against and re-imagine the things that bound us" (Endsley 2016, 57). Global girls rehearse how they might Backtalk the inequities and oppressions that bind us all in destructive patterns. Courage is required for navigating these crossroads.

Quantum Justice Leaps with Global Girls

SWP provides a vehicle that moves girls from micro- to macro-scale reflections on their lives, memories, and futures, and back again in unpredictable ways. Indigenous Futurity and Afrofuturism provide important entry points into the crossroads of the winding and knotted pathways and offer diverse gradients of light to follow. For the girl poets introduced in this beginning, their poetry indicates a quantum justice leap landing on girls' concepts of community and networking. Those leaps unfold for each girl, her poem, and her audience in multiple and rapidly changing ways even as I work to gather them here for a moment that we might examine them in stillness. The scholarly and artistic remnants that I Recognize at this beginning are foundational, but they rely on racial and ethnic identification and solidarity for application. This is of utmost importance, especially given the nuanced ways that the girls' techniques for Backtalk and their repertoire of responses to poetic echoes are shaped by racial epistemologies. I began with a Recognition of racialized embodied experience because of the specificity and localization that are inherently at work in the embodied performance of SWP, yet quantum justice theory is not singular, nor is it still. Rather, quantum justice theory *leaps* and moves beyond the scope of racialized identities even as it is energized by their properties. SWP performance is dynamic, relying on the ways that Time and space are engaged and put to work in Indigenous Futurity and Afrofuturism, and the ways racial assets mitigate experiences and relationships. Thus, engaging with these creative praxes can be understood only relationally as well. When we are propelled on a quantum justice leap, the breadth and scope of global girls' networks through performance move us to another plane.

The quantum justice leap encompasses the multitudes of directional possibilities that are available and stretches for a "both/and" reading and multimodal response to the girls' poetry; race is a critical part of that, but it is not the only part, so the theoretical foundation that coheres in this analysis also features multiplicity (Lindsey 2015). Girls are talking back to linear, singular representations of their subjectivities. Poetic echoes hold space for transnationally scoped linkages and ruptures even as we are moved internally, personally, on a granular level. Embarking on quantum justice leaps accounts for the specificities of local re-membering that demand immediacy, while simultaneously tending to the broad disruption that will inevitably occur within the girls' embodied performance. The bounds are thrown wide and portals slit open to offer the gift of traveling through the quantum justice leaps girls deem necessary.

At this crossroads we carry the sounds and practice of backtalk with us as we depart on a quantum justice leap to follow the poetic echo of contradicting conditions. This leap thrusts us smack in the middle of a new crossroads, where concepts of community are challenged and put to work. Representations of community are expanded to macrolevel disruptions of girls' decisions and their experiences in education. Contradicting conditions invite us to continue to be limber, and to show our flexibility by holding competing discourses as real, imagined, and true in crystallized moments of Time and space.

CHAPTER 2

"Understand This, and Be Happy in Life"
Contradicting Conditions, Complicating Community

As soon as creative work is performed live by girls in the local community, there is an immediate shift in their trajectory. Their pathway is altered yet again when the creative work departs from them and is sent to other girls. Once the creative work arrives and is performed at its new destination, global girls ricochet into an unprecedented and unpredictable future Time and space. After the performance has occurred, they are already in motion in a million different tiny ways that refuse to be followed, captured, or documented. Their movement is infused with energy and sets in motion changes that quantum justice theory observes. In the next round of SWP's arrival and reproduction through performance in a new community of global girls, they are transformed into audience, artist, and recipient, and then exploded through a quantum justice leap into a million tiny directions of their own. Girl performers and quantum justice theory are all about movement. Quantum justice theory moves through the metamorphoses of delivery and reproduction of SWP to test and challenge our notions of community. This poetic echo, contradicting conditions, cultivates disruption to girls' environments through the ways Time is interpreted by applications of Indigenous Futurity and Afrofuturism. How is community both cultivated and disrupted in the practice and performance of SWP by girls? How does performance strengthen connections with other girls while deconstructing ideologies of a singular subjectivity? An analysis and activism with and for girls must remain focused on their overlaps, separations, concerns, and experiences. How do the specificities of race and nation across global interpretation reorganize the function of power in transnational girl networks? Why do SWP and performance puncture the borders of these identity categories? Community must be understood as a living organism that is organic, authentic, and sometimes temporal.

The Network Makes the Net Worth: Tanzanian Girls and Community as Capital

The bottom dropped out. Clouds that had been menacing all morning seemed to coordinate their pounding fury on the rest of the world below. How were we going to climb up on the roof now? We scrambled to gather our supplies, dragging duffel bags filled with notebooks, pens, markers, and cameras to the shelter of the classroom. The dust covering our feet turned to mud that I didn't notice until after we were seated at the small desks. Indoors we could hear the loud thrumming of the rain on the roof, and steam quickly began to rise from the skin of fifty bodies in a room with no windows to open. I smiled at Zola, our translator and coordinator. "Well, I guess we will begin with some inside lessons first!" She smiled and shrugged. "It goes this way sometimes. The rain will stop soon." I dug some chalk out from the bag on my shoulder and passed it to her as I signaled my students to begin to pass out notebooks and pens to the girls. It was so quiet, and I had not intended to begin cramped indoors. I was mentally rearranging the plan and realized Zola was waiting on my instructions. "Could we . . . do you think we could find out what they know about poetry?" Zola's eyebrows raised, and the tone of her voice raised at the end of her response, indicating in that polite Tanzanian way that I was *mzungu*—thinking and behaving like an unwelcome foreigner. "Why don't we start with what the girls know best—science." Inwardly I cringed. I knew better. Poetry is my place of comfort, so I always turn to writing corporately first when I am anxious or uncertain. Then I laughed out loud, remembering where I was; the high school boasts the only STEAM-focused curriculum for girls in all of Zanzibar. Of course they want to start with science, not poetry! The girls were quiet, watching us, and barely making eye contact with my college students, who were awkwardly attempting small talk, passing out notebooks. She turned, facing the girls, and I saw Zola's no-nonsense college-professor demeanor come forth. As soon as Zola asked in Swahili, "Who can explain to us about the role of solar energy and the ecosystem here on Pemba?" no fewer than a dozen hands shot up. About fifteen minutes later, a student named Miriam came to the front and sketched the entire cycle of photosynthesis on the board while her classmate Ula described each step. Zola translated for my students and me while Ula spoke directly to her classmates. I glanced at my assistant, Penelope, who was prepared to lead the first workshop on solar energy and suitcases. She was speechless. "How old are these girls?!" she whispered to me. "They are going to end up teaching me today, not the other way around! They really know their stuff." I slipped my arm around her to give a quick one-armed hug. *Funny how often that happens,* I thought. Penelope was almost as shy as the Pemba girls.

The Zanzibar Outreach Program (ZOP) is a community-based partner organization founded in Tanzania that I worked with for this program. ZOP is highly reputable, dependable, and trusted by local community members. Most significant, the main contact and translator during my time on Pemba Island was Zola, a Zanzibari woman and professional engineer. Her experiences and willingness to vouch for my presence lent me the credibility to work with girls, who are typically highly protected from outsiders. Our workshop took place at the all-girls, all-Muslim Secondary School. The girls live in a dormitory on the campus, which positions both the school and the girls' experience as highly unusual (Decker 2007). Traditionally, a Zanzibari Muslim girl will grow up in her family home, marry a Muslim man, and then move into her husband's home (Thompson 2011). Historically, although Zanzibar boasted the first state-run school to educate girls in Tanzania, there is a cultural anxiety that Muslim girls will be seduced or enticed by education and the perceived freedoms it offers and abandon their families and traditional religion for European ways or colonial influences (Beckman 2010; Decker, Presler-Marshall et al. 2015). Although highly guarded and policed by men, girls are not always wanted as children in a family. Indeed, a proverb from Pemba Island states that "daughters are bad cargo to be unloaded at the first opportunity" (Turki 1987, 57, as in Decker 2015a, 47). The contradiction is striking. Girls are placed under security and surveillance that is extreme, and yet sons are preferred and desired by expecting parents. Girls are categorically unwanted yet protected like treasure. Thus, there are multiple reasons for the girls to board at school. On the one hand, there are social factors, like families who cannot afford either the financial burden or the shame of an educated daughter, so the girl lives on campus year-round. On the other, the school, Utaani, provides a premier-tier education, as it offers the only STEAM-focused curriculum at any high school in Zanzibar where girls are allowed to enroll.

Utaani's focus is on science, technology, engineering, art and design, and math, and only girls can board and attend at its campus. The only men who are regularly on campus are a few of the teachers, maintenance workers, and the director. The Head Mistress, equivalent to a US school principal, and her immediate administrative support are both local women, one from Zanzibar and one from Pemba Island. Additional reasons for the girls to live on campus include any combination of family, financial, religious, or cultural practices. The girls' enrollment, which already enjoys notoriety on the relatively small, secluded landscape of Pemba Island, positions them as abiding in the in-between of tradition and modernization (Decker, Tefera, et al. 2015; Vavrus 2002).

When I arrived with the group of college students I was working with, we were immediately given a tour of the grounds. The girls ushered us through the damp mist with quiet pride, and Head Mistress filled in some of the background on how Utaani came to be focused on STEAM. Utaani's campus was supplied with a few modern technologies, but they were rarely used, because the school was under-resourced. What good is a light or a fan if you cannot afford the electricity to power it? The Pemba girls who attended and participated in the GGG project were familiar with living in the borders, somewhere between home and away, girl and woman, formally educated and yet traditional. Their dreams of STEAM careers were audacious, in part because of their geography; they were not even on the main island of Zanzibar, which still experiences conflict with mainland Tanzania's governance. Living on campus ostracized the girls from the local community, yet they enjoyed public admiration for the opportunity for secondary education that is not compulsory across Tanzania. They were also secure in their housing and food, yet living away from their families meant they were not raised by their mothers, grandmothers, or aunties, who could share important knowledge about growing up and their changing bodies, or how to comport themselves as they become women (Sommer 2010). There seemed to be a disconnect between cultural wisdom and formal curriculum that made me wonder at the cost of each. It seemed the girls must exchange one for the other in this instance. I don't know if that was always true. Living in-between is never convenient. Despite the uncertainty that imbued some aspects of their lives, the Pemba Island girls shyly greeted us when we arrived for the workshop at the entrance of their campus, dressed in their uniforms. The goal here is not to conjure what Shenila Khoja-Moolji (2018) describes as "the composite figure of the Muslim woman/girl [who] emerges as an example par excellence of this backward femininity—she is threatened by religion, tradition, patriarchy, and local customs, is ill-equipped to survive in the modern social order, and is thus unable to fulfill her potential" (4). Rather, the girls enrolled at Utaani face contradictions rooted in some of the realities listed by Khoja-Moolji but complicated by the lived experiences in their unique space, place, and time. Already, the Pemba Utaani Secondary School challenges essentialized perceptions of African Muslim girls in the Global North, but also across the continent. Left out of this popular narrow caricature of Muslim girls are the subversive ways girls demonstrate everyday political legibility and disruption. Their SWP community poem leverages their words to unravel cohesive mainstream holograms claiming to represent who the girls are.

Community Poems

The community poems I facilitated with each GGG location (some to a deeper degree than others, depending on the location and practical restraints) employed Afrofuturist technologies to engage the conflict of current realities and girls' concurrent and contradictory desires. The girls' poetic chorus echoes how working through collaboration and collectivity undermines master narratives about girl-to-girl relationships.

Community poems can be constructed as follows to emphasize how we can know and understand one another only partially. They also demonstrate how our messages are coauthored by others in our community, and that we do not maintain control over our narrative; rather, it is coconstructed by others. This simple version of a community poem exercise usually prompts deeper conversations about power, privilege, and discourse maintenance within a workshop setting. These conversations are particularly important to girls who see representations of themselves populating global media that rarely reflect their daily lives. The community poem also provides an important opportunity to discuss the poetic and cultural artifact exchanges that GGG facilitates between groups of global girls.

On Pemba Island the girls composed a poem that radiates power through their backtalk to the common discourse that positions girls in competition for limited resources and for sexual attention. The contradicting conditions emphasized in their writing highlight the ways girls actively worked to recenter their relationships and coconstruct futures for themselves and the girls who sent them poems and artwork, as well as the girls who would later receive their gifts of poetry. The Pemba girls position themselves as writers of the past and prophets of the future, moving through Time, space, and imagination at the speed of quantum justice. An excerpt is below:

Hupenda tuwe pamoja, kama ilivyo jamia
Hata tukija makwenu, vizuri mutukarimu

It's always lovely to be together as family.
Even if we come to your place, you'll be generous, too.

Madawa ya kulevya, yana hatari
Vyema tukiyatumia, yatakuja kuathiri

Drugs are dangerous.
If we use drugs, their impact is inevitable.

Elimu ndio muhimu, katika yako maisha
Hili ukilifahamu, tafurahia maisha.

Education is indeed important in your life.
If you understand this, you'll be happy in life.

Usafi kitu muhimu, ni lazima tuwanacho
Usafi si lazima wa mwili, pia na usafi wa nafsi.

Cleanliness: it's important and essential to have it.
Not only for the body, but also for the soul.

This is an excerpt from a community poem composed by Aisha, Khadija, Amina, and Rhama, from Pemba Island, Zanzibar, Tanzania. The piece was written in Swahili and translated to English by Amanda Leigh Lichtenstein.

This portion of the Pemba girls' community poem overlaps the decisions that girls must make and is laced with advice for their girl audience. Their lyrics offer frequencies that were not necessarily identical but made to harmonize. The Pemba girls use their SWP as a tool to subdue and capitalize on the contradicting conditions of their community. By recognizing the people and place they are currently in community with, and yet articulating who and where they *want* to claim as community, girls resist the binary options of leaving behind the troubling parts of their homes and experiences and the people that are important to them while also asking for more. Maneuvering through social codes as a technique for any slight gain in mobility and agency can also be understood as another version of what the Maasai schoolgirls practiced when creating a new social subject to position themselves between the identity categories of girl-child and bride from Heather Switzer's (2018) study based in Kenya. When this reapplication of "cultural codes" used to constrain girls occurs through SWP performance, a girl is making moves. Making moves signals global girls' desire to create, resituate, or otherwise choreograph an alternative form of movement that will propel her socially, economically, politically, or often all three. The Pemba girls used the SWP community poem as a means of working together to send cohesive but specific advice to their global girl audience. Their advice reflects the social issues they face or that concern them as high school girls living on Pemba Island. This excerpt of a community poem offers very direct guidance for etiquette in the home, welcoming visitors, drugs, education, and cleanliness. The domestic domain and duties fall to any proper Zanzibari Muslim, and thus, Pemba girls' purview. By offering practical and straightforward advice to global girls about conduct, they are sharing what they believe will support their success in life. The topics seem to reflect how the Pemba girls "are currently experiencing the simultaneous pull-back tug of tradition, and the pull-forward draw of modernization and its (perceived) freedoms" (Sommer 2010, 132; Vavrus 2002). The contradiction of the girls' modern educational and dormitory living environment with their old-school advice presents tensions that Pemba girls face. They work to regulate themselves based on the "pull-back" that is both viscerally experienced and acquired culturally. One example of performing those expectations is in their greetings and welcoming of strangers into their community, as well as the "pull-forward" of their new exposure to experiences as first-generation girls enrolled in formal secondary education that influences their future hopes. Their coauthored SWP community poem thus creates a jointly governed "space between that reforms both the self and the other, the self and its lived relation with others" (Ellsworth 2005, 48). By rule of design, community poems signify relationship with other poets as well as the audience of the poem, who is positioned to coconstruct the poetic performance and the negotiation of the meaning behind the poem. The resulting meaning reflects and revises how the girl poets understand each other and relate to their girl audience. In other words, SWP and performance "puts inside and outside into relation" (Ellsworth 2005, 46). They position their girl audience as "family" and assume that "you'll be generous, too" when they come to visit. Their advice is not prescriptive, nor does it pass moral judgement with a clear "yes, do this" or "that is bad," but their poetry assumes a "we" is at stake in the decision-making processes of their audience. For example, "If we use drugs, their impact is inevitable," which is not to say drug users are bad people; rather, drugs have an "inevitable" outcome that will touch everyone involved. One girl's decision shifts the outcome for every girl. The Pemba girls have included themselves as audience as well, implicating their own dedication to upholding the social responsibility they advise as critical to well-being for their global girl audience. They stress that "education is important" and promise "you'll be happy in life" if you pursue it to completion. Formal education is costly financially and culturally; it is rare and precious for girls in Pemba, so this guarantee is not simply a regurgitation of GID narratives: for the Pemba girls it is true.

Their community poem inverts GID ideologies because they already understand themselves as in relation, not isolated or individualized. Pemba girls take up the familiar and necessary cultural expectations for girls like them and utilize the domestic duties they are responsible for as a means of coding their messages to their girl audience. Even if the girl audience were to read their poetic advice from a shallow interpretation, they would still benefit from heeding it because of its practicality. However, if their audience can engage more deeply, in ways that the Pemba girls count on other global girls to have the capacity to, then they will find the hidden and camouflaged meanings that are carefully embedded within the words. The girls' creative transformation is possible through SWP because it permits multiple ways of being, knowing, and relating all at once. Community SWP allows a consideration of radical relations that stretch girls' capacities for learning, changing, and becoming (Winnicott 1989). This poem and thus the Pemba girls' subjectivities crack open a transitional space that is at once fluid and yet remarkably traditional. The Pemba girls re-create the very tensions they are living within through the composition of their community poem. In doing so, their audience and their coauthors are decidedly occupying the middle, together.

"Not Only for the Body, but Also for the Soul": Being Careful in Community

The final line from this excerpt focuses on a primary concern for Muslim girls, which is cleanliness, "not only for the body, but also for the soul." On the three islands that make up the territory of Zanzibar, almost 99 percent of the population is Muslim, with Sunni Muslims making up 90 percent, and the remainder a mix of Shi'a Muslim, Christian, and traditional East African religious or spiritual practices (Boswell 2008). The reality is that some Indigenous African spiritual practices are incorporated into the fabric of daily life for Tanzanians; however, those traditions are not always acknowledged as such. Complicated colonial histories of enslavement, the Arabic and Indian sea trades, struggles for political and religious autonomy across the Zanzibar Islands, and forces of globalization striate the cultural lives of girls on Pemba Island. Girls are navigating the frictions between education, sexuality, beliefs about health, development, and control, and "transgressing Islamic gender restrictions or challenging other social limitations with regard to race, ethnicity, class or religion" (Decker, Tefera, et al. 2015, 5). The dichotomy of public and private is scripted with control and autonomy throughout colonial Zanzibari history, and girls' lives occur in spaces marked with secrecy (Decker, Presler-Marshall, et al. 2014; Decker, Tefera, et al. 2014). Schools often function as containment spaces for the embedded power relations that are normalized for Pemba girls, and their SWP reveals that although they are "protected" in the school grounds, they do not necessarily enjoy more privacy, and their bodies remain contested sites of control.

"Essential cleanliness" is part of the practical and subversive advice offered to a global girl audience for this very reason. On the one hand, Zanzibari Muslim girls are strictly required to participate in rituals of cleaning for their physical bodies and for their homes and living spaces. High standards for hygiene "even for the soul" that account for spiritual cleanliness extend to the body, determining that even a handshake with a non-Muslim is *haram*, or forbidden by Islam, although this practice is not always imposed. There is a spectrum of enforcement for such practices, and, in more rural settings where other aspects of religious participation may not be accessible, those practices that are easily performative, and thus recognizable, become more enforced, and the requirements and consequences for failing to uphold them tend to be sterner. Yet there is another reading for this portion of the community poem. Cleanliness—"it's important and essential to have it"; and perhaps the Pemba girls are issuing a reminder to examine the relationship between the inside and the outside, or the public and private, as an invitation to "be more or other than in agreement or opposition" with their global audience. Cleanliness is both personal and private and interpreted differently across cultures, and the in-between of those interpretations requires that multiple truths be acknowledged as coexisting. The Pemba girls' community poem is a double-edged sword in its stark yet coded subversive messaging, deploying an expectation that the girl audience will be literate enough to dive deeply into all the meanings the girl poets leave open for interpretation. Global girl audiences, as community members, are asked to remain open to a reconfiguration of whatever foreknowledge they bring to bear on the poem. The Pemba girls look to the past of tradition and to the present of their partial subjectivity as girls in school, to a future that echoes with the decisions made for them, and that they are making with others. SWP holds room for the modulation of identity, a social transaction that maintains a sense of the self and entertains an interest in the Other. The community poem develops girls' critical transnational literacy skills as it is written, performed, and read across global networks.

Yet systems and connections with community are not innocent. It is not safe to presume that community automatically translates to a safe, healthy or nurturing environment or group of people, even among global girls. Afrofuturist feminism and emergent strategies both center operations for social change around community, in part because collaborative work is premised upon decentralized power as a theory. Reality, however, is not always reflective of the futures we work to project. The concept of collaborative community work fails, relationships get destroyed, and power and inherited dominant tendencies are deployed to achieve goals that are unaligned. I find it important to fold in how bell hooks (1989) interrogates the term "community" as operationalized and sometimes used to intimidate outliers into silence. This debate is important, as it reminds that multifaceted experiences of groups are nuanced, even when formed for political solidarity. Personal events may not be shared by those in "community," but that should not invalidate group membership or an individual's authenticity. There is no monolith, although the easy assumption is to generalize and essentialize without accounting for difference. As hooks states, "It becomes easy to speak about what the group wants to hear, to describe and define experience in a language compatible with existing images and ways of knowing, constructed within social frameworks that reinforce domination" (14). Precarious political work with girls who don't enjoy access to the authority that adults do compounds the unequal distribution of power, which may parrot "compatible language" as a method of survival. Sometimes girls perform in accordance with dominant frameworks because they determine their livelihood. Communities and systems, like all relationships, are not absent of power, privilege, or hierarchy. Howard Ramsby's (2013) treatise on Andre 3000, half of southern Hip-hop's influential duo Outkast, offers a helpful perspective on problematic networks:

> The words "systems" or "networks" are noteworthy . . . because those terms signal the multithreaded, complex processes of guidance, influence, assistance, emotional support, inspiration, training, mentoring, failed attempts, constructive feedback, collaboration, funding, and more that make high-level artistic production possible and sustainable. Just as systems are capable of providing tremendous support, they can also enable devastating neglect and worse. (214)

In Ramsby's description of the supportive nature of "networks," he focuses on the sustainability of "high-level artistic production" and the ways that Afrofuturist discourse emphasizes what adrienne maree brown (2017) names "adaptations with intention" (70). Mutations of beneficial communities have the potential to offer lasting support. Brown suggests that "what is easy is sustainable. Birds coast when they can" (72). Swarms of birds fly in formation and rely on each other to navigate air gusts and wind that are signaled only via the bodies of their peers. For girls, such signals are rehearsed through SWP performance as auditions of behavior, personal identities, and the invocation of new worlds that those other selves being rehearsed can inhabit. The adaptations available through SWP are not referring only to the girls' shifting subjectivity but to the morphing of their environments and the places they anticipate calling home. Yet Ramsby warns us to remain engaged yet critical of systems as "they can also enable devastating neglect and worse" (214). For global girls, local neighborhoods, religious centers, and school community are often the introduction to formal systems beyond family. The concept of transnational girlhoods in relationship with each other offers overwhelming positive attributes that involve a level of accountability; however, these interactions require constant attentiveness. There is also very real danger, especially present in developmental feminism because the same power redistribution that purports to be community can quickly morph into another iteration of domination and perpetuate the very systems it claims to overthrow (Mama 2015). SWP offers one technique for addressing the persistent threat of powerful ideologies, while performance offers girls a way to identify those ideologies when they become internalized and embodied.

So, what is it about sharing intimate knowledge with other girls or connecting with community in the midst of contradiction that explodes into multiple imaginative possibilities for a girl's life? Cultivating disruption provides a way to trace, retrace, rewrite, revision, and plunge deeply into cultural production work with girls through GGG. Yet girls' disempowerment, often perpetuated and upheld by their communities, reminds us that "culture, moreover, is a legitimate, even necessary, terrain of struggle, a site of injustice in its own right and deeply imbricated with economic inequality" (Fraser 2000). Further, Western schemas of education and feminist agendas claiming to dismantle existing inequalities for global girls often work to the contrary and "conceal hegemonic tendencies, which are continuing to trivialize and marginalize women's knowledge systems, urging them to strive to be enlightened through education in order to fit in the larger society" (Swai 2010, 35). Swai affirms the knowledge and ability of girls and women to "tell their own stories in their own way," and SWP provides an avenue to explore the multiple perspectives and experiences of global girls. Listening is also how I recalibrate and examine the undergirding systems and networks that formulate these contradictions.

Kwani nyinyi wahisani, kwa binadamu wenzenu
Tena tunawaahidi, kutunza yenu mafunzo

As you've been so kind to your fellow human beings,
Again we promise you that we will heed your teachings.

UMMUEKHEIR, PEMBA ISLAND

This last excerpt from the Pemba girls' community poem calls to my mind the scripture that proclaims, "Blessed are they who have not seen yet have believed" (John 20:29 NIV), because it defies doubt and the generational trauma that otherwise suffocates, monopolizes, and manipulates our imaginations. The Pemba girls in this quantum justice crossroads of contradicting conditions prioritize current and budding relationships with the girls receiving their poetry, reconciling the past with the future. They cultivate disruption in the expectations of those relationships by keeping it real about the present and simultaneously foretelling the future. Audre Lorde writes in 1982: "We forget that the necessary ingredient needed to make the past work for the future is our energy in the present, metabolizing one into the other" (see https://www.blackpast.org/african-american-history/1982-audre-lorde-learning-60s/). Symbiosis between these iterations of Time and cocreative energy that we bring to bear upon revisions and responses to one another and to our conditions is crucial for prophesying a future worthy of us all, one that, according to Pearl Cleage (2014), the poet must both reflect and lead. SWP performance holds space for this energy, whose power is in its unpredictability. The fifth element and knowledge of self illuminates what girls can know and access about their communities. Self-reflexivity is spiritual work being undertaken by global girls through SWP, and connecting with the community through performance fuses and mutates that knowledge until the next quantum justice leap occurs. The leap will scatter energy and electrons and carry all that knowledge into unplanned synapses of relationship. Girls communicate beliefs about what is to come while mirroring a representation of their challenging contemporary situations. Their faith exercises a need to hope and to declare that victory will be coming, and we need to meet it in the roadway. To navigate her contradicting conditions, Ummuekheir is determined to heed the instructions of other global girls as she makes decisions about her future. Are we?

Emergent Strategies for Social Change

Transnational girlhoods must be considered in relation to one another and not simply as another essentialized category in which to lump groups of girls. Networks are important components of nature, science, and speculative spiritual work. The multiple institutions that underpin the inequality experienced by girls need to be disentangled explicitly so girls are not implicated as responsible for their own failures *or* successes. Emergent strategies apply to transnational relationships. Using the imagination to envision and build new futures based on alternative versions of contemporary reality offers conflicting versions and creates tensions between global girls. The writer adrienne maree brown (2017) writes about the work of organizing through grassroots community-based networks and centers the writings and philosophy of science fiction author Octavia Butler. Butler's body of literary work is the lens through which mobilizing toward social justice can be interpreted. This framework of brown's is named "emergent strategy." She writes:

> In our work for *Octavia's Brood* Walidah and I articulated that "all organizing is science fiction," by which we mean that social justice work is about creating systems of justice and equity in the future, creating conditions that we have never experienced. That is a futurist focus, and the practices of collaboration and adaptation and transformative justice, are science fictional behavior. (160)

She makes a convincing case about the ways that Afrofuturism situates marginalized communities as agentic creators relying on their own imaginations and one another. Projecting and rehearsing subjectivities for a time that has not yet happened operating within "systems of justice and equity" that have never existed before are applications of Afrofuturist methodologies. To build a collective vision using SWP as a tool of imaginative work requires that girls employ the skills of "collaboration and adaptation with intention" that distinctly command them to "chang[e] while staying in touch with [their] deeper purpose and longing" (brown 2017, 70). The systems brown refers to are exactly the global systems that constrain girls of color and how they imagine their futures in what Catherine Vanner (2019) writes of in her framework for "transnational girlhoods," when she argues that such an analysis foregrounds that oppressive global structures be illuminated (127). One key aspect of emergent strategy that lends itself to transnational girls in relationship is what brown (2017) names "shoal/Murmur/swarm" when she explains, "There is a right relationship, a right distance between them. . . . Each creature is shifting direction, speed, and proximity based on the information of the other creatures' bodies" (71). This is embodiment theory, performance pedagogy at its most intuitive and highest functionality, and it is a survival skill. SWP creates an opportunity for transnational girlhoods to be considered in community, and as a "swarm" the subjects engage with literacy practices to "read" their counterparts and respond or adjust accordingly.

In practice this facet of emergent strategy facilitates the ability to communicate with the six closest bodies of work or those most relevant to the girl without necessarily using speech to articulate exacting directives about how to respond or adjust. The "swarm" offers another take on what happens through

SWP performance pedagogy. Remember how your momma or an older woman in the family could correct your behavior or warn you with a certain look? Social literacies for girls, especially girls of color, include a fluency in reading and communicating through nonvocal body language of other girls and women. Sometimes safety and survival depend upon this literacy. Girls and women who feel unsafe in public spaces carry their bodies differently — we perform to communicate with others, and the more fluent we become in this skill, the more literate we become in our relationships and the more likely to survive (Simmons 2015). Keen and intentional attention to embodiment deepen and enrich the communications taking place in those relationships. Aisha Durham (2010) relies on community to understand a performance of praxis in her work on critical media literacy and considers how our relation to community determines our valuation of the self. The connection to what we say and do and how we are perceived by our peers heavily influences how we view ourselves. Transnational girlhoods must account for this relationship and mobility of subjectivities if it is to be useful; SWP performance cultivates disruption of stable homogeneous selves and focuses on the ways girls can be response-able for one another across Time and place. These methodologies are critical to the utility of transnational girlhoods. The performances of global girls living in disparate communities use SWP and performance to take care of one another by reading the body and reading written words.

Nature as Metaphor

Because circumstances and environment are so specific across locations where the girls in GGG live, they often turn to nature in their creative work to express their perspectives. They rely on common landscape imagery or metaphor to communicate important messages to their new friends living in different geographies. Nature, sustainability, and making choices to unite and work together make up the advice from girls in Hawassa, Ethiopia. They urge their girl audience to make decisions that will insist on collaboration and are rallied by the concept Amy from NYC shared in her SWP: "I am small, but mighty." Amy relayed her message to girls in Soweto, and by acknowledging her minuscule role, she also referenced their collective power: "It can take one drop of water to break the dam." The "one drop" might be interpreted as her existence, which alone makes little impact but when added to the "water" already filling the "dam," the pressure becomes enough altogether to overwhelm the structures in place working to contain her and her girl audience. References to nature and healing that are widely accessible and observable in natural environments are evident in Hilina's and Marjani's SWP.

> long live the girls who are hardworking like these
> long live the girls who are united like ants
> long live the girls who are symbols of peace like a bird
> long live the girls who cure like a lemon
>
> HILINA, ETHIOPIA (*Long Live the Girls: Love Rules*, 2015)

Hilina turns to her immediate surroundings to uplift girls who make choices that reflect nature's curative elements and beauty. Her friends, community, and traditional forms of healing and wisdom inherited from the women in her family and the environment are braided together to determine her advice to her girl audience. "Hardworking," "united," and "symbols of peace" are characteristics she calls forth from the girls listening to her. The reference to ants, who form colonies and rely on each other to stay alive, seem to shape the first and second lines. Her friends are "the girls who are hardworking" that she references and share that similarity with ants, who are diligent to fulfill their duties in the hierarchy of nature. To "cure like a lemon" a girl must have certain customs and local wisdom at her disposal; she must know how to prepare the lemon, under what circumstances it is appropriate to use lemon and for what ailments. Hilina relies on the systems commonly present in the natural world and the human body to link with her global audience. She assumes they will know what she knows and thus doesn't obscure her meaning as she urges them to listen to her advice. If girls, as a global community, can embody and work effectively like she describes, then Hilina believes they will represent "peace," and that is her desire. Marjani branches out from specific creatures but still incorporates common natural and environmental knowledge to make her advice clear. She writes:

> long live the girls who swim in the minds of all men
> long live the girls who shadow like big trees
> long live the girls who are complicated like tree roots
> long live the girls who are confident like me
>
> MARJANI, ETHIOPIA (*Long Live the Girls: Love Rules*, 2015)

In this excerpt, Marjani compares girls to "big trees" but to different parts with different functions. First, she says they "shadow" providing shade to others, comfort, and relief from the hot sun. A "big tree" doesn't get to enjoy its own shadow, but when it is nurtured and allowed the space and nutrients to grow big and strong to its fullest potential, others can enjoy what the tree provides.

Perhaps Marjani is making the argument that girls in her audience are not the only ones to benefit when they are allowed to grow. The metaphor allows her to demurely deny this claim if her audience disagrees. The next line draws our focus to the opposite of sprawling branches, "complicated like tree roots," and Marjani encourages girls to develop in intricate, difficult-to-trace patterns. Trees rely on complex root systems to draw up water and minerals from the earth. Typically, the deeper the roots extend underground, the healthier and stronger the tree. Marjani wishes long life to girls like her who are "confident" and yet rambling, unpredictable, untidy, and untraceable like roots beneath the surface. She applauds girls who follow her advice to always have a system beyond what the casual observer may notice, even as they enjoy the "shade." Marjani understands that being a girl necessitates subversion and that vital activity must be undertaken as part of an unseen network. Even before fruit grows or branches sprout, girls who are like these roots have been deepening their network, fortifying themselves and one another because they are interconnected in messy ways. If the "tree roots" were separated or singled out, they would shrivel and die, as would the tree they are feeding. Marjani's advice to girls is that they must work together, stay connected, and utilize the gift of their complexities and entangled reliance on one another for their own benefit. In a sense, Marjani, Hilina, and Amy use SWP to advise girls to consider themselves and their transnational relationships with a worldwide community as a form of social capital.

How might such an organic network scale up in healthy ways to reach and nurture girls across the globe? Some of the distance between their communities positions them as vastly different, and GID discourses work in direct opposition to any healthy or equitable links between global girls. GID discourses actively unravel the solidarity that transnational relationships may broker between girls. However, the poetic echo of contradicting conditions shifts the very identity categories that have been scribed with hierarchical value, proving that even the categories powerful and etched in social labels as formidable and unchanging can be subverted by girls for connection with other girls as they cultivate disruption together, globally, through SWP and performance.

GID and Contradicting Conditions: Identifying Race and Nation

Girl networks such as those described here offer methodological insights for the ways girls of color in the Global South are positioned as vulnerable, while girls of color in the Global North are equally vulnerable yet situated as saviors, and, ultimately, how these girls are defying and revising those master narratives by forging connections with each other (Bent 2013a). Relationship within and across communities is inevitably shaped by race and nation. Although socially and politically constructed as hypervisible, girls of color from the communities included in GGG are not unilaterally considered agents of social change in their home communities, nor are their experiences or input sought after in dialogues about girls in the Global South (Civil and Elliott 2017). One reason for this is that GID discourse profits from maintenance of binary exclusionary social positions that reify current fantasies, structures, and economies reliant on "third" and "first" world girlhoods.

Corporate influence and globalization shape girlhoods in disturbing ways. In 2008 the Nike Foundation launched a campaign named the "Girl Effect" that "constructs the adolescent girls as the next development 'frontier' for solving persistent global poverty, inequality, and insecurity" (Skalli 2015, 174; see also http://nikeinc.com/pages/the-girl-effect). The Girl Effect (http://girleffect.org) is a corporate campaign with the professed aim to support girls from the Global South living in poverty and provide them with "the tools and access to the critical assets they need to achieve their full potential" by promoting girls' empowerment and agency. The Girl Effect campaign frames the economic potential of adolescent girls in the Global South as investment-worthy and simultaneously reduces the systemic causes of global poverty to an individual basis (Bent 2013a, 5). GID discourse is deeply entangled in this neoliberal capitalist enterprise and continues to be perpetuated through NGOs like Girl Effect and various branches of the United Nations. Helen Skalli (2015) describes how "these foundations and their partners dangerously individualize the macro causes of poverty, erase long histories of colonial and neocolonial exploitation, and absolve global powers from any racial dimensions of past and present intervention" (176). Indeed, Marjorie Mbilinyi (2015) argues that African feminists have consistently critiqued development discourse because it is not governed by transformative feminist agendas. GID discourse is further problematized because girls of color in the Global North are excluded from the girl effect's logic, which, "though useful in drawing attention to the failure of the development community in addressing the marginalization of girls . . . recycle[s] former discourse of colonial paternalism" signified by the naturalized oppositionality between third world and first world girlhoods (Hayhurst 2011, 534, as in Bent and Switzer 2016, 7). In their theorization of "missionary girl power" Sensoy and Marshall (2010) further challenge "the discursive strategies that construct first world girls as the saviours of their 'Third World' sisters" (2). These strategies typically position girls in the Global South, always shown as girls of color, as endangered, suggesting that only White girls from the Global North can rescue them through uninvited interventions (Berents 2016; Switzer 2013). This "girl factor" represents intense international interest in girls from business and NGO entities whose investment in an imaginary and homogenized third world girl allows for an erasure of colonial histories, suspicious policy development, and further colonial violences to occur (Skalli and Persaud 2015, 177). Black girls who live in the Global North are not counted at all as participating members of the Global North collective of "empowered" girls. Amina Mama (2001) suggests that any GID agendas making feminist claims must survey the following three areas: subjectivity, personal relationships, and political economy (61). GGG was designed to address part of this agenda through a concentrated focus on cultural and political work. In this quantum justice leap zooming in on race and gender as primary factors that shape girls' lives, GGG localizes Hip-hop pedagogy through the praxis of SWP performance, emphasizing the critical importance of immediate cultural sociopolitical contexts that girls must navigate. Positioning global girls of color as agents of social change is a foundational tenet for the cultivating disruption framework, making tangible the ideologies that construct relationships between them, and the ways these scripts are under revision. The poetic echoes identifying race and nation are one way to map the girls' SWP messages to each other about their lived experiences. The contradicting conditions imposed because of their positions as girls matter within the theoretical conversation about their raced and ethnicized bodies, and how they envision and rewrite those overlaps with each other's stories.

This quantum justice leap considers what occurs when informal networks of girls are linked through their poetic echoes about the external contradicting conditions of race and nation. How does cultural context about Blackness frame "the terms of engagement" for global girls with one another (Pierre 2012, 156)? GGG further complicates the false racial binary propped up by White supremacy through primarily featuring Black girls and girls of color as participants: even though references to the Global North are assumed to mean empowered White girls, and rarely consider their racialized experiences, the US-based girls nevertheless find themselves bound by these conventions. Meanwhile, their African counterparts are bound by notions about the Global South that assume a demographic of Black and Brown girls in need of rescue. The girls' stories resist this tension, and we hover at this crossroads complicating what kinds of girls are allowed to experience vulnerability and empowerment. The poetic echoes released here are by no means intended to serve as the full and complicated representation of race, ethnicity, and nationality of all nations, especially within Africa, that are documented here. Rather, each excerpt shares a symbolic and representative glimpse into the ways girls understand their embodiedness and how their racial, national, or ethnic identity determines how, when, and if they moved through quantum justice leaps with other girls.

"I Am the Shadow": Acknowledging Race in the Global Community

From New Orleans, Milan shares, "My community is different skin tones."

And from Hawassa, Ethiopia, Marjani declares, "Long live the girls who have different colors like me and you!"

From Soweto, Tshelofelo simply states for her girl audience, "I am a black person / I live in South Africa."

From the Bronx, Lily informs other girls about the code: "unspoken rules / never support / someone who is racist and they try to degrade you because of your race."

Aynalm echoes feelings of pride from Hawassa, Ethiopia: "Long live the girls who are black like me."

Lesogo from Soweto describes herself as "a Sesotho girl / clever sweet beautiful."

And in Columbia, South Carolina, a group of middle- and high-school-aged Black girls composed the following poetic manifesto:

> I was royalty since birth I never doubted it.
> When times are rough, Black girls will fight in armor.
> Let them know how you are feeling.
> I cannot leave out of my house without seeing my shadow,
> Saying go away, go away,
> And then, no, stay.
> I'm hiding in my shadow, I don't want them to see that I'm unworthy.
> I put on a front, I am the shadow
> Broken and shattered when times get shallow
> My expressions are real, Black girls do you feel what I feel?
> I don't believe it because society is not trustworthy.
> Society kicks in and tells me, Black girls are:
> Ghetto
> Weak

Lazy
Dumb
Loud
But we can stand out between everyone!
Your past doesn't define you
Scream every word like it's your own testimony
We are:
Powerful (*audience repeats*)
Natural (*audience repeats*)
Important (*audience repeats*)
Genius (*audience repeats*)
Amazing (*audience repeats*)
Confident (*audience repeats*)
Strength is everything.
We stand together
Because birds of the same feather flock together.
Girls are powerful in the world's healing
We stand up after every beating
Knowing that you are with girls for girls
Gives me strength and tells me you've earned my trust
You can stand with us
It takes
Sacrifice
Honesty
Representation
Strength
Empowerment
Being Real
Defeating our shadows
Earning our trust
Not by force, but because you want to
Listening to our story
Taking action
Making us secure.

When facilitated correctly, the construction of community-style poems requires time and in-workshop revisions that must achieve group consensus. The girls from South Carolina represent a version of community and are special to me for several reasons. First, we have an ongoing relationship, which means I have had the rare opportunity to work with this core group of the same girls for multiple consecutive years. This is only by the design of educational and cultural mastermind Dr. Toby Jenkins. She collaboratively makes it possible for the SC girls to visit my campus for a special program planned by my undergraduate students in New York City and then to attend Girls Speak Out at the UN. Because Dr. Jenkins invites me to return to Columbia often as a part of the Museum of Education programming that she directs, and because of my position as codirector of Girls Speak Out, I can tailor our workshops to the theme and incorporate rural Black girls' Global North experiences into the space of the UN, where they are otherwise never centered or invited to speak. This is not an exaggeration. The UN space, on the rare occasion when girls are included, focuses intently on girls representing the Global South, or the Global North given the location of the headquarters in NYC. The girls from SC are the only US girls from the rural South who have been able to physically attend Girls Speak Out, and that is due to Dr. Jenkins's dedication and commitment. She ensures that their physical bodies are seated in the audience for the live performance and demonstrates critical intergenerational activism through this program. There is far greater depth to Dr. Jenkins's work in behalf of Black girls in South Carolina, but in this section I elevate her willingness to cooperate and collaborate with me because our relationship establishes an incredible extension to the network of girl performers in NYC who are responsible for sharing the SC girls' poetry. Girls in South Carolina use their SWP performance to literally call out and engage an audience, demanding that they embody through their call-and-response a small gesture of the larger structural issues faced by southern Black girls. The SC girls outline clear values and point deliberately to the emotional impact of racism that works to diminish them and wound their spirits, and they detail their requirements of the audience's specific support. The call to action in their poem provides a plan and a promise if their audience is willing to work with them. This poem was composed specifically for the audience at the UN, which is worth consideration given the topics these girls sought to amplify through that platform.

The SC girls open with acknowledging their birthright: "I was royalty since birth," but their inheritance does not protect them from the pain racism inflicts. Although they state, "Black girls will fight in armor," the next line encourages emotional vulnerability from one SC girl to another, and to the world: "Let them know how you are feeling." What is clear from this line is that Black girls do not always share how they feel, and certainly not with strangers. It is only when encouraged by someone they perceive as a peer or a collaborator that their poem continues to describe a "shadow" of being "unworthy." The shadow is a metaphor for how they see themselves at times.

The sense of unworthiness is exposed as the rhetoric of "society," which situates how the girls understand themselves to be influenced by a larger discourse in which they are constructed as less powerful, especially when they are isolated. To resist this isolation, they ask for support repeatedly throughout the poem, demonstrating wisdom, an applied knowledge that they are stronger when their poetic echoes are heard and responded to by other girls. Somehow, they know they are not alone in this struggle. First, they insist, "My expressions are real, Black girls do you feel what I feel?" This line is a form of political outreach, connecting with other Black girls, conjuring solidarity of experience for the sake of cohesion and support. They are strategic about the placement of that call because they must confront society:

> Society kicks in and tells me, Black girls are:
> Ghetto
> Weak
> Lazy
> Dumb
> Loud

In the performance of this poem, each of these adjectives is shouted by a different girl performer and choreographed with a movement miming physical harm being done to the girl, mimicking the action of being hit or kicked in their body. The SC girls were very specific in this staging request when they submitted their poem, because they wanted to "really show how these attitudes hurt us" and "how these lies about Black girls cause pain" (fieldnotes, 2019). As we developed the poem together, the girls started off seated around a table, five to each side. Platters of snacks and buckets of markers and pens lined the middle of the long table. When we were deciding which words to include in this section, my research assistant Shana asked the girls to "think about which words carry the most weight, you know? Which words do you hear the most about girls like you?" As the list of negative words was called out, I scrambled to keep up with their pace, writing as fast as I could on the chart paper we had taped to the wall. When we narrowed their initial list down to five, Tasha hopped up out of her chair and shifted her weight from foot to foot in excitement. "Yeah, this list just ain't right. These words are really powerful! It feels like someone is hitting you, you know, sticks and stones." Tasha gave us the inspiration for the physicality of the UN performance because of her energetic interpretation of what the words were doing to her spirit. The labels the girls included in their final version of the poem suggest that they are accustomed to stereotypes about Black girls from all aspects of a monolithic "society" likely represented through their interactions at school and portrayed by the media.

Media portrayal is fueled by the commonly researched topics specifically focused on girls from South Carolina that are centered on physical and sexual health and decision-making. Obesity and sexuality appear at the forefront of commonly researched topics around Black girls living in South Carolina (Bynum et al. 2009; Dishman et al. 2006; Felton and Bartoces 2002; Lock and Murray 1995; Pate et al. 2007). While there are some exceptions that take into consideration these girls' internal lives, agency, and decision-making processes, there is scant academic literature on contemporary Black girls specifically located in more rural southern scapes of the Global North (Ivashkevich et al. 2018; Lewis 2018; Simmons 2015). However, that does not mean that SC girls are overlooked by everyone: although overlooked by the academy, there is incredible activism taking place that engages them in identity work, leadership development, and social action. For example, Every Black Girl, Inc., which was founded by community activist Vivian Anderson after the widely publicized incident of physical violence at the hands of a school officer endured by a fifteen-year-old Black girl at her high school and her subsequent arrest. (See www.officialebg.org.) Many of the girls I work with in partnership with Dr. Jenkins are also involved with the work of EBG under Anderson's dedicated guidance. The mentorship they receive from these community women is reflected in their sophisticated and powerful poetry.

Also noteworthy is that in their poem specifically designed for a global platform and composed on a microscale with girl performers from the Bronx in mind, the words they list are not physical characteristics. This deliberate exclusion implies that the negative attributes of their behavior and personality are cast on them by society solely due to their Blackness and girlness. Black girls in SC have something to say about it. They pull on their "armor," as they let us know in the very start of their poem and call up their own memory: "Your past doesn't define you." And they bear witness with each other—"Scream every word like it's your own testimony"—also inviting the audience to join them in this act of prophetic declaration.

We are:
Powerful (*audience repeats*)
Natural (*audience repeats*)
Important (*audience repeats*)
Genius (*audience repeats*)
Amazing (*audience repeats*)

Confident (*audience repeats*)
Strength is everything.
We stand together
Because birds of the same feather flock together.

Again, the collective "we" is mirrored in the onstage performance and within the poetry itself. Black girls in SC understand that power can be compounded within a collective. The list of adjectives that the voice of the audience is invoked to repeat in concert are positive affirmations positioning the girls as leaders articulating who they are and perhaps who they want to be. They are cultivating disruption of society's discourse about Black girls, and they are conspiring with the audience to be involved. By joining voices, they generate energy that makes it possible for the girls who authored the poem as well as the girl performers to transition by the ending, "bringing about their own vision for an empowered girlhood" through SWP (Walters 2017, 26). They engineer further strategy by emphasizing the plurality of their connection with other girls and among themselves in the next lines: "Girls are powerful in the world's healing / We stand up after every beating." There is tenderness and a heart-wrenching knowingness embedded in the acknowledgment that "every beating" will mean numerous occurrences of various types of pain. The ownership of healing after these acts of violence—some physical and others emotional, spiritual, mental—for themselves and the whole world weighs heavy. The pressure on girls, particularly girls of color, to heal others in a world that positions them as most likely to experience violence is problematic and seems to carry regurgitated sediment of "the girl factor," which makes girls unfairly responsible for every member of the population's problems (Skalli 2015). Their word choice does not shoulder all the responsibility, however; it simply states "girls are powerful." Assuming a position of agency and political dissonance creates friction between the girl factor and what these girls from SC lay claim to. The last portion of the poem completely flips the girl factor script and unexpectedly holds their audience accountable for joining them and doing the work: "Knowing that you are with girls, for girls / Gives me strength and tells me you've earned my trust / You can stand with us." The SC girls give voice to their appreciation for the "strength" that they derive from "knowing you are with girls, for girls," because the audience has "earned [their] trust." The act of earning trust repositions the audience from simply receiving a message to active agents who have demonstrated their reliability to act "with girls for girls" and qualifies them to "stand with us." This is a new possibility for the audience, and as the girls have transformed throughout the stages of the poem, so have they transformed the audience through "training them for real action" (Boal 1979, 122). In tangible ways the audience is required to engage and coconstruct this performance with the girl performers. While the identity and racial categories of the audience are not addressed or even acknowledged, the girl poets have clearly staked how they understand themselves and how others perceive and interact with them. The risks are high, and the girls pay a cost because of their racialized identity. At the same time, the reward of this risky cultivated disruption is their strategic manipulation of the discourse around their raced bodies to achieve an end goal, even as they are multiplying its representational meanings by the knowledge that other girls are going to be performing a live version of their words (Gonick 2003; Richardson 2007). The audience is not the focus of the SC girls' SWP, but they are required to embody the message the performance communicates.

SC girls interface with their audience in nuanced ways, and create an alternative to their current realities and feelings of being "a shadow" or living up to how society has labeled them. This line echoes the sentiment of Sojourner Truth's photograph and quote "I sell the shadow to support the substance" (https://www.artic.edu/artworks/238249/untitled-i-sell-the-shadow-to-support-the-substance). Truth trademarked and sold her image, using the profits to support her campaign for the abolition of slavery, and her performances on the circuit to advocate the right to vote for African American women. When the girl poets write, "I am the shadow," it unintentionally recalls Truth's savviness and activism. The "shadow" is but a projection of their real selves, and yet the girls say the unknowable. The untextured shadow that Truth interpreted as her representation, an unsubstantial duplication, is equally reflective of who they are. It is impossible to fully "know" the girl poets, and yet they occupy a fragmented sense of self by utilizing race as an expression of solidarity and a desire to be seen. They specifically seek to connect with other Black girls asking, "Can you feel what I feel?" Then they push further at the crescendo, calling the audience to invest and rehearse new names for Black girls, defying the negative adjectives they are scribed with. Finally, the girl poets invert the list of characteristics once more, casting the audience in a future role of ultimate potential regardless of their identity categories. The SC girls' prophecy comes to pass through audience action, working the power of language to describe how their audience shows support through "taking action" that results in "making us secure." Future-making sounds like acknowledging the painful past to forecast an interconnected future that holds Black girls' audiences accountable for that outlook coming to pass.

Performance in Community: Girl Artist and Audience Relations

The writing and performance of SWP changes the girl poet and the girl performer. This piece was written as a manifesto to be performed by another group of girls, who were total strangers to the girl poets from SC and who had not yet been cast as girl performers for the 2019 Girls Speak Out at the time the poem was written. The girls did not know each other; they had only my explanations and the International Day of the Girl Summit website for context about how the process of compiling the script and then staging the performance would take place. The key component that links the writing to the staging is ensemble: the composing and performance are produced through the community of a *group* performance. The writing process for the poem was composed in a unique way that not every GGG workshop I conducted allowed for: a community poem, which is written by the entire group participating. Further, the poem was designed for the girls to send to another group of girls to be performed as a community piece. Composing SWP for a live performance produces an instrument that instantly reveals three things: structures, expectations, and stakes. SWP performance offers an opportunity for girls to showcase the ways "lived experience mediates how [they] express culture" (Durham 2010, 130). The SC girls' SWP works to disclose that which is actively "hidden and suppressed" by "the one-dimensional and caught in dominant ideology" of society, activating their work as revelatory and socially responsible (Becker 1994, xiii). The act of their performance overlays the personal experiences of oppression the girls have faced onto social inequalities (Brown 2013, 26). To pursue and dissect this fusion of individual and systemic processes, performance and SWP must be considered foremost as a relationship, which is what these art forms offer us at their core. Examining this relationship allows for reflexivity between the artist, the art form, and the audience, and these components are necessary for tracing the small moves made by girls. The synergy of words to action and back again must be diligently attended to if we are to conceptualize and rehearse useful means of creating revolution (Freire 2000, 88). Tracking the quantum justice leaps the girls are pointing toward through their creativity may just lead us all to a freer place.

Social expectations and their consequences are exposed through performance as power dynamics that scribe the relationship of the audience and the artist through SWP. There are—at least—two sets of expectations made visible during performance: those of the audience member and those taken for granted through a discourse of normative social expectations. Power carves each of these sets of expectations and, conversely, illuminates how they might be resisted. Oftentimes audience members at performances rely upon their position offstage to circumvent any participation in the realities constructed through a performance. This false sense of voyeurism is interrupted and impeded during SWP performances, because the act of performance cultivates disruption of what feminist film scholar Laura Mulvey (1975) famously coined "the male gaze." This gaze falsely secures the audience as spectators and creates a "sense of separation" between what is happening in a performance and their own participation (8). This critique is furthered by bell hooks (1992) in film studies; she extends it to specifically analyze the consequences when Black people "dare to look back" at the ways in which they are constructed in history and in popular culture, thus developing even in the worst historic moments a form of agency through the "oppositional gaze" (208). She offers an interpretation of how the SC girls demand their audience become implicated—as witnesses, critics, and analysts to their Black girl experience rather than remain passive recipients who are simply entertained but not held responsible (Langellier 1998). The SC girls don't just defy discursive narratives by representing themselves; instead, they "formulate transgressive identity" by "knowing the present and inventing the future" (hooks 1992, 220). The audience are consumers of Black girl genius and culture and are made to share citizenship within the oppressive present through the event of performance poetry. Reckoning with the ways we are also coconstructing a present that upholds systems of domination is unpleasant and painful for an audience invested in maintaining the status quo, because we benefit from systems of White supremacy and privilege. As a result, ownership and responsibility for outcomes of social change are shifted into a burden the (often majority) White audience at the UN must bear along with the girl artist. In this case, the SC girls incorporate the rages of their past, and the NYC girl performers embody those meanings and pivot them based on their experiences. The audience at Girls Speak Out reconstructs how they must claim their own share of responsibility for the future outcome of the SC girls as original authors of the SWP, as well as the NYC girl performers' reincarnation of the piece. Any new futures that are to be imagined as liberatory must disrupt comfort (Freire and Macedo 1993). Performance allows for a cultivation of what that disruption might be and simultaneously brings forth an examination of these systems, because it makes visible "the sincere, visual expression of the ideology and psychology of the participants" (Boal 1979, 137). These ideologies are multiple and contradictory. Therefore, the role of the audience during a SWP performance is one of cocreation in the meaning of the event, actors who engage the oppositional gaze and extend that gaze into action (Denzin 2003). Audiences typically resist this implied participation in both the performance and the reality it re-creates. Quantum justice harnesses that resistance as energy for the girl performers to leap further, lengthening the arc of the SWP from SC to NYC to the world via the livestream of the Girls Speak Out performance and, even now in this moment, because you are reading their words. But we can never fully know the future, because in the instance of the performance, it is still loading, still pending. The quantum justice leaps that manifest through the analysis documented here are ongoing. Our role in negotiating the "oppositional gaze" is one that is bursting with possibility; we can actively contribute to disrupting mainstream expectations by our participation in cocreating new knowledge during the performance alongside the girl performers. Or we can work to stabilize and further entrench the expectations we hold. Either way, we as the audience are complicit.

The unpredictability of the audience at a performance of SWP also reveals stakes, or who has skin in the game, literally, because performance features the body of the artist. SWP like the piece written by the SC girls provides an explicit example of an embodied act of performance that intentionally points out racial injustices through the words and the bodies of the girl performers. In this way, their SWP effectively challenges the powerful status quo represented by the audience based on their lived experience. Such an engagement assigns value to the words of the girl poets and the bodies of the girl performers, making evident their own investment in social change and their audience's complicity in choosing to join them or not. The stakes are incredibly high for girls of color, whether poets or performers. This is dangerous discursive work for an already marginalized group, and their work always carries the possibility for further disenfranchisement. No matter how empowered we would like to imagine girls in the Global North to be, the structures and expectations that are immediately revealed through SWP and performance also soberly remind us of what is at stake for the girls of color who dare to participate. Adrienne Rich (1994) observes

> When those who have the power to name and to socially construct reality choose not to see you or hear you . . . there is a moment of disequilibrium, as if you looked in the mirror and saw nothing. It takes some strength of soul . . . collective understanding, to resist this void, this non-being into which you are thrust, and to stand up, demanding to be seen and heard. (1)

Transforming the structures and expectations that confine and endanger Black girls requires the sort of joined efforts that are demonstrated through the SC girls' connection to the girl performers in NYC, and their audience beyond them. The SC girls and, later, the NYC girl performers enact resistance to authority in their refusal to enable dominant scripts about Black girls. They situate society as having poorly understood them, and their refusal corresponds with a praxis of critical performance pedagogy (Boal 1979). These are the poetic echoes that shape transformation in all its unpredictable and immeasurable extensions.

Although most of this work does not occur within a traditional schooling experience, it is important to note the overlaps with the arena of education. Black girls talking back and making decisions about race in each of their contradicting conditions and global locations carries implications for emancipatory relationships. Education scholars with a variety of specializations have argued for SWP as an effective tool for social justice in the classroom and suggest that because SWP utilizes the strengths of the community, it shifts the process of teaching and learning from a deficit-based framing to that of an asset-based approach, which is elemental to transformative pedagogy (Biggs-El 2012; Desai and Marsh 2005; Jocson 2005; Kinloch 2005; Morrell 2005; Paris and Alim 2017; Stovall 2006). Performance pedagogy demands acknowledgment and respect for the performer's body and identity, and simultaneously mandates the audience acknowledge and participate in the performance. There are potentially powerful outcomes available through SWP. Artist and audience are producers of knowledge during a SWP performance, decomposing what Deborah Britzman (1998) calls the "linear relation between teaching and learning and between knowledge and conduct" (139). Unsettling this arrangement can offer inspirational results when reinventing the position, alliances, and power that scribes socially normative expectations and the structures made obvious through SWP performance (Davies 2000). This possibility requires what Chicana feminist Cherrie Moraga (1981) writes as a struggle, which is an internal one for each of us:

> . . . for each of us in some way has been both oppressed and the oppressor. We are afraid to look at how we have failed each other. We are afraid to see how we have taken the values of our oppressor into our hearts and turned them against ourselves and one another. (32)

Cultivating disruption boldly confronts this fear as a theoretical framework rooted in performance praxis and social justice, and wrestles it constantly on behalf of the educator, the researcher, and the artist. How do we write and reflect and live to love and teach in these spaces with girls of color? How are we held accountable? How do we become "trustworthy," as the poem calls us, disassociating us from the "society" that "kicks in" with negative projections of Black girls, perhaps setting a hopeful if too lofty goal for the audience? How might White Western feminists in the Global North engage with their whiteness and their privilege even as they are positioned to advocate for the students of color they teach and work with? How can the White folks in the Global North represented robustly in the audience members at the Girls Speak Out performance in the UN headquarters engage with the conviction they are expected to respond with during the girls' performance? How does the practice of call-and-response through cultivating disruption rehearse new configurations of relationships between key players? The SC girls created their poem through a community exercise to be performed by an unknown ensemble of girl performers, putting into practice the "collective understanding" that Rich (1994) insists is necessary to continue resisting the silenced hypervisibility that they experience as Black girls. Poetic echoes provide a way to listen through, to hear the many voices of many people as well as the multiple voices of a single individual (Gonick 2003). Community-mindedness is woven in the fabric of this experience; deep listening and call-and-response are modeled through the creation and performance of SWP.

Embodying Contradicting Conditions

Eventually the SC girls' poem shared here became the second performance piece in the 2019 Girls Speak Out script. The show began, opened first by the girl performers' own "Crossroads" poems, and then they immediately transitioned into the SC girls' poem. The girl performers and I blocked the whole poem in one rehearsal, and the girls were hype. The blocking process for this piece was atypically smooth, and the girls were full of energy as we tracked the staging. This portion of a rehearsal usually takes up more time and involves more trial and error, as the procedure is stop-and-go, start-and-pause. Most early rehearsals for a theater production are focused on script readings and staging that include long pauses for "holding" as the stage managers and directors work one-on-one with actors. Not every performer is actively engaged in the scene being staged, and concentrating during these holds has sometimes proven difficult for the girl performers. After our script reading, they had strong reactions to this poem:

LUNA: Wow! You mean they wrote this—
SIERRA: Wait, how many of them were there?
AMY: This is so good, I just, I just feel it!
IVY: Yeah, I feel it too!
ATHENA: Do you think they're going to talk back, like when we need them to?
AMY: Yeah, how will they know—
CRYSTAL: Well, you will be talking back to each other, so if they don't respond, you won't need them. But if they do—
IVY: Oh, so we're showing them—
CAROLINE: Right, you're doing what you want the audience to do.
AMY: Do we give them the mic? Or—
ATHENA: I'm not doing that!
LUNA: No, I'm not doing that (laughs).
ATHENA: Can we, can we do this one again?

The girl-performers were talking over one another and across each other, loose and fast, scripts in hand. There was palpable energy in the room, zinging from their voices and flicking from their hands. The girl-performers experienced this SWP on a visceral plane, engaging the girls in what Cynthia Biggs-El (2012) suggests is the reflexive power of performance that subverts racial oppression and calls forth social justice. The SC girls' poetic echoes were reverberating through the bodies of the girl-performers from the Bronx. This evidences that Hip-hop feminism was at work, physicalizing the theoretical praxis into our rehearsal space, moving through quantum justice to shift the girl-performers into contact with the SC girls via poetry. This poem, rooted in racial identification, reminded the girls that our creative work is not abstract but involves "real places populated by real bodies" (Petchauer 2012, 30). At every rehearsal from then on, this piece anchored the girl performers. It became our anthem and guaranteed me as director a sure way of resecuring the girl performers' focus on our mission during our meetings. Through their performance, community was being created, and although the connection was a result of personal pain springing from racial injustices, the act of performing created a new world, a new stratum where the girls could commune with each other (Weinstein 2009). The girls are able to attempt multiple drafts of their racial and cultural identities only because of what they hear and learn from each other. Spiritual ways of knowing were strengthened through their embodied knowledge and rehearsal of a response to the SC girls' call.

Great Expectations:
Internalized Doubt and Conflict

I'm beautiful
I'm grateful and proud of who I am
sometime I look down at myself
I tell myself I'm beautiful but sometimes if there is just that little voice telling me this
thinking that
I have defeated it and look where I am today
I am proud
I'm proud of who I am
I'm proud to be a black African girl
I'm proud of what I have I'm proud of where I am
I am proud of being me

TSHINOLOG, SOWETO

Tshinolog from Soweto shares a very transparent piece of poetry about overcoming of internal conflict. There is a poetic echo of internalized doubt and discouragement in Tshinolog's poem that is rooted in racial identification. However, she does not cower from the interior debate that troubles her; instead, she describes it for us as "sometime I look down at myself." Tshinolog begins her poem by declaring, "I'm beautiful," before she reveals the inner voice that nags her with doubt. She doesn't divulge any specific external factors that may cause her to "look down," but that does not mean that the conflict she experiences is of her own making. Rather, her SWP serves as evidence of the maltreatment she faced due to her physical appearance, as well as providing her with ideas about how to maneuver through her downward perspective: "I tell myself I'm beautiful but sometimes if there is just that little voice telling me this / thinking that." One barrier that she perceives to her own success emerges as a result of insecurity about how she looks to others. Her internal struggle with self-esteem stands out given the lack of attention that race and beauty within Soweto have garnered from the scholarly community. South African scholars Ntombela and Mashiya (2009) conducted a comparative study of memory work about girlhood between two generations of KwaZulu-Natal women who experienced apartheid. They concluded that girlhood is subjective and not universal, yet "gendered expectations and roles remain basically the same," particularly in terms of domestic and household duties across the generations (106). Although this group of women experienced various stages of apartheid in South Africa, race or color did not warrant a mention throughout their recounted memories of girlhood. In 1994 the South African government reversed its apartheid structure to that of a political democracy after years of legislation that organized and violently enforced racial segregation in all aspects of public life, including education, politics, and social interactions between Black and White people, which created traumatic impact (Everatt and Zulu 2001; Ferns and Thom 2001; Gaganakis 2003, 2004; Kamper and Badenhorst 2010). Bhana (1999) offers historical insight into how this legacy of race in South Africa continues to be situated:

> In post-apartheid South Africa, the category of race continued to be given some salience. Race has become a powerful and legitimate category for analysis in social research because it appears to be "natural and obvious." (23)

The history of apartheid influences how Black people living in South Africa seek out community and maintain a vested interest in positive group outcomes as an underlying proponent of any individual decision making (Moosa et al. 1997). Accordingly, girls in Soweto making decisions about race are likely interested in a sense of common good for their community and rely on particular social codes and discourses at their disposal for signifying and re-membering how they want to represent to other girls through SWP (Durham 2014). Tshinolog's poetry reflects tensions she might be feeling between her self-representation, her ability to evolve, and her desire to connect to other girls.

Margie Gaganakis (2006) specifically explores the ways that South African adolescent girls living in townships construct and engage with race and why that occurs, and counters with the suggestion that "the celebration of race as a form of analysis reinforces the idea that the categories of race are necessary differences . . . predicated upon nature and discriminate on the basis of these differences, as 'self and other'" (363). Therefore, race is also a relational process deeply etched with power dynamics even as it is derived from historic trauma and thus "continued to be mobilized in different ways, both to support and oppose cultural constructions of local identity" for girls in South Africa (364). In terms of subjectivity, the meaning of Blackness morphs for girls like Tshinolog depending upon immediate context, allowing her to adapt to the landscape of school, township, and other social contexts she moves through with some flexibility. Post-apartheid Black South African adolescents typically formulate identity rooted in the values of their immediate families "wherein stable traditional values and norms [are] still forming the basis of their development" (Kamper and Badenhorst 2010, 245). Given the years of legally enforced discrimination against their Blackness and ethnic identity, turning toward family and kin provides a sense of security (Ferns and Thom 2001). A sense of collectivism, interdependence, and concern for the overall well-being of the group become embedded family values (Brown 2001).

When Tshinolog asserts, "I am proud to be a Black African girl," she summons all the one-dimensional reductiveness of a generality and its historical Otherness to invert and implode those projections of inadequacy from Western and internalized White supremacy that are cast on girls like her. This tactic is one that, following Brown (2001), Gaganakis foregrounds in her study. She suggests that the all-encompassing label of "African" should be understood as a usable political identity but one that does not discount the diverse communities with different local customs that stratify this category. Political and racial solidarity offers a complicated understanding of how girls in the Global North are reading race and the multiple ways girls in the Global South might employ or identify with it (Mafe 2010). Tshinolog engages the fluctuation of her racial identity and represents important parts of her to an audience of unknowable girls, which shows how her race and geographic location within the Diaspora reconstructs her, moving fluidly from her location and imagination to those of other girls. She has claimed victory over "the little voice telling [her] this thinking" and "defeated it," instructing her audience to "look where I am today." The act of overcoming is not attributed to external messaging. She chooses to link herself with a community that has endured a long history of oppression and continues to be excluded from access to resources and political agency, and to interpret her choice as one of belonging, inclusion, and importance. She asserts "where [she is] today" as triumph, although she remains ambiguous about why she wrestled with "telling myself I'm beautiful." Her "where" or physical location has not literally changed, but she marks her changed mind-set as propelling her into a new space, and her writing provides insight about her inner world (Mtashali 1988). Does she perceive herself as missing something, some element of beauty? We are not given any further explanation, which produces ambiguity through her poetry, leaving us, her audience, to sort out what we want to understand. Her audience is limited to their interpretation of the words "I am proud" repeated through every remaining line of her poem. Does the repetition convince Tshinolog that she is, indeed, confident? Does it persuade us, her audience, of her security? Or is Tshinolog actively working to imagine and forecast a version of herself that is swayed to believe she is satisfied and assured? These questions persist, while Tshinolog willingly embodies this "situationally specific" knowledge and reconstitutes herself out of her doubt and into her confidence (Gaganakis 2006, 362). She is not racialized until the moment she takes up her identity as a "black African girl," and the reason for her pride becomes obvious to her audience.

By conjuring the popular culture representations and GID discourses that construct her "black African" identity *and* her girlhood, Tshinolog disrupts shallow readings that position her as confined in those representations. She refuses to be read in ways that neglect to engage her in the ways articulated by the SC girls and her own immediate cultural context. She reproduces a version of herself, drawing us from her private, inner debate with doubt into sweeping, politicized identity categories. She is "proud of where I am" and "proud of where I'm from" invoking her geography in Soweto, laying personal claim to the same locations that housed Freedom Fighters and sheltered Winnie Mandela during the revolutionary resistance that turned the tides of apartheid, and yet the area remains impoverished. The legacy of brutal wars to gain legislated freedoms for South Africa do not appear lost on this grade seven girl, yet, as young as she is, she is also aware that the rights promised to citizens like her have not all made their way into the fabric of everyday life. Further, Tshinolog made an important distinction between her present ("where I am") and her past ("where I'm from"), which reconstitutes her subjectivity within a broad cultural context. "Where I'm from" may refer to this history of anticolonial resistance that is orchestrated in part from the home base of the area where she lives and goes to school. "Where I am" may indicate her personal achievements, attending a private school where she is physically located during our workshop when she constructed her SWP, and the tuition for school, which marks her family either as financially viable or, conversely, as recipients of an income-based tuition scholarship. Or this may refer to broader Soweto again, young in its current state of political sovereignty, well regarded for its triumphant upheaval, and sometimes very dangerous or unpredictable for a girl like her. Where Tshinolog currently or formerly "is" does not entirely make the point. I am led to wonder if, instead, she is reading the room; is she negotiating her location materially, physically, and subjectively, based on her reading of where and how power might be located and accessed for her? She seems to echo an acknowledgment of shame or embarrassment yet performs how she tracks the moments when she reverses and repents of those perceptions of herself.

I am also led to wonder if Tshinolog employs her declaration of being "proud" as a counter to uphold the normative expectations of her household or her school setting (Ntombela and Mashiya 2009). If identity is a basis from which individuals make decisions, then what does Tshinolog's pivotal pride mean for her decision-making processes as a girl, and what is she showcasing for the girls in NYC who she knows will be receiving her SWP? FemAl, a collective of South African feminists, have documented the ways the constitutionally promised end to discrimination from apartheid continues to fall short of the everyday lives of women and girls (2011). Their critique of the government's shortcomings extends to the schools, leadership, and other sociopolitical tenets of neoliberal patriarchal capitalism that "has contributed to the masking of power distribution . . . [that] leaves growing violence in its wake" and is fueled by racial discrimination (Essof and Wesso 2011, xi). However, art practices are one avenue of combating the injustices faced by women and girls in various South African contexts, such that "art can act as a space of encounter, where the meaning[s] of the piece[s] are constantly being reproduced by the audience, regenerating and revealing histories/herstories, sharing struggles, and proposing questions to think differently about how we relate to ourselves and our community" (xxv). Tshinolog's SWP creates an encounter of the quantum justice kind, allowing NYC girls a deep reading of one aspect of her emotional and mental self-perception and decision making. Tshinolog can reach them because of their willingness to be vulnerable to cautiously explore "the emotional risk of self-revelation" (Weinstein 2010, 19). This encounter could have occurred only through SWP and provokes an investigation of race, traces its historic impact, and offers a chance to make a different decision.

Making Decisions in the Face of Contradicting Conditions

Plaited together, these poetic excerpts represent various stages of consciousness entered by global girls together and spotlights the deep revelation and agency that SWP offers when girls can encounter one another. The SC girls instigated a movement of critical consciousness raising that flowed through Soweto, and the Bronx; put the girls in poetic conversation with each other; and provokes them to "analyze their own social and cultural practices for recognizing inequalities" (Gonick 2003, 52). Their critiques examine and deconstruct discourse about race as a natural or inevitable force, and SWP performance allows them to "abstract" and transcend the social construction of race and the power hierarchies acted through it (Shor and Freire 1987). Transcendence does not ignore the structural, institutional, and ideological nexus that works to constrain the girls due to their Blackness. Rather, it concretizes those limitations to make visible the boundless possibility that they imagine together through performance, for "words build worlds" (Cornwall and Brock 2005, 1056). Girls build and dismantle such worlds to encounter one another and in so doing multiply opportunities to disrupt again (Ginwright 2010). Together they have affirmed and critiqued one another and the larger discourses about their lives (Giroux and McLaren 1992). As girls occupy the canyons of racial identity, they are becoming the shadow and screaming their own testimony until it echoes, boomeranging the lyrics between girl poet and girl performer across community.

Even as we attempt to recognize a transnational community, girls describe how their voices are not listened to in either a local or global landscape. Geography and false borders fail them. Most girls represented in this project, even when located in the Global North, lacked access to power that could be attributed to the same reason they are so visible and yet silenced: their Blackness or Indigeneity (or proximity to either), their social position, and the rules governing their local social interactions. The highly regulated discursive space where girlhood happens is contested and misconstrued. Visibility for girls often means increased policing that results in violent punishment for any behavior that is not deemed acceptable or appropriate, and "the Girl Effect paradigm functions to constrain girls' political agency and subjectivity," further exacerbating the inequities experienced by girls of color (Bent 2013a, 4). Violent responses to hypervisible girls of color are steeped in racist histories and traditions that inform contemporary education, religion, and global media (Epstein et al. 2017). These traditions raise the question of who stands to gain from GID discourses and how girls of color are operationalizing them.

Communities are the systems and networks that reflect girls' realities back to them in stark and undeniable ways. The poetic echoes resounding throughout and across those networks disrupt the expectations that local and global communities project onto girlhoods. Decision making is considered one of the key areas determining the impact of global development on girls (Herz and Sperling 2004; Temin and Levine 2009). The poetic echo of Making Decisions was especially audible in the SWP by girls in GirlForward (www.girlforward.org), a nonprofit organization focused on supporting displaced refugee girls. The vibrations are equally legible within the microscale of localized interpretations of community, such as home or school experiences, as well as across the macroscale of the girls' global poetic networks. Quantum justice theory propels us into a local leap where autonomy and self-sufficiency tug on girls as they move, even as they are rendered as vulnerable subjects in need of protection. Within this poetic echo, girls seek to rework the categories of girlhood available to them, even as they are managed and restricted by them.

CHAPTER 3

"Always Giving Something Up"

Decision Making and Subjectivity

All the arts-based workshops I have ever had the opportunity to host happened at the informal invitations of a friend of a friend who made an introduction. I was raised not to go where I haven't been invited. Translated into my artistic practice and professional career, this means I rely on a network of other artists and educators who also straddle multiple planes, and my personal quantum justice leaps often catapult me into unknown geographic locations but familiar forms of relationship. Such connections are what I rely on to ease the navigation of unfamiliar terrain, emotional attachments, and my creative stability. Discomfort frequently accompanies a quantum justice leap because adults working with girls intentionally centering feminist advocacy should somehow shift or destabilize power in relationships. Moving in unstable environments at speeds of processes that you cannot control are part and parcel of performance work *and* authentic work with girls. The insecurity that is often generated by quantum justice work can feel discouraging, alienating, and unsettling. So can the creative process. I foreground these thoughts as reminders because the poetic echo that guides this leap lands us at a crossroads of girls negotiating subjectivity through decision making. The first section begins with the SWP and photovoice by refugee girls in GirlForward, an organization that offers programming "dedicated to creating and enhancing opportunities for girls who have been displaced by conflict and persecution," especially designed to support "refugees, immigrants, and asylum seekers" (www.girlforward.org). Girls who are refugees from communities beyond US borders who now live in Chicago, Illinois, demonstrate how existing at the crossroads of adulthood and girlhood can be simultaneously empowering and dangerous. This small, tightly knit group of friends shared easy chatter, and their laughter set a warm atmosphere during my visit. The girls were diverse in racial phenotype, and each one was eager to share her poems, design her photovoice projects, and learn more about the other girls who were a part of GGG. Two of the girls, Claudia and Esther, both aged seventeen, arrived in Chicago about a year earlier from different communities on the African continent. They were seniors in high school, and our conversations were peppered with questions about college, boys, and careers. Although girls like Claudia and Esther currently live in the US, they exist between the status of citizen and refugee and seek out resources via the GirlForward program to supplement their public education. The conversations we had throughout the workshop made it clear that each of the girls was persistently aware of the ways their status as refugees or immigrants destabilized them and set them apart from their peers at school, although the topic never surfaced explicitly in their poetry.

The girls attended the GGG program voluntarily; they showed up knowing I was coming to do this workshop, and the safe space programs are drop-in optional. In other words, the girls could receive the other benefits of the program even if they opted out of my workshop. Although not considered part of a "development" agenda because it is run stateside in the US, the GirlForward program overlaps GID goals in some ways because it seeks to redress issues that result from the aftermath of the intersecting forces of colonialism. We began the workshop with poems about what it means to be a girl. Their poetry provides examples of how girls use SWP to navigate their identities when their context changes, negotiating their diversity of experience by "forging connections among themselves to subvert the processes of political and economic restructuring that have marginalized their knowledge and agency" (Swai 2010, 4). Their relationship with one another adds a key aspect of dynamic friendship between girls onto the analysis of their poetry. Political definitions of girlhood on a macro plane offer a starting point for feminist challenges of those definitions based on the girls' poetics. From there we zoom in to the micro-plane experiences of education across global girls' communities. Girls contest the girlhood and subjectivity assigned to them and what that entails for their daily lives, and they utilize SWP to cultivate disruption of the category of "girl." Competing desires that shape their decision-making processes are audible through their performances. We started one spring afternoon, and when I first met with the girls in Chicago, I had no idea what to expect.

"I Want So Much More": Navigating the In-Between and Beyond

I could smell burnt popcorn as soon as I opened the door. The afternoon sun, warm for Chicago in April, was heating up the right side of my body and cast my left side in cool shadow. I double-checked the address and swung the heavy door open. As the warm air from inside the building enveloped me, I could hear heavily accented girl voices, rising in emphasis and then dropping back to a murmur, but I couldn't see anyone. The burnt smell got stronger as I walked toward the light in the adjoining doorway. My nose wrinkled. "Hello?" I called. Bright paint—turquoise blue and yellow—dominated the walls. Comfortable-looking pillows and couches, books stuffed into bookshelves, several whiteboards, and braided rugs with no particular design made the space feel welcoming, as if I belonged. I stepped behind the desk to take a closer look at the art on the wall behind it when I heard someone chirp, "Hi!" I nearly jumped out of my skin. I hadn't heard any footsteps, and I was a little embarrassed at wandering so deep into the room unescorted. I turned quickly and said in a rush, "Oh hi, I'm Crystal I am here to do a workshop? I didn't see anyone when I walked in and I wasn't sure . . ." A giant, bright smile lit up the face of the petite brown-skinned girl standing there, one hand on her hip. I noticed her red Converse sneakers and her delicate nose ring made of bright gold. She reached out her arms and squealed, "Hi! I'm Mariana, we have been emailing!" I was so happy, because she was reaching to hug me and affirmed I was in the right place. Her hug reassured me. This was going to be fine, right? "Come with me!" She kept an arm at my waist as she reached to carry my book bag. "It stinks in here, right? They burnt the popcorn, again!" Mariana walked me across the threshold of the door, and I could see four other girls, talking to each other. One especially tall and slender dark-skinned girl hopped up out of her seat to greet me. "I'm Claudia," she said with a small wave. Around the table the girls introduced themselves, some with more enthusiasm than others. I exclaimed, "Wow! You're all so beautiful!" It was true, and my social awkwardness made me say it aloud. Claudia looked to her friend, Esther, who froze with her hand halfway to her mouth with popcorn. They burst into giggles.

We completed the first half of the workshop, where the girls followed my prompts to compose poems. We shared them aloud, and since there were only five of us that afternoon, things had gotten personal in our discussions. The girls were at ease in an intimate setting, and we lingered over the performances of their poems, unpacking and revising their rough drafts. The girls' next task was to select the most powerful line from their poems to design a hashtag sign. They would hold the hashtag signs as part of the photovoice portion of our workshop and take portraits. "Eh eh! You want me to take my photo for these other girls? Let me make sure I look my best," exclaimed Claudia as she slipped her fingers through her belt loops to readjust her jeans, pedaling her feet. She flipped her hair from one side to another. "You look gorgeous! Like a model, anyway. Come on, I'll take yours and you take mine." Mariana rushed Claudia along. I passed off the digital camera to Mariana and turned to Sarah, who was laughing at Claudia but remained seated beside Esther. Esther was hunched over her paper, deep in silent concentration. I could still hear Mariana laughing loudly with Claudia. "It's a portrait, Claudia, not a photo shoot!" I caught Sarah's eye as I pulled out a chair across from her and Esther. "Have you decided what your line will be, Sarah?" She was so soft-spoken I had to concentrate carefully to hear what she said. "I think so. I think I like this one best." She pointed to her paper with one hand and with the other tucked her tight curls behind her ear. Vanessa leaned over the table to read upside down, the ends of her straight black hair brushing my arm. Vanessa nodded solemnly, "Yes," she agreed, "that's a good line. Hmm . . . maybe I should do mine over." Her forehead scrunched up as she inspected her sign, which was sketched in pencil. She glanced up at the GirlForward coordinator, who was seated at her desk catching up on work and not paying us any attention. Vanessa whispered, "But I'm going to make some more popcorn first." Esther, without looking up, slid the half-empty bowl across the table to Vanessa. "Yes, please. And don't leave it in for so long this time!" Sarah and I smiled. I watched Vanessa walk away and turned back to Esther. "Are you stuck, Esther? Do you want to show me what you have so far?" I toyed with the cord of the second digital camera that I was still holding. With a dramatic sigh, Esther sat back in her chair. "I can't choose just one line for my hashtag. I want the girls to read the whole thing." I nodded. "I know it's hard. That's sort of the point. They'll see your entire poem and the photo, too." "Where did you say this was going again? Somewhere in the country before New York City?" Esther asked, narrowing her eyes. I laughed aloud then. "Yes, all of your poems and photos are going to a school in New Orleans next, for the girls there. Then they will be a part of Girls Speak Out in the fall. You'll be able to see all the portraits online during the show." Esther looked over her paper. "Well, tell them they can't possibly know me in one line. Tell them even in the poem, it's only part, it's a true part, but a part. But just tell them there is more, okay? I want so much more."

DECISION MAKING AND SUBJECTIVITY

To Be a Girl Is to Be a Woman: SWP Transgressing Girlhood

SWP allows us to imagine ways to transgress the normalized discourses we participate in and can be used to create disruption to the category of the girl (hooks 1994). Claudia's poem complicates easy readings of refugee girlhood in a US-based context and provides a rich example of instances when her girlhood is oppressive and yet "worth it." She leverages poetry as a discursive tool to explore how power scripts her admission to normative westernized girlhood *and* restricts access to belonging according to which version of "girl" her home community recognizes in East Africa. This shifting between identity categories accounts for Claudia's first line, "to be a girl is to be a woman," which indicates she is acutely aware that she is not always recognized or allowed to participate in the rights and responsibilities that scribe either category, and that social categories are slippery (Davies et al. 2004). Others have the power to determine how she performs as a girl, which is obvious to Claudia because she does not always participate willingly or to her benefit in either discourse. Her partial participation demonstrates an attendance to the differences between herself and others, "finding commonality in difference while not compromising its distinctive realities and effects" (Gentile in Orner 1992, 85). Understanding Claudia's partial and unwilling participation in varied discourses of girlhood allows us to explore her cultural construct of what it means to be a girl, because culture is utilized as a tool for coping and is a hotly contested site of struggle. Leith Mullings (2000) reminds us that ideology impacts perspective and that circumstances can shift ideology. To manage both her environment and response, Claudia situates herself as a negotiator and uses SWP to explore how she will make decisions.

> To be a girl where I come from its to be an educated and also responsible woman who can take
> care of herself and family
> to be a girl is also to be able to make the right decisions and take risks
> to be a girl is awful
> to be able to care for her children
> to be a girl is also to have pride and also to serve as a role model to others
> loving Queen
> emotional, good friends, having an image of yourself
> to be a girl is to be respectful to those older or to be a girl is to be brave and respectful

to be a girl is to have a good self-esteem and be self-confident
to be a girl is to be caring and supportive
to be a girl has to say no sometime to some things
to be a girl is to be able to stand for people you care about
to be a girl is to love Korean culture like me
to be a girl is also to be able to handle and manage money
to be a girl is to love someone and to be loved
to be a girl is to be powerful and influential
to be a girl it's always say I cannot

to be a girl is to encourage others
it's having to wear things to cover
to stand-out unique outstanding confused make mistakes
to be a girl is worth it.

CLAUDIA, CHICAGO

The very first line of Claudia's poem demonstrates for us the explicit demands girls experience in the contradictory space of becoming: the overlapping social status of girl and woman. Claudia uses the terms "responsibility" and "educated" as qualifiers that determine whether a girl/woman is "taking care of her family." What are the "right decisions," and how does a girl know "when to take risks" and which risks to take? Claudia does not specify those personal crossroads; however, she is clear that the skill of savvy navigation is critical when making decisions. Her next line tells us unequivocally that "to be a girl is awful," right before informing us that "tak[ing] care of her children" is part of girlhood. Family responsibility seems to be the immediate and primary focus of what it means to be a girl for Claudia, because her poem leads with these expectations. After all, if the girls' subjectivity is coconstructed by language "in ways that are historically and locally specific," then "what something means to individuals is dependent on the discourses available to them" (Richardson and St. Pierre 2005, 961). Claudia's version of girlhood translates her experiences within the discourses through which she makes sense of her life.

The next few lines of her poem launch into other aspects of her internal attitudes and approaches to those around her: "emotional, good friends, having an image of yourself" all imply that relationships with others shape how she sees her own image. Do all these behaviors help to strengthen her "good self-esteem and [to] be self-confident"? We are not told, but characteristics like "caring and supportive" further emphasize the attention and high priority that a girl gives to others. If "to be a girl is to be respectful to those older," then how older people perceive a girl's demonstration of that respect carries consequences. I am led to wonder what Claudia means by the second half of this statement: "or, to be a girl is to be brave and respectful." Why does she associate bravery with respect? Who determines what is considered respectful behavior?

These questions from Claudia's poem mobilize a brief quantum justice leap to Tshelofelo, a grade seven primary school student from Soweto, who also writes explicitly about respect: "I respect those older than me, and my friends too." This indicates that respect for Tshelofelo is not reserved just for her elders but is given to her friends as well. Maybe a relationship of respect should be reciprocal among peers who might not ordinarily be considered deserving of it. Although younger than Claudia, Tshelofelo seems to set up rules of engagement with others in her social relationships, and this excerpt from her poem might mean that her rules apply to elders as well as girls. The performance of "respect" can take on many localized social versions, including swift and unquestioning obedience to requests and demands made by parents, teachers, or other authority figures, politeness in conversation, and other types of social etiquette. If this is true, then Tshelofelo has remixed this definition, because she would not ordinarily obey the other grade seven girls who are her friends, but she may negotiate with them. If respect can become a negotiation between girls, then Tshelofelo is perhaps pushing back against blind obedience to her elders in favor of a more equitable social relationship that includes dialogue and compromise. Such communication is what one might expect from a "friend." This pushback informs us of Tshelofelo's determination that to be a girl must also mean entering new social contracts. She makes a decision that will likely result in consequences, for it is beyond the social norm adhered to in her community. The assertion of oneself through the act of setting boundaries in relationships is another characteristic of the decision-making poetic echo for girls.

Indeed, the theme of decision making and exercising personal relationship boundaries is acknowledged in Claudia's poem through her next line: "to be a girl has to say no sometime to some things / to be a girl is to be able to stand for people you care about." Here, Claudia concedes the need to "say no," which indicates two things. First, she is aware that being a girl means she is mostly expected to acquiesce to what is asked of her. Given the current flood of social media posts that encourage girls and women at different stages to exercise their right to refuse obligations, unwanted attention, or undeserved negativity, this assumption is reasonable. Although she does not specifically name this practice as setting boundaries, what she describes is a form of doing exactly that, determining access and boundaries as part of her identity. Second, she must decide when and what to say no to; although she does not explicitly name sex, I read sexual implications in this line. Her acknowledgment of consent is clear, and her acceptance of the responsibility of saying "no" signals broader societal demands on girls' sexuality. The responsibility that rape culture assigns to girls to control or resist male sexuality remains pervasive and oppressive. I set this thought back down in this moment only because Claudia—and in fact *none* of the girls in any of the GGG locations—addresses sex or sexuality in her SWP. The striking absence of sex is not that unusual, and girls avoid the topic for many reasons that I won't attempt to unpack here. According to Claudia, to be a girl is to make up her mind and deploy her own agenda.

Part of that agenda includes action, given her next line, "to stand for people you care about." The relationships that determine so much of her experience being a girl position Claudia as responsible for herself and for others. Standing for people implies that Claudia exercises resistance against some unnamed force on behalf of others whom she "cares about." Claudia's decisions to protect or defend others are driven by her capacity to care for them. It is important to note that she protects people to the point of anonymity. Those in need of her defense remain vague, only generically described in her poem; even though girls like Tshelofelo who might later read Claudia's poetry and write according to the same poetry prompts would have no way to identify whom she is "standing for." The people she cares about deserve her defense and protection inclusive of their reputations, yet Claudia is still cautious about revealing their weaknesses. Holistically "caring for" someone gives us a clue about how relationships and girlhood should be enacted according to Claudia. Mutual protection, an exchange of bravery, is valuable.

Next, the poem plunges us unexpectedly into intimacy with a revelation about Claudia's personality, because she describes another layer of being a girl is "to love Korean culture." During the workshop Claudia shared that she was originally from Uganda, and her adamant emphasis on her "love" of Korean culture made me smile. After she read her poem aloud for us in the group, Esther rolled her eyes at this line. I laughed and asked about her reaction. "She constantly is singing K-pop! Do you know K-pop, Dr. Crystal? She is always singing, only this music, all the time!" Entering the space with my orientation from Hip-hop, I was familiar only with the most popular songs played on the radio, but I got a full education that afternoon. From the food to the music to the traditional culture, Claudia was enthralled with Korea, and she participated in an after-school club dedicated to learning more about it. It was important to her to share this personal fact about her appreciation for Korean culture within her poetry so that girls in other places would know that about her too, that she was interested and involved in something so distant from her status as a refugee yet directly tied to her as a girl.

Just as abruptly Claudia's poetry pivots us back to a practical skill that is equally necessary for girls: financial literacy. Critical to note is that a girl needs to know "how to handle and manage money," which should not be conflated with being poor. Again, Claudia seems to be resisting caricatures of immigrants who come to the US in search of social mobility but without any knowledge of how the economic system operates in their new city. She seems to recognize money management as something that is necessary, and that wealth is a tool to be used, rather than a status to aspire to. Nowhere in her poem does she articulate dreams of material success; nowhere does her poem seek to achieve the American Dream in the land of opportunity and picket fences. This is contrary to most discourse around immigration and refugee desires. Instead she claims that girlhood is about control, "handling" and "managing" a tool, but to what end we are not told.

Claudia's poem loops us back to relationships—this time explicitly about love, which distinguishes this line from the others that specified "caring," "supportive" and later in her poem to "encourage." Reciprocity is an important part of Claudia's girlhood relationships, as she demarcates in this line about love, and we are left to wonder if she means familial, romantic, sexual, platonic, or some other type of love. Claudia deliberately differentiates between the experiences of "to love someone" and "to be loved." She has experienced both and expresses her understanding that neither situation is necessarily guaranteed. What is the pain of loving someone and that love not being returned? What, for a girl like her, is the decision of being loved and choosing not to reciprocate? Her line also lets us know that she is conscious that just as she has agency to determine her love, so do others. Perhaps this is also related to how she understands the concepts of "respect" and "bravery." In the very next line, Claudia expresses her feelings of "power" because she is "influential," and there are at least two ways to interpret her choice. First, perhaps she is still referring to her agency when it comes to reciprocal loving. If this is the case, Claudia's poetry proves that love is more than an emotional response; it is a verb that requires action, and in the determination of love, girls are "powerful." What does power look like to a girl who is scripted to the sidelines in larger discourse around who counts as lovable? Under what circumstances are girls allowed to love, and what types of girls can "be loved" in return? These questions are not answered. On the other hand, Claudia's line might be read as understanding that a girl can be "powerful," but that does not mean she is liberated. The next lyrics reverberate from the larger context of decision making within this poetic echo: "to be a girl is to be powerful and influential / to be a girl it's always to say I cannot / I can't." Girls are positioned to experience the rights and responsibilities of both womanhood and girlhood simultaneously and to feel forced to make split decisions. Claudia emphasizes in two ways how she must deny others and herself, "I cannot" and "I can't," and the repetition of this phrase denotes firmness and importance. She has learned to say no "always," which makes me think she does not often want to turn down what she is being offered. Is this an example of the "role model" or good behavior that she is acutely aware of earlier in her poem? Is it simply another way that her circumstances position her between multiple demands and her own desires? While Claudia claims the decision as her own to make, we are led to wonder what the contextual expectations are that she is working to satisfy.

Near the close of her poem, Claudia acknowledges a physical element of girlhood for the first time. Her line "it's having to wear things to cover" indicates that Claudia is made to dress modestly. Whether her parents or her religion determines what constitutes modesty is not shared here, and while the large population of both Christian and Muslim immigrants who are relocated in the nearby community in Chicago might be a clue, the rules for Claudia might also be a result of traditional East African expectation that girls and women cover their bodies as a social marker of modesty and self-respect.

Claudia's SWP defies easy caricatures sketched by the discourses that construct her life as a Black African refugee girl living in a historically under-resourced urban neighborhood in the US. Yet her poetry does not present her refugee status explicitly for the other girls to read. In fact, when girls in New York looked at her poem, they nodded and agreed that "she seems like one of us" (fieldnotes, 2019). Her poetry excavates internal processes that converge into what it means to be a girl, and that these processes are a constant negotiation. Claudia is predominantly preoccupied with developing skills and abilities. The list of aptitudes is long and often at odds, weighted down with unspoken pressure when she is "standing out, confused, mak[ing] mistakes," but ultimately for Claudia, "to be a girl is worth it."

Girls in Development and Decision Making

Quantum justice theory suggests that the movement between subjectivities of girl and woman for refugee girls like Claudia and Esther can be understood as agentic navigation in the vehicle of SWP. Quantum justice allows them to leave a trail of light tracking where their energy has been expended to undergo a quantum justice leap or transformation. Shifting subjectivities are critical moves sometimes dictated by girls, and necessary for survival, and yet not registering as any large-scale assessment or evaluation tool. SWP and performance are practices of freedom that occur on a molecular scale yet provide significant momentum for refugee girls who must move to survive (Swai 2010). In their efforts to gain autonomy, global girls pursue the nimble quantum justice leap between identities, seeking out the in-between, the third space, to exchange energy and to rehearse new ways of being in this hostile world. During the transfer they can swap ideas and build with each other. Maybe the category of "girl" will shift in their favor, and maybe it won't—but girls will keep moving.

Localized contexts that are already rife with contradiction become even more complicated when migration and refugee status further politicize girls' identities. Elinami Swai (2010) effectively describes "dislocated subjectivity" in her work that honors the value of women's everyday knowledge systems from Tanzania. Cultivating disruption for global girls means using the knowledge systems and modes of communication that are unique to them. Thus, SWP performance is a key application of Swai's claims. Quantum justice theory zooms further in to explore the everyday uniqueness of the knowledge girls like Claudia and Esther coconstruct, while simultaneously recognizing the sound of the poetic echoes of girls in a transnational extension of their network. SWP inherently insists on the inclusion of multiple readings of their performances of the distinct and competing knowledges that girls construct, while quantum justice theory expansively holds the harmony and the clash in those knowledges by leaping us in and out of them. For refugee girls to be included in this framework, quantum justice theory must consider their knowledges in multiple contexts, times, and spaces. Recognizing their distinction and similarity is challenging, but we can scrunch down into a close reading of their SWP even as we acknowledge its metamorphosis occurs as soon as we make observations. The cypher energizes and shapes how we confront those dynamics continuously with each other during the workshops and beyond. Further, SWP and its quantum justice analyses expose the racial and gendered power corruptions and collaborative weaknesses within our day-to-day interactions. Quantum justice theory plunges us more deeply into an examination of revelatory moments that allow us to address and heal injustice, asserting the past and using our emotional energy to produce an alternate future. Naming an imbalance of power is the first step to rectifying it.

Girlhood is political. To be a girl is to exist in a stage of life that does not rely solely on the number of years lived; it is a political category that scripts girls' bodies and the social obligations they are expected to fulfill. Part of the colonial legacy reinforced by GID is dismantled by Oyěwùmí (1997) in her canonical work decentering Western White feminist approaches linked with missionary and foreign aid systems that essentialize gender as a category of analysis and explores the ways that "wife" and "woman" are conflated terms and wrongly assigned in anthropological research beyond the Global North. Oyěwùmí argues that this approach erroneously assumes how African societies are structured and that globalization has for centuries enabled Western researchers to perform analyses of gender without accounting for local cultural constructions that would frame the constitution of gender differently (1998). Research conducted about the discourses that determine girlhoods, especially global ones, and the social accesses that they establish are in danger of being swept up in similar ways through the broad generalizations Oyěwùmí warns against. Gender, in this case the social category of girl, is complicated in equal parts by age, race, nationality and other cultural constructs unique to the location of the US for this specific instance of the GGG project, but gender does not create the discourse that polices social access for girls. Instead, girlhood is conjured within a variety of sociohistorical and material contexts (Gonick 2003; Inness 1998; Johnson 1993; Jones 1993; Lesko 1996; McRobbie and Nava 1984; Wald 1998; Walkerdine 1990). However, prevailing discourse is in part a result of that social access and who counts or is recognized as a "girl" in each context. What it means to be a girl is revealed through the function of other identity categories that, like contexts, are fluid and can be understood as a site of critical agency, intersecting with other competing discourses that work to include or exclude girls at the juncture of many different categories (Butler 1993; Davies 2000; Tilley 2020). Identities form crossroads for girls, and SWP provides protective equipment to explore these intersections as unstable sites under construction for global girls of color. Competing discourses must be made explicit and localized to prevent replicating colonialized views about gender. In other words, girls like Claudia and Esther participate in the constructs of gender and identity but are not solely governed by them.

Dislocation and agency are joint processes. As refugee girls, they experience dislocation in a distinctive way. Contextualizing subjectivity and knowledge production works to "identify neoliberalism and globalization as transformations that profoundly mediate national policies that, in turn, shape women's life course trajectories" (Swai 2010, 4). Girls' lives are even more vulnerable to the interlocking systems that punish Black and otherwise marginalized women. Joyce Ladner's (1971) pioneering work *Tomorrow's Tomorrow: The Black Woman* sheds light on US-based urban Black adolescent girls and their understandings and expectations of womanhood. Her early work captures how a variety of contexts shaped Black girls' visions and hopes of womanhood and questions how each is "re-membered" by the other, offering new readings of girlhood through a relationship between the two (Dillard 2012; Durham 2014; Morrison 2004). LaKisha Simmons's (2015) work, applied more in chapter 6, deserves mention here as well, for she offers similar rich reconsideration of New Orleans girlhood via historical and archival research connecting women and girls through memory and firsthand documentation. Yet Ladner's and Simmons's work notwithstanding, there is scant scholarship on how girls of color not born in the US but who grow up there conceive of and experience the discursively constituted position of a girl. I most frequently turn to literary giants like Edwidge Danticat, Helen Oyeyemi, and Julia Alvarez for their exquisitely piercing stories that memorialize and fictionalize migration experiences. Their tales resonate with the performances of refugee girls that I have borne witness to.

For this reason, it is helpful to combine Swai and Ladner's insights to analyze Claudia's and Esther's poetry. Although the distinction between girls and women is blurred as Claudia shares in her poem, it is not an uncommon effect of globalization to reify a false distinction between childhood and adulthood, further dislocating girls' agency. Yet marginalized girls' knowledge systems are generated within conflicting and competing discursive constructions, and when this knowledge is honored, it activates a line of inquiry between the self and Other into how discursive practices shape and are shaped by the girls (Swai 2010). SWP by girls like Claudia explores this terrain. Swai further extrapolates the need for research to magnify how gender discourse is interrogated and transcended by "ordinary African women," and her sociocultural lens accounts for the ways that education maintains and reinforces inaccurate readings about African women. Her argument opposes easily digested and replicated power relationships and must be even more seriously applied to research with Black girls and/or girls from the Global South. She argues that binaries of "good and empowered or bad and illiterate" are weapons of neoliberalism and as such:

> [reinstate] a worldview based on colonial lines of demarcation. [They fail] to see the great gray areas in between the pretentious claim that Western women have already succeeded and the equally false statement that success of women in Africa is nonexistent. As far as I am concerned, those in-between degrees of complexity are the only ones that matter, and they should be put at the center of the agenda. (10)

The "in-between degrees of complexity are the only ones that matter" for global girls in the process of becoming, of shifting subjectivities. For this reason, SWP embarks on quantum justice leaps to "put at the center" the ways girls know what they know, how they disrupt the claims laid on them, and how they engage with other girls. The girls' meaning making occurs through SWP, and they enter this process equipped with Hip-hop feminism to make sense of the "gray areas," the middle, the state of being in-between Swai points out (Lomax 2011; Morgan 1999; Richardson 2009). Therein lies resistance to essentialized Western claims and the radical reminder that girls of color bring to bear valuable "situated knowledges" that informs their lives (Haraway 1988). The only guarantee is that global girls are multidimensional and always changing.

Adolescence is a time of psychological and physical metamorphosis that garners attention from society at large, belying the ways that girls disturb oversimplified categories determined by social constructs. Age continues to be a problematic yet widely used category to define what it means to be a girl. According to the United Nations, ages 0–14 are considered childhood, while ages 15–24 are considered "youth."

> This statistically oriented definition of youth, in turn, entails that children are considered those persons under the age of 14. Worthy of note, however, is that Article 1 of the *United Nations Convention on the Rights of the Child* defines "children" as persons up to the age of 18. At the time, it was hoped that the Convention would provide protection and rights to as large an age-group as possible, especially as there was no similar document on the rights of youth. Many countries also draw the line on youth with regard to the age at which a person is given equal treatment under the law—often referred to as the "age of majority." This age is commonly 18 in many countries; so that once a person attains this age, he or she is considered to be an adult. Nonetheless, the operational definition and nuances of the term "youth" vary from country to country, depending on relative sociocultural, institutional, economic and political factors.
>
> FROM THE UN WEBSITE,
> HTTPS://WWW.UN.ORG/EN/SECTIONS/ISSUES-DEPTH/YOUTH-0/INDEX.HTML

For girls, especially Black African girls and their Global South counterparts, these demarcations by age can be arbitrary. Age rarely equates to the sorts of social protections and rights assumed to be necessary under the purview of the UN Convention on the Rights of the Child. Moreover, it is imperative to investigate how insidious racism and White supremacy contribute to the shrinking amount of time that a Black girl in the US can enjoy the presumed innocence associated with Western notions of childhood that persist to deform that freedom for girls of color (Bernstein 2011; Dumas and Nelson 2016; Sharpe 2016). Claudia and Esther, who have experienced girlhood in Black bodies in localized contexts of both East Africa and North America, offer keen insight to how age is both arbitrarily and specifically applied. Venus Evans-Winters (2017) reminds us that girlhood in the US, much like Oyěwùmí's argument about the category of "women" in Africa, is raced and classed in such a way that any discussion of gender norms automatically assumes a White Western middle-class sensibility formed in opposition to patriarchy. The categorization by the UN is intended to reflect "age of majority" and "equal treatment under the law"; however, the paradox of government assurances about enforcing protections and the realities of Black girls globally being treated as adults is despicably unjust. Often, White Western feminists further replicate this injustice by attempting to "do the right thing" that maintains a White savior complex and employs charity to reify a one-dimensional caricature of Black girls from the Global South as in need of intervention (Sensoy and Marshall 2010, 7). Global girls are using SWP to cultivate disruption of these popular narratives frequently employed in the nonprofit sector or political campaigns at the UN.

Claudia's poem provides keen insight about her personal strategy for countering this script. She shares "to be a girl is to say no some time to somethings" and that "to be a girl is to be powerful and influential" while simultaneously admitting that "to be a girl is to always say I cannot" and to "make mistakes." In her determination Claudia utilizes SWP to disentangle from a one-dimensional reading of her girlhood by asserting her agency via the apparent contradictions that involve her. Claudia formulates her own agency like what Swai (2010) suggests African women are already and always doing: foregrounding their context and subjectivity. For Swai, dislocation and agency are inseparable processes and function as tools of negotiation:

> Juxtaposing them reminds us, however, that a woman is always an active subject, making meaning of who she is and what is expected of her, while accommodating societal demands and repudiating others in order to achieve her goals in life. (5)

For Claudia and her peers at GirlForward, the inseparable processes of dislocation and agency are even more important because of the ways that their access to actual power is diminished through their position as girls. This quantum justice leap charts a pathway for Claudia and others to configure and ascribe meaning to their lives and to the decisions they make by focusing on the conflicting expectations placed on them. SWP shifts our readings of Claudia's dislocated subjectivity and agentic identity as a girl. Aimee Meredith Cox (2015) makes the case that girls might "use our displacement as a starting point for regeneration and the creation of new lifeworlds and spaces that affirm our collective humanity" (27). Cox urges against working toward "inclusion" and aims to generate instead, suggesting that creative acts can be a fruitful site of transformation (27). Claudia's SWP engenders change when she postulates that "to be a girl is also to be able to make the right decisions and take risks," which positions her experiences somewhere between Swai's (2010) inseparable processes of dislocation and agency and the hope of Cox's (2015) "regeneration." Her desire for transformation is not fully conceived as complete or finished, perhaps because her identity is under negotiation. Process matters. Quantum justice theory operates through SWP and performance to conceptualize the caretaking of process; rehearsal prior to a performance is integral, as it allows and encourages girls' comfort with auditioning new ideas, ways of being, and their hopes for the future, even as they acknowledge the strictures working to regulate their lives. Dislocation puts demands on agency that quantum justice makes evident for Claudia: although she has no control over how her dislocation happens to her, quantum justice insists we read it instead as a performance of her agency. In this very specific, granular translation of Claudia's performance of her agency, quantum justice reframes her dislocation because our recognition and observation of her experience transforms it. Her very act of performance reframes the circumstance and experience of dislocation from permanent to temporal—quantum justice clarifies this shift in materiality and form, making it observable to us, and invites new readings of Time and the process of becoming. Quantum justice leaps like this one are possible primarily through SWP because such rehearsals of new ways of becoming, of negotiation, of creating and re-membering might also be engaged with as prophecy. By rehearsing through SWP performance the "lifeworlds" that affirm who she is and whom she wants to become, Claudia reenacts the past, acknowledges the present, and prophesies her future through her SWP. The quantum justice leaps that bring us as her audience into her regeneration also delve deeply into a reflective moment on our participation in girls' regeneration (Cox 2015). Are we supporting these rehearsals of new and multiple girlhoods? Are we cultivating the disruptions necessary for global girls to create and freely imagine? Are we also transformed?

Back to Reality:
Refugee Girls and Education

Black African girls with refugee status in the US face a unique situation. Claudia, Esther, and the other girls in Chicago did not divulge any revelation about these challenges beyond their SWP. Their silence about their refugee status is interesting to put into dialogue with scholars from the fields of psychology, medicine, women's studies, and education, as doing so further enriches concepts about "dislocated subjectivity" (Swai 2010). Broadly, scholarship describes a process of "acculturation" wherein refugees work to acclimate to dominant culture, and girls with refugee status experience intense levels of discrimination, powerlessness, and academic struggle that result in poor mental health (Ellis et al. 2010; Fox and Johnson-Agbakwu 2020). However, there are studies that challenge the shortcomings of acculturation as a one-size-fits-all for refugee girls and suggest what Jacqueline Mosselson (2006) terms "cultural hybridization," which highlights coping strategies adolescent refugee girls develop to succeed academically and maintain general well-being (22). Fostering trust between refugee girls and institutions of learning, while a highly recommended method of ensuring health and well-being, is a test given the racism and nationalist attitudes prevalent among teachers and healthcare workers who interact with refugee and immigrant populations in the Global North (Fox and Johnson-Agbakwu 2020; McBrien 2009). Claudia's poetic prophecy is not only about a not-yet-attained future; she juggles understanding the practical duties she is expected to expertly fulfill such as "manage money" and "care for her children" and her less tangible aspirations "to be a role model" or "to love someone and to be loved." Claudia and Esther are neither here nor there as subjects in the world they must navigate; they are in-between and not involved in the conversations that take place about them, although those conversations center their legal status, nationality, Blackness, and other identities (Cox 5). Their subjectivities are not easy or tidy, and their existence implicates those in power, no matter their geographic location: for them, each identity category obfuscates another and threatens the validity of a different power source in their lives. Their status as "girls" is further complicated because of their status as refugees upon their arrival in the US, which exacerbates their experiential differences at school in Chicago and with their families, who presumably carried African standpoints into their new US environment. Responsibility to family remains a priority at their homes, while their peers in high school in Chicago likely assume they have the benefit of social freedoms typically associated with adolescence and being nearly eighteen while still enjoying the advantages of a more carefree, although equally complicated, girlhood.

"School success" remains a commonly used marker to determine whether adolescent refugees acclimate to their new environment, and as a tool of assessment for gauging feelings toward their homeland (Mosselson 2007). The institution of school sometimes functions as a "space of transformation" where a refugee identity morphs significantly for adolescents (26). Education is often equated to social mobility, which is widely understood as an opportunity for refugee girls to expand the discourse they are permitted to participate in on a spectrum from Otherized to American (Popkewitz 1998). For example, if they perform well in school, then refugee students can supposedly shed the difference that positions them as perpetual outsiders and become socialized to the normative mainstream, smoothing out their interactions with their peers. This assumption conflicts with what the GirlForward girls expressed. When refugee identity is seen as a status to be grown out of, acculturation and academic success seems to suggest that refugee adolescents categorically view their in-between status as entirely negative and seek to hide or at the least mute their refugee identity. Yet in their SWP the girls did not distinguish between being a "refugee" girl or a citizen, which suggests that both social positions were equally fraught with a combination of positive and negative experiences. What emerges from their poetry as a focal point is that being labeled a girl has rendered them in a subordinate position and the discursive power of gender subsumed their other subjectivities in everyday life. Thus, gender was the only reading of their identity category that they chose to specifically write about. Given their apparent disregard for fitting in, and contrary to this scholarship on refugee adolescents, the girl poets produce SWP that does not seek integration but adaptability to face changing and contradictory definitions. Acutely aware of the political nature of their physical presence in the US, as demonstrated by their enrollment in GirlForward if nothing else, the girl poets did not seem particularly interested in changing any laws or engaging with politics. They were instead very concerned with the day-to-day happenings of their lives. In every single CCC community, the girls always wrote about love. Whether they were refugees or citizens did not warrant further distinction in their poetic messages to other girls.

Quantum justice theory holds space for the experiences and desires of girls like Claudia who experience girlhood as an internalized set of decisions and actions that they must make. Using SWP, Claudia hatchets through the binary of imagined "ideal and failed girlhoods," expressing her disappointment and frustration as well as her matter-of-fact ability to survive through commonsense skills not taught in formal education (Khoja-Moolji 2018).

Her subjectivity as a girl is mobilized by her choices, limited as they may be, through the difficult process of being a girl and being a woman. These processes persist and are in part responded to through the poetry of girls like Claudia and Esther. Esther writes:

> to be a girl is to stand out to be a girl is to be unique to be a girl is to be outstanding among the standing
> to be a girl is to be sometimes confused
> to be a girl is to be a role model in your own way
> to be a girl is to be challenging
> to be a girl is to smile often
> to be a girl is to be ready to make sacrifices
>
> to be a girl is to exhibit pride and even self-confidence
>
> to be a girl is to be soft-spoken
> to be a girl is to keep trying
> to be a girl is to help others when they need it
> my community is filled with welcoming people and all sorts of support it is a place to come and feel comfortable
> with the laughter love and happiness flowing friends turned family
> a large form of cooperation
> We Are One
> fun can be another side attraction like the saying all work and no play makes Jack a Dull Boy
> diversity is seen at every corner
> new skills learned
> promotion of confidence and Justice
> We Are One
> never letting anyone down no matter how long
> we are here for them we never give up standing strong with hopes High
> a little bit of problems here and there but you know nothing is perfect
> we are one
>
> ESTHER, CHICAGO

Esther and Claudia were attached at the heart, and their tight friendship was evident from the moment they entered the GirlForward space on my first afternoon with them. In the same way that Claudia's opening line compels me as I read, the refrain at the end of Esther's piece has a similar effect. "We Are One" she writes, three times over as if a chorus, careful to capitalize each of the words to add extra emphasis. "We Are One" comes at the portion of her poem that is focused on her community, so I assume they are who she means—many bodies into one. She describes her community as:

> filled with welcoming people and all sorts of support it is a place to come and feel comfortable
> with the laughter love and happiness flowing friends turned family
> a large form of cooperation

In this excerpt, Esther describes a physical location, with "welcoming" "support" where she and others can "come and feel comfortable." Because she doesn't go into further detail about the physical and geographic structure that defines her community, we can assume those aspects of the spaces are mutable. The phrase "friends turned family" exposes how family is prioritized for Esther and that the status of family members and friends can shift depending on their participation in the "laughter, love, and happiness" that make up a place where Esther can "feel comfortable." She ends her description of family with "a large form of cooperation" which tells us that to her, family is a group that works together toward a goal. This action-oriented description of friends who are counted as family gives a new reading to her first statement in the repetition of "We Are One"; we can be sure that her concept of "oneness" is shaped by "fun," "diversity," "learning," and "justice." Esther's writing contains an energy and a sense of excitement about the bustling activities that take place in her community. This is a breathing place full of stimulation and options for its members. For her, the "promotion of confidence and Justice" shows us that self-confidence and self-determination are present when "Justice" is there, and that is something she expects from community.

Esther closes her poem with lines that explain how relationships are negotiated within her community:

> never letting anyone down no matter how long
> we are here for them we never give up standing strong with hopes High
> a little bit of problems here and there but you know nothing is perfect

Esther's lines adamantly insist on an ethical standard in her community; this standard implies endurance, reliability, and presence as relationship agreements for members of her community. Although the trials that she faces with her "friends turned family" are not detailed, her poem explains that enduring through time to support others is a social commitment that Esther sums up as "we are here for them." Reliability means that she not only "never give[s] up" but will remain "standing strong with hopes High." Esther is determined to have a positive outlook buoyed up by hope not only for herself but for others.

To be a girl, Esther insinuates, is to be present with optimism during trying times. The last line of Esther's poem offers an honesty that is likely to link her poetry to the girls who receive it. Admitting to "a little bit of problems here and there" means that Esther understands that relationships are complex, even as she declares, "We Are One," yet that does not preclude their being powerful or working together. Esther models collaboration through her description of community, rounding out a unified front. She reminds the girl audience "you know nothing is perfect," assuming they have lives scarred with blemishes just like her. Their problems will be different, because they are not refugees, because they are not living in Chicago, and for many other reasons, yet, because they are girls receiving her message, she calls up the difficulties scribing that shared identity category to ensure that they interpret her correctly. I wonder if her last line, a lowercase "we are one," is intended as an invitation to the group of girls whom she is composing her poem for, giving them permission to join in as part of her imperfect family of friends.

Education, Adultification, and Subjectivity

What Claudia and Esther share via their current localized context adds an important layer to the issue of adultification for Black girls in the US. While the responsibilities they describe as being expected to meet seem extreme for a "girl" under the age of eighteen, because of their specific context, their poetry cannot be engaged solely through this Western lens of girlhood. They likely experience the negative impacts of adultification, particularly given the dismal record of sexual discrimination Black girls face within Chicago public school districts (Gholson and Martin 2014; Henry 1998). However, they complicate these generalizations given their nuanced lives as Black African girls who now reside in the US. Neither girl explicitly discusses her schooling experiences, although education is mentioned, and the practical skills for everyday living are loaded with value within their SWP. Meanwhile, the expectations of their traditional East African families are predicated not upon their race and appearance but on their position as girls within the family structure. The reconfiguration of that family structure once they arrived in Chicago after displacement is unclear, and we are not provided any specific reference to their family organization in their poems. Perhaps this omission is telling as well.

Ultimately, their identity is simultaneously constructed as girl and woman, which they have been able to employ as sometimes advantageous, but is rife with danger. Black girlhood scholars call this process "adultification." Scholars in the fields of education and public policy have written about the adultification of Black girls and the resulting excessively harsh punishments they receive from teachers and administrators in schools and subsequently through the criminal justice system (Crenshaw et al. 2015; González 2018; Morris 2007; Nunn 2018; Toliver 2018; Wun 2016). Monique W. Morris (2015) is at the helm of a movement to address the dangers of this institutionalized phenomenon known as "school pushout" and examines the "educational, judicial, and social disparities facing Black girls" because of being assigned excessive punitive discipline by school administrators and teachers. The 2019 documentary film *Pushout: The Criminalization of Black Girls in Schools* features Black girls' powerful testimonials, and the website and resources offer ways to advocate for new legislation, hosting watch parties to raise awareness, and other avenues of action to redirect the tide of education. These important works shed light on the ways the system of education continues to endanger Black girls in the US. Punitive consequences impact girls' lives beyond the schoolyard as Black girls encounter what Lara Adekeye (2019) sums up as "to be a child without the protection of innocence" in her dissertation of the same title. Adultification of Black girls has led scholars like Venus Evans-Winters and Jennifer Esposito (2010) to sound the alarm for the transformation of educational institutions through a radical shift toward equity and justice, and new methodologies that will address and put an end to these harsh inequalities. The in-between subjectivity of Black girlhood, adolescence, and womanhood is not a linear path in the Global North. While there is an age that legally marks the end of childhood and beginning of adulthood, there is no agreed-upon cultural ritual or rite that signifies to the rest of a community that a girl is ready to be a woman, and this renders girls who are refugees like Claudia and Esther vulnerable to a new set of dangers in an unfamiliar landscape with unwritten social codes, expectations, and assumptions. These codes are enforced by adults and sometimes by other girls who are invested in upholding normative discourses about whom they ought to become. The impacts of adultification are echoed in the poetry between Claudia and Esther and girls in New Orleans, Louisiana.

SuperGirls and Schizoid Girlhoods: Movements but No Justice

"I'm from New Orleans," Clarsey shouted in front of the classroom, gripping her loose-leaf page scrawled with poetry with both hands.

"Where you ain't never safe!" hollered back the rest of her class, all twenty-five of them.

I sat in a desk in the audience section of the classroom and struggled to maintain a neutral facial expression when I realized they were quoting an edited version of Ninth Ward rapper Lil Wayne's (2011) verse in "Rolling." The song is a swagger-filled track that promotes predictable mainstream southern rap narratives of money, misogyny, mayhem, and, because it was Lil Wayne, New Orleans pride. Clarsey was sharing her poem in front of the group, and strategically incorporated this line, knowing full well the response she would get from her classmates would be raucous and total. Slowly the girls had warmed up to performing for each other, and as they grew more comfortable, those waiting their turn in the audience became increasingly interactive. We were in the cypher portion of the workshop for the day when all the girls were reading their newly drafted poems aloud. I glanced over at Louise, my teacher and administrator friend, who invited me to offer this workshop and who was born and raised in the outskirts of NOLA. She rolled her eyes at me and pursed her lips as if to say, What can you do? But she did not shush the girls. Knowing Louise the way I do, I was half surprised she wasn't rapping along. During Clarsey's performance that afternoon, I couldn't help but laugh, because I had not expected this outburst from the class, and while they had grown more vocal in their support of one another during the cypher, this call-and-response was on another level. These beautiful girls, so prim and coordinated in their Catholic school uniforms of skirts and crisp blouses, had started our session off on the quiet side. The girls began the afternoon wary of me, a newcomer to their classroom, and a bit shy to participate in a spoken word workshop to begin with. Now half of them were on their feet, dancing to the beat of a song playing in all our minds, called up by Clarsey's lines. Clarsey cleared her throat in an overly exaggerated way, signaling the other girls to quiet down to hear what else she had to say. Clarsey is a savvy poet, manipulating her knowledge of the localized aesthetic to solidify the group as one before disintegrating them back into separate entities. Her performance reflects and reminds her audience that they are all in this, differently but together.

School is a stage where much of a girl's life is performed and rehearsed. Nia Nunn (2018) explores the "Super-Girl" phenomenon in her application of critical feminist theory within educational spaces, named thus to represent the imbalance of "strength" and "sadness" that Black girls in the US work through because of gendered racism (Perry et al. 2012). Nunn conceptualizes this effort as "self-defined feminine power that fosters resilience and on-going decision-making" countered by "historically rooted pain, sorrow, and sometimes debilitating current conditions and experiences" related primarily to schooling (240). Imani uses SWP to reveal examples of the "Super-Girl" imbalance and how it is played out in this quantum justice leap through the following excerpts:

> I come from turning my pain into a positive outcome
> I come from hurting every day to trusting in God
> my community supported through good and bad times
> my community has its way of putting on a front
>
> IMANI, NEW ORLEANS

Imani's poem opens with reference to emotional pain that ultimately, she claims to transform "into a positive outcome" by "trusting in God." She gestures to her own agency, pointing to her decision to trust as a move that alleviates her pain. Imani claims credit for her choice and her action in the phrase "turning my pain" as a way of asserting and acknowledging her commitment and process, and more importantly, her ability to transform. She can and has shifted her status from one state of Nunn's (2018) Super-Girl to the other, and Imani assumes control through self-determination to do so. Imani is astute enough to point out and value her navigation through "strength and sadness as structural constants and individual experiences," although she does not explicitly identify what provoked those states of being for her (Nunn 2018, 248).

At first glance, it might be tempting—especially for educators—to read Imani, Claudia, and Esther's SWP performances through the superficial lens of a "wider popular cultural consciousness" about who girls are supposed to be, which would only allow for a highly popularized version of two mixed-race girls from the Ninth Ward who will achieve success because of their access to private education (Ringrose 2007, 474). But the girls complicate the problematic "optimistic stories of overcoming" and revise neoliberal "redemption narratives" (Cox 2015, 148–149). Imani, like Claudia and Esther, demonstrates subjective agility in her SWP. Their words situate themselves within this discursive fiction to acknowledge the support from those who have helped them, drawing strength through an Act of Recognition, while simultaneously leveraging that widely accepted "successful Super-Girl" narrative to confront its expectations. They require accountability from the systems that rely upon the easy deception of such stories to groom a "Black girl [who] is expected to fly without seeking redress or leveling accusations" (Cox 2015, 149). SWP disrupts narratives that demand gratitude be paid to oppressive systems that form the root cause of Black girl subjugation in the first place. Quantum justice protects and holds space for the tension between desires for mainstream success and connection with community, healthy boundaries, and stories from girls who live beyond the limits systemic-isms impose. SWP links girls in the margins to each other, encouraging flight or stillness and sometimes both.

Girl subjects are conditioned to strive for an impossible neoliberal ideal of perfection that pervades public discourse and "[creates] massive contradictions for girls" (Ringrose 2007, 474). The contradictions are pointed out, not within the girls' reflections of themselves but in their articulation of the environments they must move through. Imani names her community as complicit in sculpting the paradoxical landscape she is expected to succeed within, because although they "supported through good and bad times / my community has its way of putting on a front." Putting on a front might mean that members of Imani's community are consistently present, but they are acting, or presenting a facade with ulterior self-serving motives. It seems that inconsistent support from her community is part of the landscape for Imani, and she would prefer that they were more cooperatively minded. On the other hand, putting on a front may be a form of protection for members of her community; in other words, the front is what makes it possible for them to "support through good and bad times" because outsiders can't tell when they are going through the "bad times." The pressure of such expectations pushes her, which might mean that the others' opinions of her hold powerful consequences in her life. What Nunn described as "Super-Girl" binaries are evidenced in the lyrics of the girls' SWP and demonstrate the "interplay of [the] external and self-evaluations fueled by . . . representational . . . labels" (Cox 2015, 10). If "sadness" or "strength" is the only option made available to Black girls, even when they are viable options, what happens to the girls who are not as adept at transferring between the two? Emma Renold and Jessica Ringrose (2011) describe this struggle between subjectivity performances as the "schizoid pushes and pulls [that] operate as one of the new normative conditions" girls are expected to nimbly manage (393). We see girls who want to be "Super" like a hero, who desire to be seen and acknowledged as exceptional, who are discursively set up to strive for impossible goals and yet resist that narrative through the shortcomings and significance of their communities. The use of the term "schizoid" to describe a state of girlhood is disconcerting because of the way it frames people who suffer with this mental illness, and because of the contradiction it represents given how we are typically socialized to perceive and relate to girlhood—as smooth and cohesive innocence during the coming-of-age experience.

Scaling the terrain of subjectivities carved by the violent turns of "schizoid girlhoods" discourse is nimbly conducted through the projection and performance of the girls' SWP. Their honesty about such experiences, even when their perspective casts others in a negative light or unmasks their subversion, shows us how the girls do the work of cultivating disruption. This form of truth-telling is known as "keeping it real" and refutes social ideals through an interesting contrast; the evocative imagination of SWP Futurity praxes and hope-filled prophetic work of the girls invoke realness and dreams all at once (Richardson 2007, 797). The girls' poetic exchange represents their experiences with making decisions. They engage with "ambiguous practices of identity," which are important when undertaken by Black girls who, in the process of subjectivity negotiation are neither "agent" nor "compliant" yet are expected to perform in "normative, socially constraining and often contradictory spaces" (Gonick et al. 2009, 6). Though they straddle many worlds—refugee status, urban living, the Diaspora, the overriding concepts restricting their girlhood—these girls can acknowledge and discern between the contradictions; they "accommodate and repudiate" as they make decisions for themselves in their navigation of the world (Swai 2010). Transnational girlhood is complex, and the specificities of each girl's experience offer multiple rich and tangled interpretations.

Local and Global Girl Effects and Hip-hop Feminism

Reconfiguring and remixing the dialogues of dominant discourses is integral social justice praxis, and emerging girl poets must be permitted the time, space, and safety in which to identify issues, sort out and audition possible solutions, and negotiate who they are and how they want to be represented (Endsley 2018). The transnational experience of refugee girls offers us concrete engagements with these guidelines even as they complicate them. Performance work offers girls the chance to experience what it feels like "being in motion across the porous boundaries between self and other in ways that reconfigure" (Ellsworth 2005, 65). Brown (2009) defines Black girlhood as "the representations, memories, and lived experiences of being and becoming in a body marked as youthful, Black, and female that is not dependent on age, physical maturity, or any essential category of identity" (1). This definition is important and useful, yet I keep returning to Claudia's poetic summation, "to be a girl is to be a woman," and Brown's definition explains why this lyric echoes within me; I also understand "to be a woman is to be a girl." Her lyrics help me account for the entrenched investment I have in curating spaces for the nuanced richness that SWP performance invites us to tenderly explore and untangle. Reconfiguration of ourselves as subjects can be painful and never provides a tidy ending. Some categories of identity stricture the girls' lives, but they contend with their differences by learning strategies across transnational networks. The fifth element is an ongoing cypher, and through SWP Claudia scrambles Western concepts of time, age, place, and space to present how pervasive mainstream discourses continue to be in the lives of Black girls like her. Feminist research that engages with African women and girls must cross the boundaries and borders of institutions, nations, and knowledge praxes (Mama 2001). To effectively meet the possibilities that manifest, cultivating disruption ensures that we must also face the conflicts, the poetic echoes and consequences of making decisions and how we are implicit in reproducing those effects even as we yearn to be free of them.

Transnational activism with girls requires intentional action and analysis, driven by girls, and focused on their concerns and experiences. Advocacy and activism invested in facilitating opportunities for global girls to form community in politically affirming ways is difficult, yet the arts offer a unique starting point for centering girls' experiences while connecting them across borders. Catherine Vanner (2019) writes, "Girls in different countries must speak to each other, whether it be in person, through virtual networks, or by responding to each other's work . . . to build moments of solidarity in which they learn from each other and challenge global patriarchy" (127). The poetic echoes initialized by refugee girls in Chicago to a girl in Soweto chart the discursive discrepancies about what constitutes a "girl" in varied sociohistorical contexts. The poetic echo we can trace through New Orleans further demonstrates how girls are using educational settings to build through the essentialist ways they are read. Girls continue to show us that "girls themselves are often best positioned to describe experiences within these systems" (Vanner 2019, 122). Sometimes they benefit and other times suffer from socially dominant readings. We make multiple attempts to reconfigure because we long to see, and make, ourselves even as we see and make others.

CHAPTER 4

What Girls Want

Dreams and Desires

"Do you remember me?" "Girl, please. It wasn't that long ago! Yes, she remembers you." I opened my eyes to look around the museum conference meeting room where we were gathered. I had leaned back in a chair to close my eyes just for a moment before the girls arrived for our workshop. The calm quiet air was laced with Toby's R&B YouTube playlist, and Jill Scott was living her life like it was golden. I sat up with a smile and recognized two familiar faces: Synthia and Reese, fourteen and fifteen years old, peering over the table, looking at the materials we had laid out for the day's work. I jumped up and gave them each a big hug. "Of course I remember y'all! I want to introduce you to my student who is helping out today. This is Shana." It was my first time having an official research assistant, and I was so excited for her to join me. The night before, I pulled my car up in front of the small Columbia airport, and Shana climbed in, wearing a deep blue lounge suit, her platinum curls wrapped in a scarf, looking glamorous and cosmopolitan. She had taken at least one course with me every semester since her arrival at college, and not only was she bright, but she was also energetically committed and excited to work closely with the girls in South Carolina.

Now we were about to get started, and after I introduced her to our early arrivals, she smiled at them both. "I'm so nervous!" Shana told the girls. "Nervous for us?" asked Synthia, feigning shock, drawing one hand up to her chest. Reese ignored them; she was still looking over the packets and reached for a snack. "Can I have one? Or is it too early?" Shana looked at me, and I winked. "Sure," said Shana. "Take as much as you want. We won't get started until the other girls get here." Reese was already digging through the basket, looking for something she liked. "Dang, girl, you act like you didn't eat breakfast!" said Synthia, giving Reese a playful push on her arm. Synthia picked up the other basket. Reese looked up and put one hand on her hip. "You just saying that, but I know I'm gonna make sure I get what I need . . . and what I want!"

Showcasing the Word:
Blackout Poetic Transcription as Method

Desire and satisfaction, agency and autonomy, all matter to girls. Often, girls who articulate their desires place themselves at risk of being ostracized. Other times girls are not exposed to tools adequate to express or explore what they might want. Because they are marginalized and rarely tuned in to by the mainstream beyond an appropriation of their language and looks, global girls' SWP requires alternative representation as data but must also be considered beyond data. The form of poetic transcription opens possible alternatives to the traditional Western ways of knowing that position the creative and artistic as less rigorous or serious than the quantitative. In the fourth stage of cultivating disruption, the "remix" of the data must be implemented. Remixing requires that a showcase of the analysis be re-represented in a new format to deepen, refresh, and further reconfigure the audience as they consider the findings. Tony Keith (2019) describes his "Blackout Poetic Transcription" (BPT) methodology as a critical race method he developed inspired by Hip-hopography (the study of Hip-hop) and blackout poetry (a form of literary art), for his research about spoken word artists (poets, rappers, emcees) and Hip-hop educational leadership (Keith 2019; Keith and Endsley 2020, 56). Tony designed BPT for his dissertation research and has since expanded his project to incorporate the stories and histories of what he names "Ed Emcees"—educational leaders and practitioners who teach using Hip-hop methods in higher education (56). We have published on the impact of BPT as an arts-based qualitative research method for undergraduate students, and Tony continues to pursue further research on Ed Emcees (Keith and Endsley 2020). The method was developed as an extension of poetic transcription (Denzin 2003; Glesne 1997; Langer and Furman 2004). According to Byrne (2017), the process of writing poetry from data is distinct from that of the poet, because "creating poetry from the data reveals the researchers' involvement more clearly. . . . The primary intent of researchers is to represent their data in alternative ways, . . . Poetry is not their aim but a means" (41–42). In this chapter I present a BPT remix, by taking up what Corrine Glesne named "poetic transcription" to invoke not only the "essence of the coded theme[s]" that I sorted through the girls' SWP, but also "to convey the emotions that the

[data] evoked in me" (206). Quantum justice ensues as a means of revising dominant readings of the girls' subjectivity through the re-representation of the data in the form of poetry, even as it is enacted by the girls themselves in their everyday lives. The data and the representation of the data are both functioning as disruptions to discourse—on the plane of the girls' embodied experience, and then again on the intellectual analyses that I am sharing here through their poems. I created remixed poems from the collection of girls' poems. These layers enable the reader to slow down, and the poetry operates as a reflexive tool for the subject, the researcher, and the scholar-artist. "Poetic transcription can open interpretive space to deepen understanding and bridge experience . . . to concentrate on the felt-sense or embodied knowledge that poetry privileges" (Durham 2014, 104). As a Hip-hop feminist researcher invested in social justice, I make use of poetic transcription for these reasons, because as Durham reminds us, "It enables the researcher to carve interpretative space . . . eliciting the emotive from experience" (105). LeConté Dill (2015) suggests one of the strengths of generating research as poetry is that the presentation of "poems-as-data" can allow a diverse set of audience members to engage with the research, including but not limited to artists, youth development professionals, and policy makers. The remix stage of cultivating disruption also works to broaden the reach of scholarly findings, breaking down the entrenched hierarchy of who counts as knowledge producers in Western academia. According to Glesne (1997), poetic transcription effectively blurs the accepted boundaries between art and science. The in-between-ness of this method offers an exploration of "intersubjectivity," and allows us to examine issues of power and authority through poetry that "creates a third voice, that is neither the interviewee's nor the researcher's, but is a combination of both" (215). Gloria Anzaldúa (1996) describes the ways that women of color must shift as the enactment of imagination and adaptability. Elizabeth Ellsworth (2005) also names the ambiguous "third space" that is uniquely accessible through SWP and performance (Endsley 2016, 2020). Ellsworth insists that third space is critical, because "we must be able to access something external to our own projections and identifications; otherwise, our entire reality would consist of our own dreams or individual delusions" (30). Engaging with "the middle" is essential when we work with girls, because "if they rely on socially determined assessments to define their self-worth, they would be exiled from their own bodies and any home spaces they might establish for themselves" (Cox 2015, 29). However we encounter the in-between space, we must enter it to create. Poetic transcription is powerful and necessary in creative social justice research and work that claims to be transformational, because as Anzaldúa (1987) reminds, it is through our inhabitation of the in-between that

"we beg[i]n to get glimpses of what we might eventually become" (1029). SWP sculpts malleable futures in the in-between even as the girls represented here articulate their present and collective past. BPT translates global girls' prophetic utterances in new ways.

BPT, then, is a specific practice and extension of poetic transcription and blackout poetry, which is created by using a black marker to redact words until a poem is formed from a piece of text (Brewer 2014; Kleon 2010). In Keith's (2019) project, the data or the text that is going to be "blacked out" is pulled based on interviews with his research subjects. He codes the interview transcripts for themes to ensure they align with his research questions. I have worked with Tony in the capacity of a spoken word artist and scholar, and we have traveled the world performing together for the past fifteen years. I trust his experience as an artist, and his friendship is precious to me. I always learn something new when we create and perform together. He is gifted, and he pushes me to live without fear. We Zoom regularly to check in and cut up. During one of our conversations, I was sharing with him how overwhelmed I was with the sheer number of poems I still had to analyze. He laughed at me, sucking on a mango seed in his Washington, DC, kitchen, and said, "SpongeBob, why don't you try some BPT? It's Hip-hop, it's feminist, it's spoken word. Also, it's brilliant, if I do say so myself." I sat back in my chair, holding my cup of coffee. "Did you just gather me together like that, Dr. Keith?" Tony had just matriculated with his doctorate a few months prior, so every chance I got, I addressed him as "Doctor." Tony popped his tongue. "You tell me. I mean, if you feel gathered and such. Go on and be yourself. It's time, it's past time." With this encouragement, and with fresh excitement I saw the girls' SWP in a new light.

> Blacking Out is an agentic action and focuses and re-directs the readers' attention to key points. The power dynamic between the researcher and the subject ceases being solely an intellectual concept and instead is viscerally experienced and thus made real for the researcher. (Keith and Endsley 2020, 70)

In this series of quantum justice leaps, data poems have been produced through BPT from the global girls' SWP. The data poems are a manifestation of crossroads that are both the destination and the point of departure between global girls and the poetic echo of What Girls Want. The figure below provides an example using Alem's SWP of how I executed the process. The left column contains Alem's original SWP. The right side is the Blacked Out transcript. Below the chart is the final version of the "data poem." This example demonstrates the process I used when working with all the SWPs that revealed overlapping themes and echoes with what girls want.

SWP transcript	Blackout Poetic Transcription
the beauty of being a girl is when there is respect for her when she learns effectively with pride when everyone shows her the right direction with that she is going to be powerful with her people and for her country but if you are make her ashamed and burden her she will not make happy her husband or her country she will never make you happy not even her child if she is given good opportunities She is the beginning of civilization respect her rights that happens when you let her get educated she learns and then she will educate you she will be wise and creative boys know gender equality between men and women when they are children they learn equality then we must live it	the beauty of ▮ a girl ▮ respect for her ▮ she learns ▮ pride ▮ everyone shows ▮ direction ▮ she ▮ powerful ▮ her people ▮ her country ▮ make her ashamed ▮ burden her ▮ not ▮ happy ▮ husband ▮ country she will never make you happy ▮ ▮ her child ▮ given good opportunities ▮ beginning ▮ civilization respect her ▮ ▮ get educated ▮ she will educate you ▮ be wise and creative boys know gender ▮ men and women ▮ children ▮ learn equality we must live ▮

DATA POEM — ALEM, ETHIOPIA

the beauty of a girl
respect for her
she learns pride
everyone shows direction
she
powerful
her people her country
make her ashamed
burden her
not happy
husband country

QUANTUM JUSTICE

she will never make you happy
her child given good opportunities
beginning civilization
respect her
get educated
she will educate you
be wise and creative
boys know gender
men and women children
learn equality
we must live

Five blackout poetic transcriptions follow: "Sweet Dream or Beautiful Nightmare," "Feeling Myself," "Feeling Afraid," "Chains That Bind," and "Hurting Girls." Each of the data poems represent a quantum justice leap that was repeated through call-and-response within the poetic echo of what girls want. SWP from girls living in every location that participated in GGG have been incorporated into each poem. There was remarkable overlap and repetition of key words and phrases across communities within this echo. As a method, BPT resists providing additional context for the poems to situate detailed background for your consideration as you absorb and interpret these representations. An important component of this form of poetic transcription is its insistence on reflexivity, not only between researcher and subject, but between the audience and the artist. How are your power, identity, and subjectivity projected onto these data poems, dear reader? Which girls do you imagine writing these themes? Why? What role do you play as you read this work? How do you observe my role as researcher and poet? What soothes you? What frustrates you? Why? Sit with these thoughts. Sit with what global girls of color are facing and how you benefit from their suffering. What girls want is always nuanced by what girls are subjected to, and what they are permitted to desire. Following the data poems, I close this chapter with SWP by South Carolina girls that encompasses these echoes and deploys solidarity between global girls as a salve and salvation that is made available through their relationship with each other.

SWEET DREAM OR BEAUTIFUL NIGHTMARE

long live the girls who are loved
always happy like Jesus
sweet like candy
who are dancers like me

I'm pretty
dark Beauty
proud daughter
golden child an ocean
I love myself and you who is reading this
Dream, I
singing and dancing
grateful to God with my mom and dad
a black person
worshiping God
they make me happy
confident
reminds me how I love them
my passion in life

cool smart talkative
a good listener
drawing
the craziest
when I'm done everyone cheers
a beautiful voice I
take me far when
I finish my studies

community is a network
uplifting
supporting people
who understand
who love me for me
trust
can count on
I can tell anything
not be betrayed
very few people because it's hard to find

FEELING MYSELF

people spoils me
pretty long hair
girly
my heart been broken

QUANTUM JUSTICE

I didn't deserve
I make somebody understand unconditional love
New Orleans grew up in the 9th Ward
where I was being taken for granted
I forgot how pretty
and spoiled
a strong black woman
raised me

my fun joy and laughter come from
party that's what I do
a strong black woman made me
who I am today
Shopping and getting cute is not a problem
girls who are beautiful like me
prays like a priest
sing like a bird
live patient like a chair

girls are heroes
big like the Earth
live sweet
like sugar the girls are fast
a train

I am a girl who is forgiveness
I'm good
plaiting baking and singing
I'm so quiet at class
I'm beautiful
I forgive too much evil
forgiving
someone be loved by God
like I am
I Can't Let Go

to forgive
is to love my friends
they are my community
no one will take them away from me

without them there is no life
beautiful girl
a silence girl
grateful
I am wonderful fun smart thankful joyful enjoyable

fun is what I enjoy
I'm thankful
people around me don't get bored with me

my community is best place
I love people
when they share
we share

FEELING AFRAID

Bittersweet moments of a broken home mistrust
a place that I thought was full of love
a broken home where only mom loves me
I see bad things happen
a place of confusion and hurt
that has stretched me
stripped me of my identity
of who I really am
a broken home isn't a home at all
full of laughter
good
memories
can sometimes be a place of sorrow and fear
strong and full of Future Leaders
my community is a place where you can be whoever you want
my community is like a home
a family
royalty
my mama whose kitchen smells like gumbo around Christmas
that blue and white house
God herself
whose hands shaped me
from a broken house
where I hear the tears I cried

QUANTUM JUSTICE

come
my father's saying
I have so much glow left
a dark place
my innocence is taken from me
young

I consider my sisters
outspoken
community keeps me strong
keeps me grounded

CHAINS THAT BIND

my community has had so many protests
and War
people were killed
yes
a dangerous street
at least you know your family is always by your side
I come from Darkness
God
different backgrounds oneself broken pieces
pain shaped me
the sound of Fury
yet silence I can no longer hear
from my mother's struggles
Father's shame
used as a joke
to intimidation
to others
dying to sleep
no food to eat
fake friends and family
I came to an end
the grace of God
I am still here

breaking every time you look
Raging
tears falling from my face

dark
with nowhere to turn
left me all alone
brought me depression
Pain
fails to show me the right way
filled with the anger and hatred
of my family
for each other
lost
No One tries to find me
only hide me
looking for the real me trying to understand my hurt
shocked
for the smile you see is a brave face to hide away the true pain
violent
everyday we lose a brother
the Police Department is hiring
but that won't stop the sirens
some take a stand
While others let it slides
when they see the son and nephew on the news
it's stand up for violence
get better
and no war lines
our prison is overpopulated
I'm tired of hashtagging

to be a girl
doing jobs that supposedly only women can do
getting married at an early age in some states
protected by parents
over
protection
treated as weaker than boys
one of many
girls in the family
challenges
a lot of black on black violence
police brutality

capable of so many things
reliable trustworthy scared of the future
a big sister
more than my short curly hair
that has so many times
define me

I am adaptable
I don't complain in the face of change I adopt
go on the journey
reliable
because you can always count on me to get the job done

scared of the future
there are so many things happening
expectations that I'm scared
I'll let someone down
I like to get out of my comfort zone and seek new experiences
I am a strong person
all the stereotypes
still
I am careless
I don't care what anybody say or think about me
I am shy when I'm around
people I don't know

the tears Market
that was closed yesterday
the people did not come
they look for Treasures
everyone has tears
too many
and I
who kept knocking on the gates of the market
and the people did not open
they cry with dry eyes
and a silly smile
they go out to collect donations
tears in the streets
with sealed hearts

DREAMS AND DESIRES

I come from a
strong woman
who has been hurt
drug use
abused
the abuser who suffered
I come from the dirt that blows in the wind
The Sounds you hear at 3 a.m.
from the smell of cold air
I am proud
living in the streets
I faced daily challenge
walking to school but I achieve my goals
being an astronaut
I know the challenges
and I make a stop to that
in society

my kind
would share food
water
and even clothes
we would love a neighbor child
would die for a person
they are loving and generous
very loud
they like gossip
about houses Lifestyles and can judge people
it's always fun
they don't have thieves
they like to fight
but I love it
they have to fight abuse and people that are selling drugs

HURTING GIRLS

people I love
the people who make me feel welcomed
the ones I trust
full of people who try to tear me down
who are insecure

so they point out my flaws
includes my so-called friends
the ones who claimed they had my back but in the end they was all just whack
my heart been broken
where I didn't deserve to hurt . . .
June 4th
I lost my best friend who died in a horrible way
I hurt
I live

to see the smiles of my friends love
we have fun
my little sister happy and be there so she won't hurt as I did
loyalty runs deep

my love is the foundation
my fun joy and laughter come from
my faith
my friends won't let me down
Unity
is perfect
something they need

they have to watch out
when they are playing
there are strangers where we play
if we are at school,
there is supposed to be secure
from a dark place
my innocence is taken from me at a young age

Openings, Not Closings

I must end this section with the poem "The Game of Life" written and shared by Black girls in South Carolina for the 2018 Girls Speak Out. Their poem issues a demand for what girls want and is also threaded through with what hurts girls, dreams and desires, feeling myself, feeling afraid, and the chains that bind. The piece ends with a declaration of self-determination that these

Black girls from SC wanted the whole world of girls to hear and respond to; ultimately it interferes with the status quo. This poetic echo resounds with evidence that SWP "relate[s] to the girls, connect[s] the state and the personal, and address[es] the usual problem and a differently proposed solution," because when global girls are connected to each other and performing their experiences alongside possibilities for resolution and growth, SWP becomes "effective as a method of solidarity" (Brown 2013, 149). SC Black girls composed a poem about life, about the games and strategies for winning, and most of all about the transformative possibilities that girls learn for themselves and teach each other. Their story has not yet been told!

THE GAME OF LIFE

I'm misunderstood
left in the background
told I'm difficult, never enough
for the world around me
being looked at differently
being underestimated
treated unfairly
doubted on
in need of justice
LEAVE ME ALONE
I'm not finished, I'm still living to tell my story
when you feel like you are nothing to the world
remember, you are everything
you are the past, present, future
love the person you are becoming and who you already are
be the new person
this is who I am—an African American southern girl who is not ashamed
    of my skin
I will stand proudly
as if it were a first place gold medal
don't let anyone change your mind
remember the feeling of being worthy
I am the past, present, and future—a new generation that is untold!

SOUTH CAROLINA BLACK GIRLS, 2018

CHAPTER 5

"My Shining Makes You Glow"

Motherhood and Girls from the Future

There is a poetic echo with a burden of energy and expectation in its call-and-response through the girls' SWP: Motherhood. The theme of motherhood is a quantum justice leap that stretches us simultaneously into futurity and history for global girls that is complex, exciting, and painful. The fifth element is at once personal, universal, spiritual, and embodied through motherhood; for girls, this poetic echo is also infused with urgency. Decision making about becoming a mother is a girl's responsibility but not always her choice. The value and punishment for mothers who perform against social expectations are extreme, and as Claudia reminds, "to be a girl is to be a woman" who is unfairly held responsible for children. Worldwide, the expectations and privileges of motherhood are at the forefront of girls' time and attention. For example, at Girls Speak Out, Sophia's speculative strategy based on the symbolism and reality that motherhood would and has come to pass was rooted in Indigenous Futurity and raised awareness about why girls are concerned about their gendered roles. Power and degradation converge here. At once, Time is inverted and reversed and raced forward for girls. As a result, I examine two quantum justice leaps focused on motherhood; one represented in chapter 5, which propels us to consider motherhood as the future for girls, and the second in chapter 6, which will vault us through the past, reflecting on the mothers of the girls who share their SWP. Both quantum justice leaps resist any easy or superficial attempt to smooth or avoid disruption to how motherhood is operationalized in the lives of global girls. Motherhood is not a monolith. Global girls understand the gravity of this theme and echoed it to give advice to other girls, to rage with them, to pay tribute, or to stoke their desire for motherhood.

Love Is the New Money: Hawassa, Ethiopia

Even feeling the most pain
Sickness, and putting me in a coma
Please give me love that never costs you
Feed me when I am hungry and give me something to drink when I am thirsty.
When I feel, who will hold me and say I am at your back?
That's the one who I can say is mine.
By giving love and avoiding discriminating.
If you hate me, go far from me.
I have a silent gun inside my heart,
Love and strength to kill all those limits you give me . . .

Roza needed no encouragement to perform. She spoke in a clear voice, and although she was reading from her notebook, she looked up, making eye contact with girls in the audience earnestly to emphasize her points. We were seated on the ground, and as Roza continued, the sounds of "whew!" teeth sucking, and hand claps and snaps could be heard from the other forty girls seated around me. Encouraged, Roza began to pace back and forth in front of us, growing louder and emphasizing her points with great emotion. She clutched her free hand to her breast on "when I feel, who will hold me and say I am at your back?" Wrapping that same arm around her slim waist, she tipped her head to one side, ear almost touching her shoulder. The more animated Roza's performance became, the more physical and vocal the responses from the audience grew, shifting in their seats, leaning on each other, calling their sympathy to Roza. When she finished, she bowed deeply as the other girls clapped loudly and cheered her name. Almaz couldn't contain herself and leapt from her chair to meet Roza as she returned to the audience. "We have to include that one in the play!" Tegnane leaned over to me and repeated herself to make sure I heard her. "We have to!" I nodded, not taking my eyes off Roza's energetic performance. She was captivating and fearless. After Roza regained her seat, I called out, "Okay, who wants to go next?" The girls looked at each other, and some shook their heads. "Oh, so no one wants to follow Roza? She was that good, right?" Roza, now back to herself after leaving her performing persona at the front, stood again where she was. "You want I should go again?" she called, teasing the girls, knowing she had completed only the one poem. Claps and laughs rose from the other girls until Roza bowed again with a flourish and a silly smile and sat back

MOTHERHOOD AND GIRLS FROM THE FUTURE

down. Tegnane rolled her eyes dramatically, again draping her arm over my lap to make sure I saw her. "I will go next. Someone has to." She straightened and stood to make her announcement, hugging her notebook to her chest. "I will go next!" she called out. "Tell me what you think. And I hope you do like it." Tegnane was exceptionally good as a poet; she had a flair for drama, and she was a strong writer, so I was excited to hear what she would share. I looked over at the faces of the other girls in the audience. They were all turned up toward Tegnane, waiting. After checking to make sure everyone was watching her, Tegnane looked down and began to read.

> World . . . listen to me.
> I am a girl who can be a mother
> I am a girl who can be a best wife for my husband
> I am the one who is the mature sister
> I can be the one who is the best leader and follower
> I believe that you love your mom/sister/wife so I am who can be these all the basis of all nature.
>
> but why do you want to limit me?
> cover all my shine and damn me.
> please don't.
> my shining always makes you glow more makes you all more powerful.
>
> but now I understand:
> to fight for myself and bring you to this kind of thinking
> to hold your hand and see a better world together.
> I am confident together we can all change.
>
> TEGNANE, ETHIOPIA

Tegnane appeals to the sense of familial relations between herself and her listeners who, according to her, are the whole "world." Tegnane understands the connectedness between herself and her bodily autonomy as it impacts the relationships of all girls in the world. Specifically, she lists the roles of "mother," "wife," and "sister" that overlie and inflate her social value. These relationships position girls as full of potential but as valuable based only on how they might perform as contributors to others. Tegnane makes a plea, staking her own safety and future on the hope that her audience—the "world"—loves or at least respects their "mom/sister/wife." She bargains with her capacity and personality as "maturity" and "best" and reminds that girls like her are fruitful "as the basis of all nature." She positions girls as the source, the life-givers, the origin story of "all nature." Tegnane carefully decided to approach her listeners as people who are capable of love in an immediate relational sense but not for girls they aren't related to or for girls who are conceptualized as an abstract category of human being. She positions herself beneath the "world" and requests that they reconsider girls by reminding them of girls' contributions to their lives. Tegnane is wise at playing up dominant scripts and demonstrates a clear understanding of how she is socially perceived. She is strategic in her tactics to achieve a goal; she seems to understand that proving her value will ultimately provide her with the platform she wants. That platform allows her to teach. Indrawatie Biseswar (2008a) succinctly reminds us that "feminism is strategizing for political confrontation that aims at transformation" (129), and Tegnane is performing a radical version of feminism through her limited agency as a girl subject in this SWP. She decides to "bring you to this kind of thinking" because she is "the best leader and follower," and her plan is not to leave but to "hold your hand," and to fight for herself by teaching.

Tegnane relies on her knowledge that the "world" includes her immediate community, and those people organize social power according to a normative ideal of subjecthood and gender, a "socially organized set of achievements," and thus a performance and not a set of defined characteristics (West and Zimmerman 1987, 129). The social hierarchy values her girlhood only as it relates to her potential to become a "wife" or "mother" and to her role as a responsible "sister." She is clear that those who wield power do not view her, or any girl, as valuable as a girl alone: girls must perform or excel at "doing gender" in a way that appeases the powerful (West and Zimmerman, 1987). Thus, to achieve her goal—"to fight for myself and bring you to this kind of thinking"—she begins softly, by appealing to their investments in her current position for their own benefit: joining her ultimately improves their own lives (Oyowe 2014). Had Tegnane not been able to conform to these dominant power relations, or should she fall outside of their version of potential girlhood for any reason, she would have no basis for her persuasive argument. Judith Butler (1993) posed the question "Which bodies come to matter—and why?" (p. xii). Tegnane matter-of-factly answers in the first stanza of her poem— maybe mothers matter, but not girls.

Refracting Identities

As an Ethiopian girl in Hawassa, Tegnane is always performing more than she intends or can control. In so doing she pits competitive discourses against each other to re-create the tensions that forged her girlhood, perhaps in the hopes of repositioning herself. She "understands" that for her not-yet hopes to come to pass, she must assist the "world" with arriving there, a conflict-ridden site, and she will play the role of "mature sister" and "mother" and "wife" with care as indicated by "take you by the hand." She is willing to acquiesce to these social norms "together" in her present so that she can be "confident" that her future will "change" before she arrives. Patriarchy regulates the ways girls continue to be valued only in their relationships with men or proximity to Whiteness or compliance with the GID discourses of properly scripted third world girls as victims. Tegnane plays up her intention to adhere to these harmful scripts that embed her body within a rubric of political economy such that she is worthy of producing but not of any value beyond that (McFadden 1993; Peoples 2008; White 2011). She mirrors the mainstream colonial, global, national, and patriarchal demands that propel and coerce Black African girls like her to imagine themselves worthy only when they are commodified and in alignment with ideologies that reproduce Black African girls' bodies as objects. It is by virtue of their future transactional value that others in power consider them in the present. Tegnane wants to be recognized in the present, for "girls are not merely 'women in waiting' but members of our communities today . . . citizens with a full set of rights and expectations right now" (Kirk and Garrow 2003, 6). In her SWP, Tegnane places enormous value on her role as a "mother" because she is "the basis for all nature," but she does not see the responsibility of motherhood as a limitation. Rather, she presents herself as a girl in process, in between, at the axis of all the roles and subjectivities she incorporated into her poem.

Tegnane's performance troubles the status quo for girls like her. From this perspective, the use of future tense, identifying as "women" while legally and physically being limited as girls, invokes protection and futuristic potential for girls who don't always have control over the responsibilities they must bear, which are adultlike in their seriousness. Black African girls are genius at refracting the light to illuminate the sights they want others and outsiders to focus on. Such a refraction occurs when girls are navigating the available social positions, passing, taking up and putting down the identities that will afford them the most social mobility with the highest potential for their security. Switzer (2009) identifies such an example in her study on the narratives of education by Maasai "schoolgirls," and she notes that identity categories can be created and rejected by girls "to protect them from the conventional exigencies of being female" (4). In the case of Switzer's project, the Maasai girls position themselves between the social and cultural categories of girls and women by identifying as "students," which affords protection from early marriage and simultaneously acquires the vulnerability of girlhood. The girls in Hawassa have a keen sense of survival and use the various written and visual artwork they create as a means of "pitting one social category against another in an effort to find the most room for maneuver . . . using cultural codes once used to define them in limiting ways to define themselves in liberating ways" (10). Tegnane explores these categories and possible avenues for flexing her agency through photography, poetry, and performance.

Tegnane refuses to be consigned to objectification, and her SWP performance functions as a tool to assist her cultivating disruption to local institutions and global GID scripts. Tegnane becomes a producer of culture, already competing with normative neoliberal agendas but primarily concerned with her immediate daily life. Tegnane seems to agree that change must occur across the immediate intimate relations of a girl's life if broader social and political shifts are to be made. Her performance theorizes and practices a politics "that could be employed in not just naming [her] current experiences but also in experimenting and modeling ways of being that are now unimaginable" (Cox 2015, 63). Although material equity continues to be denied to girls and women, there are related areas of life that are slowly improving. South African activist Mary Tal (2011) insists that "we can't work in isolation" and suggests that the immaterial improvements she has witnessed are of critical importance for girls and women, just like the tangible things such as money and property ownership. She shares: "They came with no self-esteem; they couldn't even introduce themselves. Now they are confident. Now they stand up in crowds and advocate for women's needs. This has given me great courage" (30). As a grassroots activist, Tal points out an important component that is often overlooked: the instability of process and the ways that change connects the internal and external lives of girls.

Tal illustrates the complicated relationships that SWP encourages girls to navigate with skilled maneuvering. Tegnane tackles a huge undertaking: she must persuade the "world" to value her position, to cease their "limit" of her and "cover" of her "shine," and appeals to their self-serving mainstream appetites to "shine more" and to be "all more powerful" for her to achieve her objective. Tegnane's approach to convincing the "world" about why she deserves to be free parallels other African feminist organizations' frustrated attempts at convincing the patriarchy to change. Tal (2011) argues:

> We come from a society where if you don't have a husband, you can't have respect or dignity; where you are not a woman unless you can have a child; where a woman who has a girl child is despised and hated for not being able to provide a successor for the husband. (32)

Tegnane struggles with the modesty expected of a girl like her; the tension of submitting and at the same time owning her shine, in service of her "world." Tegnane authors herself, all the while knowing that her "world" will likely not be able to read her, rendering her illegible, *except* to her girl audience. She relies on the assumption that other girls are also inhabiting spaces where they are read only through dominant discourse and thus models a way to achieve more recognition if that is their aim, like her. Just because she is a recognized member of the dominant discourse by the "world" that rules it does not mean she always or wishes only for identification. Instead, she manipulates their expectations and risks her acceptance within social norms by "fighting for [her]self and tak[ing] you by the hand." Her struggle is a pedagogical one—and SWP is the critical pedagogy that positions her students, the "world" that is "listen[ing]" to her, as coconstructing the meaning and knowledge of the master narratives, the normative subject positions, and the discourses that she occupies. Tegnane's SWP is an example of the ways she understands the instability of the master discourses that produce her as a subject. Although pervasive, they are socially constructed. Her desire to teach and learn with her girl audience and the larger-scoped "world" expresses that she is keenly aware of both processes occurring at once and the conflicting ways they pressure her to articulate herself. There are contradictions within an ever-evolving but always overbearing discourse that dangles an impossibly smooth and cohesive subjectivity just out of reach for girls like Tegnane. When those discourses are compared with the processes by which she, as a rural Ethiopian girl from Hawassa, is always under social construction, it makes the terrain she must navigate slippery. She strategically embodies this knowledge referring to her physical form in the poem itself, and then again in her performance. She understands that the social subject positions available to her will shift depending on where her audience is located, historically, geographically, and politically, and so relies on those shifts to make her imagined future subject position available.

Throughout her poem, Tegnane journeys through a negotiation of herself as subject first, in the future tense as inhabiting the identities of "wife," "mother," and "sister." She then pauses with a question to her audience: "why do you want to limit me." This suggests that she can possibly become more or that she already is creating her life outside of these imposed limits on the social roles she can play (Oyowe 2014). Tegnane gestures to her own subjectivity and challenges how the "world" is invested in maintaining those tidy categories for her, and the lived realities of what it means for her to "be recognized by others and recognize oneself as a girl" (Gonick 2003, 10). In her multiple and unfinished identities, she uses SWP to demonstrate the ways that she is already living beyond the story being narrated about her, in the present and the future (Britzman 1998). Tegnane's poetry allows her to prophesy and invoke the imaginations of her "world" in a way that legitimizes her desires beyond what history (the past) and society (her present) currently allow for her to inhabit.

Discourses about Ethiopian girls in particular function to produce and restrict not only Tegnane's imaginary girlhood, but the social conditions that shape it for her. Her SWP calls up and aligns with the dominant discourse in her quest to subvert its circulation. Tegnane's performance of her gender, her girlhood, and her poetry does not end with a call for her "world" to make a social change only for her sake. Her SWP is radical, and in its performance Tegnane dares to imagine herself as a teacher so that her audience, the "world," becomes her students. She bravely reaches beyond what she has experienced and, after acquiescing to the roles determined for her by her community, explains how they would also benefit from sharing resources with her. Tegnane's poem is put to work and performs triple duties, as resistance, as a revision of girlhood, and as performance pedagogy. She situates her "world" acknowledging her status within it, appeals to change it, and in so doing already subverts the discourse. Finally, she explicitly states her understanding that she must "fight for [her]self and bring you to this thinking." She is the teacher-artist, experiencing the audience-student and "world's" resistance to learning new things and interrupting ideological patterns through her creative performance. Tegnane is already engaged in the struggle of resistance and seems to be dedicated to "see[ing] a better world together."

Her rejection of normative discourse is evident when she pleads, "Why do you want to cover my shine and damn me? Please don't," for she understands that who she can be and how she can participate in social interactions is beyond her individual control, regardless of her personal decisions. She is ultimately still at the mercy of the powerful, who can choose to recognize her or not. Tegnane engages bravely with this act of interpellation, appealing to the overwhelming discourses that call her into being and produce and construct her as a subject. She knowingly outlines her strategy—"bringing you" so that you "see" her kind of thinking . . . together"—and thus draws attention to the existing dynamics in engaging the potentially dangerous processes of producing herself by speaking her way into existence, and admitting to the power applied through regulatory demands of normative discourses (Hall 1996 as in Gonick 2003, 10). She wants her life to change and understands that the cultural forces shaping her life must also change. Tegnane also understands that those forces "limit" her and "cover her shine" and will "damn her" to a life beyond repair or restoration, beyond what she currently views as limited and unlivable. She seems to have had experience with these outcomes or witnessed them, which clarifies why she is so accommodating to the "world" at the start of her treaty. Tegnane's critique of the culture must be cloaked in gentleness, grace, and soft words to protect her from further harm. Her tenderness with a "world" that has so wrongly abused her does not lessen the revolutionary call for action she issues—in fact, her calmness strengthens it.

Tegnane is socially literate in the extreme. Her ability to navigate and her fluency in how she wields agency, although limited, benefits her in remarkable ways. Her astute reading of the discursive limitations imposed on her by the nation, the law, and tradition, and reinforced by her family, is what equips and enables her to survive, seek protection, and possibly access some means of social mobility. At the same time, she relies on the ability of her girl audience to read the messages she is conveying subversively within those bounds. Tegnane knows that Black girls around the world must recognize themselves in the other (Durham 2014; Moraga 1981). Weaponizing her nimbleness, she wields agency through these same relationships that bind her to limited available subject positions. SWP is an outreach to her global girl audience. Her ability to recite the historically empowered discourses that situate her limited accessibility as a girl show us what matters most to her. Tegnane reveals those entrenched boundaries and exposes the discursive territory she is permitted to explore. The way she consciously chooses to navigate that space partially reveals her desires to us.

Tegnane has assessed her living situation, her realities, and the options offered to her through normative discursive constructions of her identity and decides to use her SWP to ensure a disruption to them, so she is properly recognized. Tegnane tells multiple truths through her poetry and embodies the contradictions that she examines in her performance. Reaching far beyond her individual agency, she remains mindful of the power dynamics through which she will be read. She seeks new opportunities for her otherwise imminent future, looking for chances that occur beyond the boundaries of truth her SWP represents. In her efforts to be "more than," she shapes and reshapes herself, decidedly occupying the contradictory, appealing to those who subjugate her, and simultaneously refusing their interpellation of her positionalities within the discourse of girlhood. The specificities of Tegnane's identity, of how she can achieve recognition, calls to mind the People's Poet, the powerful June Jordan's (1995) claims about how poetry functions, as "a political action undertaken for the sake of information, the faith, the exorcism, and the lyrical invention that telling the truth makes possible" (Muller and Jordan, 3). Through SWP, she re-produces culture and knowledge, which necessitates inventing new alternatives to replace the deconstruction of the social and cultural practices that are raced and gendered. Her success and hopefulness may be distracting us from her own investments in her nation's and family's current social norms. Tegnane stands to lose dangerously or to tenuously gain, depending on the success of her investments.

"If Water Falls" Cycles for Mothers and Daughters

Ethiopian girls have been expertly finding ways to manipulate their subjectivity in the hopes of altering their contextual circumstances long before any scholar from the West was paying attention to them. Marjani's SWP is one such example:

> I didn't understand
> why my brother learns when I stayed home? when my mother sends my brother to school she says to me—work at home
> clean the house make food.
>
> once my uncle came from the North
> he wanted to see me and my brother
> he just became angry and shouted at my mom
> he says what's going on with your mom? why didn't you send her to school?
> why didn't you send her?
> why you just put her at home?
> so you want her to be like you staying at home?
> then my mom feels sad.
> then she starts to send me and my brother to school.
> but I know now my enemy is my mom
> if she never let me stay at home I never taste this bad life the same thing that happened to her happened to me
> when she didn't make not history what repeats on her
> if I regret now I can't change nothing
> if water falls you can't just collect it
> I can't take it back
> now I will educate my girl
> not to repeat my own story with my daughter
> it started with my mom but won't go on with my daughter
> not making my girls stay at home

MOTHERHOOD AND GIRLS FROM THE FUTURE

I will let her out to go to school
never will happen to her what happened to me
to make her visions and reach her goals let mother live forever

MARJANI, ETHIOPIA

Marjani's poem is written in reflection of her experience with her mother and brings sharply into focus the conflict that occurs when a family must make decisions. Her SWP reveals "the larger dynamics of interlocking privileges, visibilities, powers, and . . . consequences" beyond intellectual debates in women's and gender studies, GID discourses, and governmental policies and enrobes those abstractions in real-life flesh and blood (Cox 2015, 6). Marjani's SWP propels us deeply into cyclical familial dynamics, especially her relationship with her mother. There is an unfortunate legacy of neglect, "a history here" of failure to respond to Black girls who face danger, and who are ignored (7). While there is published research that covers the quantitative statistics of underage pregnancy, sexual activity, and other health-related phenomena for Ethiopian girls, there is a dearth of any published work that brings into focus the relationships between mothers and daughters (Berhan and Berhan 2015; Boyden et al. 2012; Ibrahim et al. 2018; Mitiku 2011; Presler et al. 2016; Semela et al. 2019; Stark et al. 2018). What does it mean for girls in Hawassa to occupy the identities of a daughter and a mother? Why does Marjani blame her mother, writing "now I know my enemy is my mom"? Even as she acknowledges "the same thing that happened to her happened to me," Marjani's anger is directed only at her mother for continuing the cycle that forced her into early marriage and motherhood. Although Marjani shares a story that seems at first to repeat narratives on the persistent dangers of early marriage and subsequent forced childbearing, her performance also creates opportunities to problematize the dangerous terrain of this experience along with her. To disentangle this complex story, we must hear a difficult narrative, one that at first glance appears to undo the work of postcolonial feminisms and troubles SWP as political texts (Sensoy and Marshall 2010). There are many points of departure from these tropes, and her poem is multidimensional—just as she is—layered and complex. Her SWP offers multiple pivots that deviate from GID discourse, three of which I explore below. First, decisions are made on her behalf by her mother, and she situates her audience amid that difficult relationship. Second, the power and influence of men and the ways they dictate even mother-daughter relationships is exposed. Third, we are thrust into Marjani's own decision-making process and how she, like Tegnane, strategizes a future to spite her present, vaulted by momentum from her past experiences. The poetic echoes between motherhood and making decisions converge as important, if under-researched, forces across these two poems by girls in Hawassa.

Gendered Threats and Challenges

Structured as a linear story that traces major decisions impacting her life, Marjani's poem chronologically follows three of these choices made by her mother: staying home instead of going to school, attending school, and early marriage. She opens her poem by making us immediately uncomfortable, as if we are accidentally present during the private family argument that has obviously happened many times before. According to Marjani's SWP, her brother can attend school, but she is made to stay home and obligated to take care of domestic duties. "I don't understand," she writes, why he was allowed "to learn" and she was required to "clean the house make food." Such domestic duties consume Marjani's time and likely do not permit her any free time for leisure or recreation (Pankhurst et al. 2016). Although she does not explicitly mention physical abuse in her poem, a recent study shows that Marjani has a 90 percent chance of being exposed to violence.

> Most girls have to prioritize domestic work over school. Balancing household and school responsibilities can lead to a cycle of violence for girls at home and at school, and they are punished for under-performance in both locations. (Pankhurst et al. 2016, 10)

Although boys are equally exposed to physical violence, the same study later shows that they begin to torment girls physically at a young age in ways that girls do not reciprocate, and this violence is connected to other health dangers at home and in the workplace for girls (Dereje et al. 20145; Roba et al. 2015; Teshome et al. 2013). Additionally, due to the extreme poverty in rural Ethiopia, many girls migrate to urban locales or cross national borders to gain employment and support their families. As they enter the workforce, they are made vulnerable to abuses in workplace settings (Gonsamo 2019). Every single one of the girls who participated in GGG shared that they had experienced varying levels of street harassment from boys, from sexual comments to physical assault and rape. Every single one of them had elected not to report it or to tell their family, for fear of reprisal. The collaboration for the Hawassa workshop was made possible by three grassroots organizations: Long Live the Girls!, Breakarts, and Action for Youth and Community Change. Part of our outcomes included the publication of the girls' creative work in a book for them to keep (*Long Live the Girls: Love Rules* [2015] was locally published in Hawassa by Breakarts and Action for Youth and Community Change), locally designed and printed T-shirts with our logo and theme for the girls, and colorful glossy stickers that read, "Long Live the Girls! Love Rules" in English and Amharic. We initially brainstormed an app for cell phones that girls could use to mark geographic locations as safe spaces for girls to be or to post warnings if they had encountered danger somewhere in town. This idea had myriad issues, the first being a practical one of limited access to wi-fi and the fact that not every girl in the program had a cell phone to use. The second problem was one that the guest facilitators and the locally based director had repeated issues with, which included limited access to internet websites and the dangers of doing what might be interpreted as speaking out against the national government. While we were in Hawassa planning and organizing, we talked through these issues, because the girls' safety was our major concern. We understood our work as deeply political, but we did not conceive of our work with the girls as threatening or protesting the government administration, because this would have potentially endangered the girls and our partners at AYCC. We quickly learned that poetry and performance by girls that were interpreting decades-old policies intended to protect them were perceived quite differently by local men and business owners. After the T-shirts were designed and made, the girls proudly wore them, styling the simple black T-shirts with gold sparkly letters with their traditional Ethiopian woven skirts and scarves, or Western shorts and pants. During the program several of the girls wore the shirts and were accosted because of the slogan "Long Live the Girls!" They were not hurt but were threatened by groups of boys and men as they walked and carried out their daily routines. Our thought was that if it wasn't safe for the girls to even wear their shirts, then we could not think about developing an app. News of the journalists and young people known as Zone 9 online bloggers who had been imprisoned because of their digital activism had spread, and we realized that we must proceed with utmost caution (see https://www.hrw.org/news/2015/04/23/ethiopia-free-zone-9-bloggers-journalists). Digital space was unsafe, and so were the actual streets of Hawassa.

In place of the app, we decided to print stickers. The stickers began to serve as a discreet way of tagging space, like graffiti artists' work. Girls could add the stickers to public spaces without any personal identifying information and without being seen or recognized. They would still understand the code of the stickers, but they would be more likely to avoid physical harm or harassment. If the tools we were hoping to design for LLTG had potential to trigger the exact types of harm we were working to talk back to through SWP performances, then what were we doing? We worked with the girls and within our already tight budget to adapt as best we could. Varying levels of violence from boys and men continued to occur during the workshops. The congregation of girls' and women's bodies outside the home provoked such strong reactions. Men were shocked to see non-Ethiopians in Hawassa, and total strangers with no familial relation to the girls were suddenly very concerned with them, expressing a paternal protectiveness by giving them attention that was prompted only by the presence of non-Ethiopian women. One day I asked Tegnane about the catcalls and rude comments. She saw me walking to the workshop and ran to meet and walk with me the rest of the way to the AYCC. "Are they always like this?" I asked. "Who?" she asked, linking her slender arm through mine. It was hot and dusty on the unpaved road, but I was glad for the easy comfort of her touch. We strolled by the local snack-food spot—not a full-blown restaurant but good for a smashed avocado with hot spice and fresh-baked bread. Three teenage boys looked us up and down and laughed with each other. I averted my eyes, and Tegnane didn't seem to notice. "These boys. They are like this where I live too. Sometimes they follow you and won't leave you alone and say nasty things. I get so tired of it. It makes me mad." I was speaking too quickly because I was so frustrated. Tegnane shrugged. "You get used to it." She was nonchalant. I took a deep breath and shook my head. *Let it go*, I thought to myself, *just be here. Who do you think you are, anyway?* She pulled my arm suddenly, almost tipping me over, and reached for my bag, slung across my body to try and alleviate my chronic back issues. "Did you bring music today? We can dance again!" She was smiling and pulling my bag around to the side she was walking on. She flipped open the flap and spotted my USB drive that had current club-worthy tunes saved to it. We had so much fun the previous afternoon, dancing until all fifty of us were out of breath. Reaching for the USB drive, she unwrapped her arm from mine. "The music is here!" She started walking faster, leaving me behind. "I will go ahead," she shouted, waving to me over her shoulder. "I will tell the others!"

Street harassment and the spectrum of gender-based violence was common and frequent. Violence was so insidious that girls like Tegnane responded with a shrug. In the locations I would later visit for GGG that were not hosted in school settings, girls shared similar experiences, whispered in a confessional tone. I include this information here as a point of clarification—although the poem being centered in this section is from a Black African girl, *all* of the girls in this project, myself included, have felt rage and fear resulting from patriarchal rape culture that allows and encourages girls and women to be controlled and threatened in this manner. To dismantle oppressive systems and to write against the violence acted out on girls, it is essential to underscore clear connections between the failures of sexist and racist institutions and the endangerment of girls' lives.

Make-Ups to Break-Ups: Love Rules

Marjani's SWP enlightens her audience to how those critical failures, which have been touted as final triumphs by policy makers at the UN, remain disconnected from the lived realities of Ethiopian girls, thus further disenfranchising them. SWP and performance provide unique lenses for legislators to understand girls like Marjani. She illustrates her embeddedness within the systems that governing bodies uphold and create, which could provide the adults in charge with an epistemic advantage. If girls like Marjani were heeded prior to the formation of articles or consulted on policy development and implementation strategies, there might be a major shift; revisions to family articles of the constitution might position girls as rights-bearing subjects, or the extreme reduction of the national government's financial support for any community-based grassroots NGO receiving funding by foreign organizations might be repealed (Jones, Presler-Marshall, et al. 2018, 70–71). Currently, the Ethiopian People's Revolutionary Democratic Front national government maintains the controlling practices established by its prior Dergue military regime, which lost power in 1991. Although organizations such as the Ethiopian Women Lawyers Association have made radical progress on behalf of women and girls in the judicial system, Biswesar (2008) reminds "confrontation with the state, however, is carefully maneuvered and avoided" (135). In accordance with the girl factor, agencies with good intentions or feminist aspirations must focus on dodging relentless state control to advocate for social change (Skalli 2015). Subversion remains a survival skill that is advantageous for advocacy and activism for women and girls. As a result, critical aspects of life such as sexuality or sexual activity of girls remain heavily influenced by religion and regional cultural context and are thus constructed as inappropriate or personal. Campaigns and research studies that target African youth frame them as if their individual behavior is the key to institutional policy change, when in fact the governmental paradigm itself needs to be shifted (Kalipeni et al. 2007; Nyanzi et al. 2001; Ricardo et al. 2006; Taylor 2007). This approach creates more crises, and it is difficult to respond beyond triage or to unravel on a grassroots or community-based level, but there are activists advocating on the ground working through these thick tensions.

During LLTG, we were able to host Miseret Roge, a gender specialist at the Hawassa City Administration Bureau of Women, Children and Youth. This was an incredible honor for us. During her formal presentation to the girls, she discussed gender-based violence, but very little discussion followed her talk. I wondered how she experienced life in Hawassa, given her rare position and unusual job title. I understood her work to be comparable to that of a social worker in the US, responsible for providing support to the women and children she encountered because of the high occurrences of domestic violence. As soon as her presentation was finished, she left to quickly return to her office. Despite the threats and "calculated state control," women in local-level bureaucratic positions continue to do the heavy lifting in the struggle to advocate for girls (135). Roge's intergenerational efforts on behalf of the girls in Hawassa are monumental, as are her challenges; LLTG girls benefited from her attention that afternoon.

Marjani's SWP secures her validity among her global girl audience, beyond her skilled maneuvering around the local arm of the existing national power structure. Because Marjani has granted us access to her world through SWP, we are presented with an opportunity to reconsider how we operate within it. The epistemic advantage she claims through writing and performing recreates and revises how she understands herself and her possibilities within the world, which leads to insight we would not otherwise be privy to (Narayan 2003, 315). What role do we wish to continue to play within her world? It is obvious that the position we enjoy is privileged, as we are an audience to this performance rather than the subject of it. However, we are already also shaping the world, because SWP inherently incorporates its audience as knowledge producers. Part of the genius in her poem is that Marjani bluntly critiques her mother's participation in the institutionalized systems for a shred of protection, positioning her mother as both well-intentioned guardian and guilty perpetrator. Her poem demonstrates the challenges her mother confronts as she faces the same patriarchal systems. Laws or no laws, policy or not, gender-based violence remains at epidemic proportions. What would happen if average girls and women were consulted about the development of policy that is purportedly put in place to protect them before it is passed, rather than discovering it later, if at all? Marjani's poem cannot be reduced to a teenage rant rebelling against her mother: she demands change even as she acknowledges the sacrifices and abuse she will likely face as a result of her refusal to participate in gendered norms. Although an increasing number of women across the continent of Africa, and specifically within Ethiopia, are entering and participating in higher education and other vocational opportunities, the perpetual lack of basic support and resources largely contributes to the repressive daily social lives of most girls and young women (Ampofo et al. 2004; Biswesar 2008; Mama 2011; Mulugeta 2004). In other words, contrary to neoliberal GID propaganda, education and economic leverage have *not* miraculously dissolved the dilemma of gender-based violence. The opposite, in fact, has happened; it has illuminated a localized cultural backlash against human rights for women and girls who try to attend and partake in some of these enterprises, marketed as available and promising social mobility. Biswesar decries the institutionalized marketing of GID agendas because of their focus on "emancipation in terms of their active participation in state-directed policies, programs, and intervention areas. Women are expected to support the state agenda and any deviation from this is not tolerated" (141). Specifically, Swai (2010) argues against the "empowerment agenda" that promotes an assumption that education equates to accessibility to resources and self-determination for women and girls such that "their superiority renders them always more empowered than their less educated peers" (33). Formal education does not automatically induce social transformation for girls and women. Instead, such interventions often cause more instability and fail to be implemented in the daily lives of girls.

While the change in national government in 1991 began a new era in legislation for the rights of women and girls, and statistics since national reforms in 2005 and again in 2018 reflect some quantifiable improvement, the top-down approach to shifting customs and ideologies remains ineffective at best and, at worst, has provoked increased danger for girls (Jones, Tefera, et al. 2018). Statistics do not reflect the average girl's experience or story. The uptick in violence is instigated and reinforced by national policies and state actors (Biswesar 2008). School and work, the two purported solutions for stopping human rights violations, have also created environments where violent behavior toward girls is normalized, socialized, and rehearsed (Burman 1995; Croll 2007; Fennell and Arnot 2008). Although the particularities may vary on an individual level, this issue remains institutionalized and culturally pervasive for most girls and women.

Because violence is inflicted by men and boys and internalized and perpetuated by women, the next stanza peers into an interesting familial dynamic between Marjani's uncle and her mother. She writes:

> once my uncle came from the North
> he wanted to see me and my brother
> he just became angry and shouted at my mom
> he says what's going on with your mom? Why didn't you send her to school?

Why didn't you send her?
Why you just put her at home?
so you want her to be like you staying at home?
Then my mom feels sad.

Marjani's uncle intervenes on her behalf when he "became angry and shouted," asking "why didn't you send her to school?" which repeats and emphasizes Marjani's own question from the first stanza. He pushes further, asking "so you want her to be like you staying at home?" which indicates how Marjani might also perceive her mother, refusing to allow her to "learn" like her brother because she wants Marjani to follow her path, a more traditional life, instead. Why does her "mom feel sad" at the end? Is it because her own vicissitudes of life have entrenched her in tradition? As Marjani later refers to being forced into early marriage, many questions about her mother's life emerge. How old is Marjani's mother? How much control or say-so is she able to access or exercise? Elizabeth Ngutuku and Auma Okwany (2017) probe into the intersecting demands on the lives of youth and mothers, in their comparative work with adolescents as coresearchers in sexual health studies in Uganda and Ethiopia. Their work reminds that in East African contexts, the responsibility for sexual activity rests on girls' bodies and decisions "without regard to how their status as young and dependent on adults (age, gender power relations) influences this gate keeping" (Ngutuku and Okwany 2017, 74; Okwany 2016). Marjani's personal drama plays out against this political context. Her mother's real and perceived access to sovereignty is made murky. What were her mom's motivations? Marjani never mentions her father's role in all of this, yet we assume that he is present or involved and providing for them all, since there is enough money to send both children to school. The mother-daughter relationship is a frustrated one, perhaps because Marjani expects her mom to be on her side and to advocate for her to have what she perceives as a more liberated life via educational opportunity. The options available to Marjani's mother are unclear; the strains and pressures she is perhaps shielding Marjani from or grooming her to endure may be reflected in her determination for her daughter's young life. What is the status of the school near Marjani's family home? Is it safe for girls? Is the route between school and home safe for her to travel, or has harm befallen other girls who attend school? It is easy to assume her mother has only reputation or cultural norms at the heart of her refusal of Marjani's enrollment, but what might her reasons be? What are the discourses her mother is operating within? Could she know something Marjani doesn't know, or is she facing threats or working to prevent other potentially more vulnerable positioning of her daughter? Why does the uncle who "came from the North" (meaning he lived far away) have so much sway over Marjani's mom? The second stanza and this "shouted" interrogation of her mother reveals conflict beyond a simple mother-daughter squabble.

After identifying her "mom as [her] enemy," because "if she never let me stay at home I never taste this bad life," Marjani blames her mother for not changing the historic cycle that is repeating its pattern within their family. Early marriage, early childbirth, and daughters who bring shame when they are born all factor into her rage. Marjani's subjectivity is muddied, and the ambiguity frustrates her. We are left to ponder a line of inquiry that is frequently neglected in studies about girls and mothers, namely, "which categories of young people are structured as non-youth (married or parenting youth) due to normative notions of who is an adolescent and who is not" (Ngutuku and Okwany 2017, 74). Marjani inserts herself deliberately as an actor on her own daughter's behalf:

> if water falls you can't just collect it
> I can't take it back
> now I will educate my girl
> not to repeat my own story with my daughter

The only future hope she expresses is for her own child. Marjani perceives herself as an agent, imbued with the ability to change the circumstances for her own daughter. "If water falls you can't just collect it" powerfully illustrates the depth to which she feels her mother has ruined her chances at a different outcome. Marjani shares that after becoming mothers soon after marriage, girls "can't just collect" their resource, their "water" symbolizing what they have lost; "I can't take it back," she writes. Her girlhood, her potential, is gone forever. Instead of remaining in a state of regret, Marjani determines "not to repeat my own story with my daughter" and declares that she will chart her own path through motherhood. She tracks the pattern for girls like her and declares she will change the narrative; "it started with my mom but won't go on with my daughter." Her poem is prophecy and links temporal echoes of the past, future, and present.

The last lines in Marjani's SWP prophesy over her new baby girl, projecting a future for her daughter that she will not attain. It is unclear whether the structural and sociocultural transformations will have taken place so that her world will externally support the efforts she makes "to make her visions and reach her goals." The language of her closing line is a conundrum, as she ends with immortality—"let mother live forever"—that seems to give a nod to the name of our workshops, Long Live the Girls!, while simultaneously subverting the organization's claims. Perhaps because Marjani is now a mother, and therefore no longer identifies with girlhood, she alters the title and includes it in the last line. Perhaps she still craves participation with us or wants to be identified with the innocence of girlhood or a more carefree life she enjoyed prior to having the responsibility of her own baby. Perhaps Marjani is critiquing us, her audience, or me as a facilitator, reflecting the hypocrisy of an organization's name that relies on Western identity category constructions that are determined by age parameters she still falls within yet contradict her cultural identity as a wife and mother and therefore woman. Although during our workshops, the "girls" revealed to us that at least two of the participants were in their mid-fifties, and had their own grandchildren, they joined us consistently as an act of reclaiming their girlhood. The Hawassa girls' interpretations of who counts as a girl, who is named a girl, and the differing consequences of being either girl or woman came up often for us in discussion. I was single, unmarried, and had no children, so according to most of them, I was still a girl. They wanted to know how I was able to convince my father to let me travel abroad all alone. They laughed at me: "But you are so old!" "But why are you not married?" "You are small like a girl. How can you be a doctor?" Different versions of the same conversation took place over and over. I was supposed to be aspiring to be a mom and a wife, and I admitted to them, sure, I wanted a fuller life, but, "If I had my own babies, I would not be here with you." They seemed more satisfied with that practical explanation than with any of my other attempts to assure them that I was fulfilled, even as a nonmother. "Let mother live forever" may also be Marjani's grudging respect or affirmation of love to her mom. Another interpretation could be that she is the "mother" and is speaking into existence the longevity of a legacy she is crafting and building. Motherhood, as revisioned by girls from the future, is a remix of their inherited past as girls, cultivating disruption to their present status and the futures they project.

Within Marjani's critique she uplifts her own mother, loving her and submitting to her commands while opposing her as an enemy. Her poem situates her Global North girl audience to interrogate why a woman would not wish advancement for her daughter via the familiar and heavily marketed route of Western education. There is also unmistakable urgency that infuses Marjani's writing; her girl audience is refused a tidy happy ending, even if Marjani's daughter gets to go to school. Her life will be different from Marjani's. She may have a greater chance to "make her visions and reach her goals," but that does not in any way hold the local community accountable for supporting her, nor does it indicate what those goals may be. There is no definite reconciliation with her mother, and she endured child marriage and adolescent childbirth, which limit her mobility. The realities portrayed through Hawassa girls' SWP are yet to be remedied and may seem hopelessly in support of GID discourse about girls in the Global South, yet there is vital insight about mother-daughter relationships in Ethiopia and serious political and cultural critique laced through both girl's poems. Each girl provokes more unraveling, picking at the seams that stitch together a cohesive ideal of daughters and mothers.

Reading Together and Pulling Apart Boundaries of South and North

Tegnane and Marjani shared two poems symbolic of how girls conceptualize mothers, how they are making decisions about motherhood, and how they desire that those decisions be understood. There is a large body of literature that centers the negative social ills that position girls as lacking, in deficit, and policy is then formed as a reactive solution to a girl-based problem. Girls' bodies, which are not only hypervisible but muted in this discourse, are conceptualized as incomplete objects even while expected to fulfill roles of responsibility not only for their own salvation but for that of their communities. Tegnane and Marjani, alongside their newly connected peers in the next chapter, work to dismantle and subvert these top-down approaches through SWP performance, often at their own physical risk and endangerment. Their exposure to SWP rehearsals and ensemble work was not natural or easy to accomplish; it took effort for the girls to feel comfortable enough to perform what they had written. Girls like those in Hawassa are frequently seen, studied, and not heard, and therefore not accustomed to being engaged with as speaking subjects about their embodied experiences, reflections, and observations (Okwany and Ebrahim 2015). Taken seriously, the girls' SWP pushes against this narrative and refocuses their everyday knowledge and evolving cultural activities as central. While local customs must be unpacked for contextual relevance, the girls' SWP jointly rejects "essentialized notions of culture that view culture as an immutable set of negative traits passed down from generation to generation as explanations for inequality" (Mullings 2000, 19). Inherited inequality must be extracted from the everyday normalcy that orders girls' lives. Policy makers and local enforcers interested in a renovation of gender equality need to "acknowledge [girls'] activities and knowledge and look for ways through which they can be applied in school and development policies" (Swai 2010, 14). Swai further contends that scholars interested in pushing back this narrative must refocus on conceptualizing "current conditions of ordinary [girls] in Africa" and how those conditions interplay with the social and governmental institutions working to dislocate them (13). The gaping disconnects between girls' lives in Hawassa, such as the hardships they face nuanced by intimacies they enjoy, problematize an easy reading of their poetry. Quantum justice further challenges the current lack of implementation and shortage of accessible local resources. While I worked to ensure a complicated representation of girls in Hawassa and their lives to the girls who received their work in the Global North, and again here in this text, there are multiple ways this project could be strengthened. However, even with the weaknesses in organizations like LLTG and GGG, there is important data reflective of motherhood within the SWP of girls from Hawassa and New Orleans.

The contextual and historical background that accompanies the poetry and photographs by the Hawassa girls produces sensitivity and savvy about the implications of motherhood. They are daughters, so their lives are shaped around bearing children. Meanwhile, the girls in workshops located in the Global North struggled between engaging with a specific critique of governmental policy and their allegiance to their own mothers. Even in expressions of disagreement with the decisions of their mothers, the girls in New Orleans could not suppress their gratitude. They were extremely sensitive to the ways sacrifice altered the decisions their mothers made to prioritize them. Or, as Amy from New York City shared with me during our discussion about difficult family dynamics, "My mom makes tough decisions, so I don't have to." Girls in Hawassa issue a poetic call about motherhood, one that projects their future. Girls in NOLA respond to that call with an echo that reverberates back to their own mommas, one that lingers in the past, not in their own child-bearing potential. Our next quantum justice leap remains in the poetic echo of motherhood but sends us back, back into Time.

CHAPTER 6

Too Close for Comfort

Motherhood and Girls Revising the Past

I arrived at the high school in New Orleans at the gracious invitation of my friend and coconspirator in education and community uplift, hoping to explore how girls make use of SWP and performance to counter master narratives and challenge dominant political agendas. I made the mistake of thinking I knew these girls because they were the most familiar to me. What I learned was a valuable lesson about how quantum justice works—control is always an illusion. It's not that my questions were wrong, but the girls had other things on their minds. In the complicated, post-Katrina, public education world, I wondered what politicized function poetic performance might offer girls during these times. Why are poetry and performance effective exercises of survival, resistance, and joy at the intersections that emerge throughout girlhoods of the rural South of the US yet in the Global North? The crossroads of these questions are what I wanted answered. However, the girls responded in ways I failed to foresee. I never predicted their SWP would share that they tangle with ideas about motherhood. Motherhood is taken up as an inheritance of generational blessings and trauma, and the spiritual work of revising this past is vitalized by quantum justice and embodied through SWP performance. Hawassa girls engage the theme of motherhood as their present, while NOLA girls invoke it as their past.

Contemporary reverberations are evident from LaKisha Simmons's (2015) rich history of Black girls in Jim Crow era New Orleans, which details the rules of movement enforced by nuns at a local school. She writes:

> One had to understand personal geographies of the body (bodily comportment) and geographies of segregation (the city and streets). . . . In

this way, the Sisters taught the students to find a comfort within themselves, in the space of the French Quarter, and in the larger city. (41)

Simmons's description of the nuns who "obeyed the bodily rules of segregation by knowing where not to go just as they disobeyed them by walking confidently and claiming a sexual modesty for black girls and women" at school in the 1930s provides critical insight about how ethnicity, geography, and morality were perceived, subverted, and socially scripted for Black and Creole girls (41). Safety was a primary lesson, and the three aspects of "bodily comportment," "geographies of segregation," and a sense of security "within themselves" served the girls in Simmons's research with navigational tools for moving through systems of the city, their own bodies, and their local neighborhoods. The rules that regulate behavior and mobility for Black girls in present-day New Orleans are about more than respectability and representation, although they are influenced by those ideologies too. I'm especially struck by the disobedience of the nuns who performed confidence by subverting racial and ethnic identity categories and the performance of religion and respectability, while determining to be secure within themselves. This legacy overlaps the experience of NOLA girls I love whose poetry is in these pages. There are obvious poetic echoes: this workshop also took place at a Catholic school, although not entirely staffed by nuns. Learning and teaching how to destabilize systems is always a part of girlhoods of color, even when operating within a restrictive religious order.

    I couldn't wait to see how NOLA girls were cultivating this legacy of disruption. I am from Louisiana, but the far north—I was not raised in the Crescent City. There is a distinction. New Orleans has its own heavy history and culture that is specific and personal, adaptable but easily recognized. My closest friends from graduate school boomeranged back to south Louisiana after we departed university in central Pennsylvania. They are currently in or have held long careers within the public, private, and charter K–12 school systems in South Louisiana, entrenched within the charter school systems that spread like disease, mutating and changing the color of the educators through New Orleans, especially, but reflected throughout the whole state (Dixson 2011; Dixson et al. 2015; Henry and Dixson 2016). Hurricanes Katrina and Isaac wrought devastation that the state is still recovering from, with Black folks receiving the least state-sanctioned support for recovery (Phillip 2015). When I first formed the plans for GGG, I did so imagining my friends' schools as my starting point in the US, because they were the closest to me, and in dire need of free support.

    Reality met my ideas with a twist. The humidity laid its heavy arm across my shoulders as I walked to the front door of the school building. I knew better than to expect any additional relief once inside. My friend Louise's office door was pressed shut to preserve the slightly cooler air that labored out of the window unit. The bell rang and she led me down the hall, steering deftly between the flood of students in uniforms. I am always amazed by her dexterity; Louise is brimming with elegance but never stuffy. So few can negotiate that balance that she assumes without fuss, especially under these circumstances, which is one of the reasons I have always admired her. There is a minimal budget at this private all-girls Catholic prep school, and it's staffed with instructors and administrators who are so worn out they might come to work and then again, they might not. All employees play at least two roles on this campus. Louise's role is curriculum advisor, so she is technically an administrator. Realistically, her position should also include the titles—and paychecks—of counselor, college advisor, vice principal, personal life coach, and mediator, but there is so rarely acknowledgment, much less pay for that hefty and very real emotional labor. In the fifteen minutes since my arrival on the first day of my visit, two parents, one teacher, and the assistant principal tapped on her office door—mostly curious about why it's shut—and needed Louise's input on some issue. "It's always like this, huh?" I ask, sliding her an iced coffee across the desk, wiping the water droplets left behind on the dark wood with my sleeve. She leans back, bright smile rimmed with flawless neutral lipstick, and says "I'm so glad to see you."

"She Get It from Her Mama": Praise in the Midst of Disaster

"Katrina kids." "Hurricane babies." Each of these phrases was used to describe the first group of NOLA girls that participated in GGG. Global girls are often named by their trauma. They were elementary-aged children during the storm, and suddenly motherhood was personified by a natural disaster they were intimately familiar with. Mothers are characterized as the fearless or the fearful. Whatever is to be learned about motherhood for girls in New Orleans, it is that the position of the mother teaches the daughter about identity transitions: between girl and woman, and girl and child-bearing woman, and disaster and comfort. A momma has impact, and the landscape is never the same after she touches it. Katrina wreaked utter devastation on so many lives, particularly in impoverished, historically disenfranchised communities, and caused total wreckage of property when over 80 percent of the state of Louisiana was flooded in 2005. What does it mean for educators to refer to these girls, their students, as offspring of the worst natural disaster of the decade? What trauma and its impact are part of the girls' DNA now? After all, we can teach what we know, but we reproduce what we are.

There are complicated entanglements that throb throughout this personification of Hurricane Katrina as the Momma of the NOLA girls. Each of the girls hailed from one of the parishes near the school where I hosted the workshops. All of them were heavily impacted by the storm, and the school system itself reflected similar traumatic responses—NGOs and civil-sector organizations were overwhelmed afterward. Lisa Overton (2014) worked specifically with adolescent girls post-Katrina and draws important connections between the failures of "post-disaster" programs to support girls and adolescents. Overton connects sexual identity, gender performance, adolescent girls, and disaster response programming and "explore[s] why young women and adolescent girls have been largely absent from all phases of disaster research and activism" (215). She argues that gendered programming within the field of global risk management typically addresses women only in connection to the ways they benefit the family structure when accounting for their participation—if they account for women at all. Relief programs consistently overlook the needs and concerns of critical masses of girls because they are focused on economic gains as a singular means of empowerment and thus engage only with women; even so, they "often reduce women to maternal roles and/or caregivers" (Bradshaw 2002; Overton 2014, 215; Holzmann and Kozel 2007). While Overton's study provides insight into the important ways that disaster relief programs require reformation, there are few additional studies that center girls' responses to emergency events globally, or in NOLA specifically (Coalition for Adolescent Girls 2012).

The hurricanes hurt girls from NOLA, and my friend shared that some of the children had been so traumatized by the storms that any threat of bad weather triggered them in an emotionally devastating way. Because of their fragility, I did not incorporate any disaster relief data or policy into the GGG workshops with them. NOLA was my first stop for GGG, so I had less experience conducting the workshops in the confines and time constraints of a traditional classroom setting (Endsley 2018). The school allowed me a great deal of autonomy in determining what topics we explored, but I had less flexibility during the actual program, because it was built in as part of the school day. The NOLA girls stretched me to a new depth as a facilitator and taught me how to connect GGG with existing curricular parameters to ease the burden on my community partners—in this case teachers—and that this adaptability could be achieved if the girls were responding specifically to data and historical context. Although the workshop's format and structure grew to be nearly unrecognizable between NOLA and the Hawassa girls, both groups wrote and performed in ways that unexpectedly resonated with the other, and their approaches to emotional expression and content seemed to parallel, overlap, and underwrite one another despite the logistical distinctions. Quantum justice permits us to analyze their poetry simultaneously as dialogue and monologue. The NOLA girls were not building SWP from specific political documents or legislation, yet in an uncoordinated move, they voluntarily elected to weave their mothers through their SWP, creating a powerful quantum justice leap that intersects with the Hawassa girls' focus on motherhood.

> I come from mixed races
> I come from dignity
> I come from stubborn mindsets
> I come from life's trials
> I come from a strong black woman
>
> CLARSEY, NEW ORLEANS

Davionne seconds Clarsey's acknowledgment of her formidable mother in this excerpt from her poem:

> I come from a loving mother who isn't scared to show her love
> I come from a peaceful neighborhood
> I come from a believing woman
> I come from a strong and powerful mother who isn't afraid to tell her story.
>
> DAVIONNE, NEW ORLEANS

There are marked differences between these poems about mothers, and the poetic echoes carry a different pitch than those by the Hawassa girls. Tegnane's and Marjani's disruption to the discourse around girls as mothers relies on the immutable fact that they are valuable because they are available to bear children. In NOLA the girls never refer to themselves as future mothers, but nearly all the poems acknowledge the good qualities of their mommas, as well as their legacy of pain. NOLA girls implement the Act of Recognition through their SWP and center their mommas' pasts to undermine and interrogate concepts of motherhood (Brown 2013). Simmons's work demonstrates this past in a broad scope, and I highlight key parallels between girls' interviews nearly eighty years ago and those of the present-day NOLA girls. The poetic echoes are undeniably similar: outside expectations; social pressures to be "good" with haters are all around, waiting for a downfall or scandal; but the girls claim to be "determined" (111). Respectability surfaces as well, because ultimately a daughter's idea of worth and reputable behavior is perceived as "a reflection of her mother's and vice versa" (Simmons 2015, 127). The social stakes are high, but if we listen carefully, there is subversion humming within the NOLA girls' SWP. First, the NOLA girls discussed only their mommas as separate from themselves, rather than their own capacity as girls to become mothers, or as girls in process to motherhood. Second, their mommas are positioned as agents who make their own decisions, which marks a clear if unintentional rejection of the southern Mammy characters rooted in "controlling images" from "ideology of the slave era" defined by Patricia Hill Collins (1990) as "reflecting the dominant group's interest in maintaining Black women's subordination" (72). Instead, mothering is taken up as a verb by the NOLA girls and the characteristics of the Mammy are invoked to be revised. Given the frequent conflation between the category of "woman" and "mother" in policy and popular discourse, it is not surprising for mothers, Black mothers in the southern US especially, to be constructed as maternal caregivers. However, the NOLA girls reject one-dimensional tropes of their mothers as mammy caricatures cast from historically racist shadows of the media and perpetrated by the ever-present legacy of slavery in their city. Instead, the NOLA girls express awareness of their mother's dual roles. Although they never explicitly mention sexuality, the duality of their own hidden pleasure and fear is explored through a reflection on their mothers (Simmons 2015, 177). Quantum justice acknowledges that NOLA girls call and respond to a past beyond their immediate family. The poetic echoes of mother-daughter roles are ringing into previous generations, too. Finally, what their poems underscore as a chorus is the complete absence of men or boys in their narratives. Although we did not discuss specific topics about violence or intimate relationships, all the girls totally omit the presence of men. Instead, the NOLA girls cover other concerns in their SWP.

A Rose Is Still a Rose: Race and Culture

At first glance, Clarsey's SWP does not appear to be about her mother at all until the final line. However, there are signals laced throughout each lyric that crescendo to her closing tribute. Clarsey begins by letting us know "I come from mixed races" by way of introducing herself to her global girl audience. If you are from anywhere but Louisiana, then this first line may be a turnoff or signal misplaced assumptions about Clarsey's racial pride. In Louisiana race is messy, and categories shift depending on the region and the era. The only certainty is that the appearance of whiteness usually holds more legal, social, and historic value. There are obvious race-based divides even while proof of the ways race is socially constructed is evident in the mixed-race bodies of folks who claim Creole and Cajun ethnic identities. Physical features are exceedingly diverse across both Creole and Cajun cultures, which are themselves remarkably similar and often indistinguishable; they are identified by various combinations of French, Native American, African, and Spanish, and other European heritage and intimate relationships, traditions, foods, music, and language as well as geography. While the two cultures are very similar, the labels of Creole and Cajun have highly politicized histories, and locals apply these designations based on the era, perceptions of Blackness, and urban or rural hometowns (see Cleaver 2020). Class, race, and place are contested, and conflicting claims about who counts as what persist. Yet Cajun and Creole families are evidence that race is a social construct because of the variety of physical traits in family portraits that defy easy categories and contradict the "science" or biology of race. The ideology of racism was enforced to create a material binary between Black and White women, specifically for the purpose of obscuring any shared oppression they faced at the hands of White patriarchy and the institution of slavery in Louisiana. Even the labels used to identify race and ethnicity, such as "colored" or "African American" or the desire to distinguish between "Creole" and "American Black" reflect shifting and unstable identity categories, which, although always racialized no matter how they evolve, are usually dictated to reinforce the dichotomy of Black and White. Such ideology pointedly refuses to acknowledge the reality of multiethnic and multicultural families constituted by various combinations of multiple racial and ethnic categories (Simmons 2015). Ambiguity and in-betweenness make people uncomfortable, and there are consequences for nonconformity to socially imposed and racially organized power. Safety, survival, and economic opportunities are determined by the perception of the powerful and the performances of the powerless. Color, caste, and social survival and mobility are often determined based on a girl's ability to navigate the city and neighborhood, and their own embodied identity performance. For girls in this milieu, "respectability was closely aligned with geographical location and ethnicity" (111). Girls in Simmons's archival and oral histories designate who was a "nice" or "respectable" girl based on a combination of factors, including ethnicity, geography, and cleanliness or morals. Acknowledging these overwhelming inheritances and generational patterns of desire at the start of her poem positions Clarsey as aware and literate in these discursive power moves. There continue to be severe and immediate rewards and risks for identity performance, and the legacy of such efforts at racial distinction, categorization, agency, and performance is critical historic context.

Colorism in the South Louisiana community is centuries old, is legislated, continues to cause emotional strife, and still enforces very real material conditions for dark-skinned or light-skinned women of color and Black women. Racial ambiguity is constructed and employed as a privilege that is appointed with access to resources and material benefits across the racial spectrum. Racially and ethnically ambiguous women in NOLA historically engaged and employed their skin privilege to gain access to wealth via powerful men, and thus perceived financial security, safety, and resources were granted to them because of their physical proximity to Whiteness (Long 2007; Sublette 2009). Historically, these privileges were put to use in a multitude of complex ways: fair-skinned women often enslaved Black and other multiethnic people. When such women succumbed to the desires of the powerful, they were again objectified and leveraged to further dichotomize Black and White, or dark and light. But sometimes these women gained access to material wealth and then manipulated the ideological systems to control and influence economic and political resources on behalf of the Indigenous, Black, and racially mixed community, and poor White people. But sometimes mixed women tried to quietly survive and protect their children by participating to gain very minimal social mobility in the larger social context. But usually mixed women did all these things, and then some more. Skin color in Louisiana signifies complex and painful histories, social hierarchy, and intersectional class status. The assumptions and prejudices about light and dark women are perpetuated through popular culture narratives and acted out via personal relationships. We, all of us across the spectrum, internalize the narrative that it is better to be exotic, a mix, an unknown, a mystery. We punish and privilege one another accordingly. The effects assigned to racial ambiguity have positioned many women just barely, temporarily beyond the assured grasp of poverty or hard labor, and they have subjected many others to a lifetime of loneliness and shame. The thing is, mixed women are born and raised, but we don't always consider that part. We don't examine the mixed-race and multiethnic family through a lens of love often enough. This is the seductive danger of White supremacy and its ideology: we are lulled to forget that pleasure, autonomy, and oppressive systems occur and are enforced simultaneously. White supremacy ideology and the privilege of Whiteness offer a deceptive, easy narrative that ignores and actively erases the complex in-between spaces of social relationships and the nuances in families, especially those that are phenotypically different. When we uphold these fables, the oppositional forces that maintain the status quo are also upheld. Accountability and liberation are processes that are directly tied up together. Re-membering defies these oversimplified binaries. We don't remember the times when class status had everybody working together or that when socioeconomic status sits at a crossroads with race, one gets hired for a specific job and one does not (Simmons 2015, 130). To re-member forces us to reckon with the ways we betray ourselves and each other and the ways we exclude or include new people we meet. To look too closely is painful, because it wrecks the discourses about race that we have bought into and make a living out of, about what is and is not possible or permissible. We reenact the ways that we have been excluded, all while claiming liberation theory by cutting off others based on their racial phenotype rather than their consistent actions. I needed quantum justice theory to reckon with these unknown emotional landscapes, to fortify me to look at my own family history and how it contradicts the spiritual beliefs I was raised with and the values I strive to live by. The tensions of in-between and internalized conflicts are the point of this analysis, and working with the NOLA girls was a tender place to start; I wanted to go home — to belong again. I relished the sense of fitting in and simultaneously braced myself for unbreachable valleys distancing us. The problems I wanted quantum justice to solve were as personal for me as they were public for this project and the girls: how do I revise and rewrite my legacy of abuse, denial, resistance, and deep love? How do I explain that both pleasure and pain come from the same source? Poetics were echoing deep for me with the NOLA girls, internally, in secret hollows of my heart and soul, and those sounds muted the longer echoes through Time and SWP themes. How do I reconcile rejection with revival? This is why connection with community, networks, and understanding the scientific as well as the spiritual is critical for cultivating disruption: being held accountable can occur only through relationship, when endorsed as a way to experience love. It equips us for working in the dark and exploring the shadows. The global girls connected through this project demonstrate accountability in action and reaction to one another. My intent here is not to oversimplify the impacts of colorism and racism, because that is a lie too. Globally, we desperately need each other to get free, and physical appearance is not always a reliable way to identify who is for you or against you. Racial essentialism is a master deception, because there are healthy and happy multiethnic families. Families are always complicated, no matter their racial makeup, and yet it is often easier to subscribe to tempting dominant narratives than to resist or unpack them. It is easier to follow the overwhelming current than to question why we do so.

In NOLA's context it is not unusual to have immediate blood-related family members who do not look alike. When Clarsey states, "I come from mixed races" at the start of this excerpt, she is inserting her experience into a historical narrative about the Time, space, and place where her daily life occurs but goes unacknowledged. She names her inheritance to call up this entire complicated history and rich culture for her global girl audience. Clarsey positions herself racially, first. Even though she does not parse out exactly what races she is mixed with, perhaps she shares this weighted yet vague introduction because this detailed information positions her for her audience. If "positionality refers to the way in which people are ranked in society and this ranking transcends larger structural systems and follows people into their places of work, classrooms, and how they see themselves and their relationship to others," then Clarsey's matter-of-fact statement informs us not only that she is racially self-aware but that she also knows that it will instigate a reaction from her audience (Hill 2014, 162). She is fully conscious that she will be categorized based on how she is read racially, and she bluntly refuses to confine herself to a category and resists a comforting read of her body. Her embodied SWP performance is another indication about how Clarsey is scripted; she is aware that she may be read as either "Black" or "ambiguous" to girls who are not from NOLA, and for whom these identities are fiercely political, and thus acknowledges her background. She employs racial categories to disrupt them and chooses to deliberately maintain some unknowability from her audience. Through the tool of SWP and the act of embodied performance, the creative works of Clarsey, Davionne, and Jhaire, all boldly refuse this narrative about their mothers through their SWP. Partially through their uniform omission of any physical description of their mothers beyond race—but a singular reading of race was of primary importance for their mothers. Clarsey does not simply lay all her personal intimate details out for the audience to examine up front. She requires the audience to determine and decide what those "mixed races" might be and then plays with that interpretation throughout the remainder of her lyrics, which positions her audience to claim and be accountable for their assumptions about her raced body. She critiques these assumptions based not only on the physical characteristics the audience projects onto her but also on the qualities and values they ascribe to those characteristics. As a result, the audience must then examine and critique their own values and the validity of their assumptions by the end of her performance.

In a countermove, she follows up with, "I come from dignity." After allowing her audience to absorb her racial identity and then position her accordingly, Clarsey uses the descriptor "dignity," which is unusual because she immediately informs her audience about how she perceives herself given her racial context; she allows them to make up their minds about her race and then follows up with her own valuation of it. Clarsey instructs our perception of "mixed race" people because of how she further positions herself in relation to her family. She accesses her knowledge of self and commands her audience in the fifth element praxis. The next two lines draw us closer into the focus of her attention, her mother, even as what she describes grows more abstract: "I come from stubborn mindsets / I come from life's trials." Again, Clarsey is intentionally ambiguous. She does not provide detail about how she knows the "stubborn mindsets" won't change, nor does she specify "life's trials." We are not told how she arrives at these conclusions, but we are given a clue in her last line, "I come from a strong black woman," where we are looped back to her first line about "mixed races." She lets us know that her mother, the "strong black woman," can be understood as such because of how she thinks and the tribulations she has faced because of others' judgments. Clarsey nimbly positions her mother as an intellectual and strategic woman who has faced conflict and reasoned her way through it. Her mother's ability to think her way out makes her "strong."

Clarsey's poem ultimately uses ambiguity to ask us to reflect personally on relationships and positionality. She is aware of the ways she may be read, racially, by global girls outside of NOLA, who have little awareness of the patterns that shape social life and norms where she lives. Her performance layers Clarsey's SWP with added detail. Her body may be read in a different way than her subjectivity, and she prizes her inheritance from her mother, who passed down to her the "stubborn mindset" to survive "life's trials." Clarsey foregrounds struggle in these two lyrics. Because she "come[s] from a stubborn mindset," she is informing us in her final line that she indeed "get it from her mama" as the song says (Juvenile 2001). This is another way of saying that once her mind is made up about something, there is no changing it. Anita Jones Thomas and Constance King (2007) studied the impact of Black mother-daughter relationships on racial socialization and found that "self-determination and pride" were central, as "mothers seemed to feel that it is important for their daughters to not allow their gender and race to serve as barriers for identity development or for functioning as adults" (140). Could Clarsey's "stubborn mindset" be a claim to self-determination? Clarsey's SWP is an experiment in auditioning her independence. Firm ideas, even those ideas that lead to conflict, are a part of her mother's identity, as is being slow to change her mind, and thus are a part of her legacy. Making up her mind is critical to how Clarsey conceives of her relationship and reflection of her mother. She wants other girls to know that she is experienced in facing the trials imposed on her by the raced and gendered life she was born into. Clarsey denotes pride when she chooses to end her poem with a complimentary line describing her mother as "strong" and "black" and, in so doing, lays claim to her birthright. She is different from her momma but also encompasses her. She is both yet she is neither (Endsley 2020). Clarsey stands on her own, divergent yet interlocking with whom she comes from. By recognizing her mother, her respect reverberates back to the women from Simmons's project and honors the intergenerational home training that benefits her in the present day (Brown 2013).

Revising the Past: Quantum Justice and Reversing the Curse

The girls' SWP in Hawassa and NOLA demonstrate that the performance of motherhood is an integral part of girlhood, whether as a future or as a past. Social norms enforced through patriarchy and White supremacy offer limited roles for Black women, who are considered only when they are mothers striving to meet standards that are impossible and undesirable (Collins 1990). Black mothers who fall outside such strictures of motherhood are disqualified as women, while girls remain either overlooked or hypervisible. Girls who needed support post-Katrina were mostly ignored, and if their mothers did not fulfill the social norms that matched policy regulations, they were ignored as well. Most contemporary natural-disaster response policy is based on research and scholarship that continues to recognize women—most of whom are Black and Brown and living in the Global South—as the only viable category for analysis of female populations affected by these events. When women are recognized, it is only because they perform the role of mothers or caretakers of their families. While GGG focuses on global girls, global mommas are bound up with them, and the designations between these groups are blurry and indistinct in everyday life. It is urgent that we cultivate disruption to the scholarship that justifies the dispersal of fiscal and community support based on limited representations and understandings of what it means to be a girl and/or a mother.

The embodiment of prophetic SWP invites revision to such policy and research through an infusion of power and provocation. Critical formations of White supremacist ideologies about Black women's sexuality were historically constructed as binary, functioning to distinguish them from White women and to prevent solidarity and relationship between women across the racial spectrum. In her work establishing the field of critical Hip-hop literacies, Elaine Richardson expounds on Collins's pioneering theory about the various "controlling images" that are operationalized as shallow two-dimensional caricatures of Black women perpetrated in particular ways through the media. Maintenance of this hierarchy preserves power and is "pivotal in the creation of interlocking systems of social inequality such as racism, sexism, classism, and capitalism" (Richardson 2007, 78). Although evolved, the figure of the

Mammy as always smiling and "self-sacrificing" is insidious and therefore must be addressed as we consider Clarsey's SWP, because this stereotype is specifically rooted in southern imagery and imagination around slavery and constructed to debase Black women as mothers (West 1995, 794). A perpetuation of the Mammy acquiesces to White mainstream media expectations and predicts Black motherhood to be performed in service of White propaganda. Meanwhile, White mothers in the South who are poor are represented in media in similar grotesque ways, but with a primary focus on how their poverty is individual. Their shortcomings are caused by personal moral or ethical dilemmas, and they are portrayed as redeemable at the minimum, by virtue of their Whiteness. Richardson (2007) reminds us that although tired, these racist tropes linger, and they are perpetuated through cultural production invasively shaping social beliefs and legislation, and we must be equipped to critically examine, read, and counter them. NOLA girls' SWP vigorously disrupts past discourse by invoking it in the present with the purpose of reckoning with its generational trauma for the future. Qualities like "self-sacrifice" are praised by the girls, and Clarsey claims "dignity" as her inheritance, subverting the narrative on behalf of her momma. She revises this projection, past and present, of the Mammy by uplifting her own mother. Revision of the past always shifts the trajectory of the present, and Clarsey takes aim in both directions with her words. Natural disasters like hurricanes that are easily accepted when characterized as mothers are a direct result of the disproportionate inequities in infrastructure grandfathered in through enslavement and colonial history currently traumatizing Black and/or poor children (Collins 2004). This fact remains an important link between the lack of research around postdisaster work focused on adolescent girls of color and the negligence in local policy when it comes to meeting the needs of Black girls and mothers.

Disparities in the healthcare industry are another effect of inequitable discourse. The overwhelming research about physical health, specifically, for Black adolescent girls emphasizes the gaps between scholarship and the implementation of care in the same areas. Most health research focuses on causes and effects of obesity for Black girls. This is disturbing but not surprising, given the historic outlook of the internalized oppressions around physical attractiveness and race that may occur, especially around the developmental years of adolescence (Brown et al. 1995; Cohen et al. 2006; Treuth et al. 2005; Vorhees 2005). This juxtaposition demonstrates another way that Black girls are socially construed as already existing outside of the scripted social norm, which is to say White standards. The scripted social norm is used to evaluate health and success as an individual competency rather than the resulting impact of interlocking systems that are historically informed and politically enforced. As a result, Black girls are punished for their deviation from an impossible social script that serves master narratives about bootstrap success and affirms the ways neglect and punishment of Black girls are perpetuated within educational and healthcare systems with the support of governmental policy and procedure. These social issues form part of the lived reality for Black girls and their mothers; however, policy and research fail to make obvious the ways that a deficit needs-based assessment can be traced directly to the demonized archetype of the Black family infamously published by sociologist Daniel Moynihan in 1965. This report supported the development of much of the racist policy around economics, housing, and education in the US (Davis 1972). Policies backed by racist research and scholarship dehumanize Black mothers, girls, and families and depict oversimplistic, one-dimensional representations incapable of complex emotions and intellectual processes.

Such research continues to be roundly critiqued by Black feminists such as Bonnie Thornton Dill (1980), whose work analyzing parenting strategies proves that Black mothers deliberately aim to build up self-determination as a characteristic when raising their children. Scholars Jameta Nicole Barlow and LeConté J. Dill (2018) curated a special issue of the academic feminist journal *Meridians* dedicated to Black women's health, including a call for Black girls' ways of knowing to be heeded in the public health field. Critics of Black literature have examined a multitude of slave narratives and works of fiction and found a breadth of representations of Black motherhood that counter the narrow depictions of controlling images (Hansberry 1959; Jacobs 2009; Johnson 1993; Troester 1984; Wright 2016). In her work on the subjectivity of Black girls in literature throughout the nineteenth century, Wright (2016) reminds that in the US Black girls are undermined and underappreciated. She also imparts the hope that "strength, determination, an ability to strategize in creative ways are also a part of Black girls' heritage" (165). Creative critiques such as Wright's continue to reconfigure social scripts and remain paramount to the disruption of this narrative. Because institutional shortcomings have been recast as problems rooted in Black girls themselves, liberation requires the deconstruction of the systems upheld by these justifications.

Although quantum justice leaps provide us with tools to disrupt and revise dominant historical narratives, Time continues to refuse a straightforward, tidy solution. Revising the past is critical, yet in the present, Black girls in the Global North are completely excluded from consideration for policy as they are not women nor mothers, and the NOLA girls have used their experience and invisibility to defy this ideology by re-writing it. More specifically, girls in NOLA must contend with extreme amounts of negative attention via popular culture stereotypes and yet remain ignored in public policy when disaster strikes. Yet the NOLA girls position their mothers as agents, as decision-makers, delegators, and fear-facers. Although they continue to be exposed to competing discourses around race and gender that fail to support their agency, girls cultivate disruption to the dichotomous iterations of Black and White motherhood and their roles in those relationships. Their mother-daughter relationships deserve attention, and this quantum justice leap invites deeper listening. Through their SWP, the NOLA girls position themselves, their audience, and their mommas in multiple and contesting stories.

You've Got to Show Me Love: Expression and Beliefs in Mother-Daughter Relationships

Indeed, Davionne describes where she comes from by opening her poem with her mother's complex emotions: "I come from a loving mother who isn't scared to show her love." Immediately her audience is posed a question that she answers in the same line. Davionne's assuredness about the fact that she has a "loving mother" is because "she isn't scared to show her love." The expression of her mother's love positions her as fearless in Davionne's eyes. Her SWP begins immediately tracing her lineage to the everyday knowledge that to express love can be scary. Why is love shaped by fear? We are not told. There could be a million responses to that question, and Davionne doesn't deign to provide specifics. What she does instead, is position her mother as a woman who "isn't scared" and who is expressive, affectionate, and demonstrative. Love in a mother-daughter relationship can take on different manifestations. In this instance Davionne does not provide examples, but the key takeaway is that she is aware of her mother's love and acknowledges the courage required to show it.

Davionne's SWP functions as a direct assault on the perpetuation of lacking maternal images. Deficit framing of Black motherhood includes research focused on drug addiction and mothers' influences on addictive behaviors (Schinke et al. 2006); low-income single Black mothers (Elliott et al. 2015); illiteracy and literacy practices (Pellegrini et al. 1990); school success and academic achievement and beliefs (Stevenson et al. 1990); disciplinary measures employed by Black mothers (Kelley et al. 1992); and the comparisons between Black and White girls and self-evaluations (Ridolfo et al. 2013), among others. Carolyn M. West (2008) connects these harmful singular stories and stereotypes to real-life implications in her work; she argues that such stories deny the reality of Black women who take on multiple roles out of necessity because of the impossible demands they endure (290). West suggests addressing social and economic inequalities as leading solutions to alleviate the ways Black women are burdened, especially "addressing unmet emotional needs" (294). Although West focuses on Black women and mothers with a finer analysis, her characterization of and resistance to this depiction of Black mothers is reflected in Davionne's perception of her mother.

Her next lyric might be a clue as to why she describes her mother this way. "I come from a peaceful neighborhood," she writes. "Peaceful" invokes many different situations when used as an adjective to describe a NOLA neighborhood post-Katrina. Does she mean nonviolent? Does she mean quiet? Does she simply mean she feels safe there? Identity, fear, and feelings are key indicators for what constitutes "peaceful" for NOLA girls. Simmons (2015) reminds us that "feelings, such as pain, fear and anxiety make abstract words like 'power' more meaningful: who had the power to make black girls fearful? What produced their anxieties" (121)? Emotions like fear and desire are frequently the content and substance of girls' SWP, and when applied through Simmons's lens of geography, that means global girls' SWP provides insight into these pressing questions about power. Who has the power to invoke feelings of "peace"? What does safety look like? What does danger look like? If Black girls' emotions shade the terrain of their geographies, then quantum justice allows us to glimpse their perceptions and self-protection and to ultimately understand how they engage power. This information and analysis are critical for reading the performances of poetry and identity that global girls of color embody.

Safety is key to emotional and physical well-being—it is key to being loved. For the first two years that GGG took place in NOLA, the number of victims to gun violence steadily increased (Associated Press 2005). Many NOLA girls wrote about firsthand experience with gun violence. Therefore, when a descriptor like "peaceful" is used as an adjective for a neighborhood, it is often interpreted to mean the socioeconomic status of middle- to upper-class income brackets for costs of living, and, to be blunt, that income bracket means a majority-White neighborhood. In addition, the private Catholic high school setting where I met Davionne means that tuition is getting paid but not necessarily that her mother is the sole provider. It is not uncommon for tuition assistance or scholarships to fund girls' educations in Catholic high schools, especially one that services an underserved neighborhood. Separately, these facts would situate Davionne's school community space as vastly different from where she lives in the city. She seems to be pointing out that although she and her mother are Black and her school serves a Black demographic, her neighborhood is either wealthy and White or nonviolent; in either case she is using the space of her community to attribute value to her mother's character, relying on the geographic literacy of her audience to map the terrain of her momma onto her neighborhood. She may appear to skirt around race by specifically avoiding the limitations of racialized categories, but her SWP offers a rich reading because the demographic of her neighborhood is left up to her audience. The singular facts about private school costs may imply the possible sacrifices or work ethic of her mother to keep her enrolled. On the other hand, her Black mother may defy another assumption by subverting the historical positioning and narratives about impoverished women of color. Her ambiguity here plays with the audience's investment in racial discourse about mothers like hers and reflects our assumptions back to us. Why do we position Davionne and her mother the way that we do? What does that say about us and our biases? Her SWP provokes self-reflexivity. Davionne offers us an intense critique of ourselves. What do we think we know about Black girls in NOLA? As her audience, we are pushed into a quantum justice leap of our own. She is performing about her momma, but she is indirectly asking about her audience. What were you raised to believe about girls like her? Who taught you that? How has your own momma shaped you? For Davionne, SWP operates as a critique on her audience's investment in stereotypes about Black mothers and Black girls as it uplifts them. Through her ambiguous praise, Davionne extends a gracious invitation to us to join her beyond mainstream discourses about what, exactly, she gets from her mama.

Davionne's choice to include this line also brings to bear the realities of gentrification and displacement that occurred post-Katrina as well. Long-term residents of NOLA must contend with greater policing, closure of neighborhood institutions, and the erosion of cultural traditions tied to the land and space because of tourist-based urban development postdisaster (Gladstone and Preau 2008; Parekh 2015; Van Holm and Wyczalkowski 2019). The spatial fixity of tourism and gentrification converges between the global and the local, much like the girls involved with GGG. Culture and regional experience combine and clash with globalization and international corporations and economies. There are further conceptions of gentrification that explicitly tie the displacement of poor or working-class people of color to reformed policies determined by the federal government, and by predatory corporate financiers who can afford to purchase larger swaths of real estate in urban locations (Gotham 2005). This results in immediate effects on the local long-term residents of cities like New Orleans, who are already experiencing various forms of income and housing precarity but have strong localized social networks and knowledge. These diverse communities know how to make a living where they are, but that same knowledge is not as valuable if the landscape shifts or they are forcibly moved by disaster or corporations. The involuntary face-lift that NOLA has experienced over the past decade is fueled by competing interests from corporations, tourists, and residents who produce and consume rival versions of the spatial scape of NOLA. Somewhere in this mélange are the girls, who love the city that raised them but see potential for improvement as well.

If Davionne wants her audience to know she comes from "a peaceful neighborhood," then she is intentionally distancing herself and her upbringing from the violent reputation associated with NOLA's statistics, and the media's depiction of rioters and looters during the hurricane's devastation (https://www.nola.com/news/crime_police/article_46a99a39-986e-503d-be4b-e32ae071a9d4.html). There was widespread misrepresentation by the media that depicted Black people as looters, which resulted in misinformation and police and military violence during the crisis. This bias was pointed out too late by a variety of investigative news sources. The photographs and video recordings that washed over the internet and the news outlets portray New Orleans and its people as anything but calm. NOLA girls were sensitive to these negative portrayals and tender toward their classmates who experienced violence on the streets or in their homes. Why do we love and fight for what doesn't always love us back?

Given these possibilities about what "peaceful" means, Davionne's reference to her home is an important gesture to her mother's dedicated work. Black mothers are associated with the domestic sphere, home life, and upbringing. The important life lessons passed down from mother to daughter are taught within the space of the home, and Davionne's poetic reference is another compliment to her mother's efforts at keeping her safe, no matter the cost—literally. Financially and emotionally her mother has paid a price. On the one hand, her neighborhood's rent or mortgage is likely high, and her private school tuition means that there is a hefty financial price tag attached to Davionne's "peace." She is socially astute and aware of the costs for the access that she enjoys. She acknowledges the decision-making agency of her mother who has chosen to maneuver her family into these spaces despite the monetary obstacle or the time and work commitment it likely poses. Davionne's acknowledgment of her mother's sacrifice on her behalf is a tribute and not a trope. We can be sure of this, because her next lines offer a multidimensional look at her mother's humanity and spiritual vastness. Davionne's momma sacrifices but as a choice, an application of her autonomy, inverting the meaning embedded in the characterization of the Mammy. The price she paid is obvious to Davionne , and that same sacrifice makes her mother "powerful" and not subservient. Giving generously is a position of power and not fear. Her mother's wisdom is agile, and Davionne attributes this in part to her mother's faith. She writes: "I come from a believing woman / I come from a strong and powerful mother who isn't afraid to tell her story." Once again Davionne's mother is "strong" and "powerful" and "isn't afraid" to express herself, this time, articulating her own life experience. What is her mother's story? What might make such a story require a "strong and powerful mother" to share? These questions and more pepper the mute air like spice in a gravy. Davionne acknowledges the power and risk inherent in storytelling, especially when that story contradicts master narratives. The broad strokes portraying Davionne's mom do not provide the details I crave, as I am trained so often to be satisfied with an ending to every story. Maybe it is not my business, as Davionne lets us know, in that way only southern girls from NOLA can, by saying less to say more, by giving a look and a purse of her lips. Maybe Davionne wants to furnish her momma the respect that Clarsey provided hers and shushes her poetic echoes here to provide her momma the "dignity" of silence. Whatever the case, this is Davionne's momma's story to tell, and she will let her tell it.

Walking the Talk: Money and Mommas

The power of belief is incredibly important for Jhaire as well. She writes:

> I come from a beautiful woman that shows me unconditional love
> I come from a smart business woman was determined to always do what
>   is right
> I come from a baker who definitely puts her love into every sweet treat
> I come from a God fearing woman who isn't scared to worship the Lord
> I come from a sassy lady who speaks Her mind
>
> JHAIRE, NEW ORLEANS

Jhaire's mother is described primarily by the decisions she has made and the actions she has taken. Jhaire's SWP idolizes her mother's abilities to act, such as "show[ing] me unconditional love" and "always do[ing] what is right." Her mother is positioned as a "smart business woman" and "a baker who definitely puts her love into every sweet treat," so it is clear that her successful career outside of the home has inspired Jhaire to infuse what she defines as "love" into her own work as well. In her study on working-class Black and White women and their daughters, Melissa Swauger (2010) suggests that the most important messages mothers hoped to instill in their daughters encompassed perceptions of the girls' future and a host of pragmatic priorities, including "the issue of caregiving; the desirability of living near family; and the importance of establishing financial independence and security" (49). Practical, everyday concerns and skills center their conversations.

There is obvious conflict between the roles of "caretaker" and the demands inscribed in a social status that determines "financial independence." It is exceedingly difficult to accomplish both endeavors at the same time. Working outside the home, especially for Black mothers in the Global North, has historically never been optional. Enslaved Black women were required to care for all children, whether they had birthed them or not, in addition to completing the duties assigned to them outside of their homes and families (Davis 1981). Further, White exploitation of Black mothers and their reproductive abilities was carried out by incentivizing the priority of children over any other relationship, including marriage or romance (Collins 1990). As such, Black women were entrusted to care for White children and discouraged from pursuing capital-building business enterprises not related to their sexuality or domestic life. Motherhood is interlaced with survival in unique ways that complicate the NOLA girls' inheritance: "The relative security that often accompanied motherhood served to reinforce its importance" (Collins 1990, 51). Economic conflict is institutionalized through the discourse of motherhood, and girls' autonomy within the Global North is at the center of this ancient struggle. Cultural control and domination cast long shadows across future renderings of motherhood and survival for girls at young ages.

One such shadow materializes as the "successful girl" discourse that Jessica Ringrose (2007) interrogates and Sarah Projansky (2014) illuminates. This discourse promotes illusionary individualistic independence and self-making through the exclusion of girls of color in the Global North whose mothers are impacted by this history and the systems that reward its maintenance. Economic stressors incite the sorts of social judgment and public shaming uniquely weaponized against mothers who are subjected to comparison against ideals of perfection. They straddle the home and the workplace, facing dichotomous discourse that reinforces tropes of "good Mammy" and "bad Black matriarch" cast by the White imagination to operationalize blame under the guise of respectability and denigrate women who are unable to overcome social and historical barriers (Collins 1990, 74). Tiffany M. Nyachae and Esther O. Ohito (2019) suggest that these troubling binaries are extended to Black girls as the limited discourses available for their participation. The dialogues result in the social maintenance of an inaccessible "successful girl" trope that needs to be disturbed. In their analysis of extracurricular after-school programming designed for Black girls, they found that the dissemination of these binaries means "participants may believe that they, as individuals, are culpable for their subjugation, which, in the context of schooling, is exemplified by exclusionary discipline practices" (20). Nyachae and Ohito call for multiple transformations and revisions of girlhood to be incorporated as a means of disruption to the internalization of such culpability. The stakes for raising Black daughters continue to be high.

And yet Jhaire's SWP testifies to her mother's ability to cultivate disruption of this stereotype. She opens with her awareness of the "unconditional love" her mother has for her, then immediately praises her mother's business acumen and integrity. Her mother's capacity to share her gifts and talents with the world and be compensated fairly for her efforts are qualities that Jhaire admires. She writes that her momma "definitely puts her love into every sweet treat," which places her workplace clearly in the kitchen. This line presents yet another stereotype subverted through SWP. As a dessert chef, a "baker," Jhaire's mother willfully engages in domestic labor, but the gag is that she subverts stereotypes and enjoys economic gain from running her own business enterprise. The NOLA girls' SWP identifies this genealogy and challenges "spectacular girl" attitudes that remain prevalent and can function as extensions of controlling images in the media that focus on Black mothers (Projansky 2014). Based on Anita Harris's (2004) "can-do girls" analysis, Projansky describes a girlhood that is portrayed by the media to promote master narratives invested in reproducing "a narrow version of acceptable girlhood: the impossibly high-achieving heterosexual white girl who plays sports, loves science, is gorgeous but not hyper-sexual, is fit but not too thin, learns from her (minor) mistakes, and certainly will change the world someday" (1). Projansky further assesses how girlhood is mediated into either the "spectacular girls" who take on the characteristics described by Harris or "at-risk girls" who fail to achieve these claims and devolve into spectacles of vulnerability and victimhood. Girls like Jhaire are confined by media representations as having only these two limited versions of girlhood available, and Jhaire, in a quantum justice moment, moves like her momma, and refuses them both. Defying the parallel systems that work to constrain her girlhood in mimicry of the dichotomies of Black motherhood, Jhaire models her identity development after her momma's rejection of the controlling images claiming to represent her. Confronting the root causes of generational trauma to heal and thrive requires strategies that make use of what is at hand, subverting social expectations to succeed. Jhaire's SWP turns the "successful girl" trope inside out; the "both/and" of Hip-hop feminism is put to work because she understands the historic patterns and is counting on her legibility to her audience

(Lindsey 2015). Her momma's savvy social literacy has provided economic opportunity and inheritance of financial value to Jhaire. The fifth element forges a relationship—knowing others to know the self and employing both intersections of who girls like her *were*, and who they *are* to the eyes of the world. Jhaire understands she can inhabit that ideal and meanwhile pursue her own autonomous goals. Her momma has drafted the blueprint. Quantum justice can project possibilities but cannot dictate the desires Jhaire might develop as she chooses her path.

Whichever direction she takes, love must guide her. Jhaire identifies that the "unconditional love" that her mother showers her with can also be shared with others and that the quality of her love is what makes her mother's business prosperous, not just her recipes or book smarts. The costs of such a love are investments producing a return of intangible richness and spiritual strategy in daughters: Jhaire's momma was a prophet also. Jhaire appreciates the "unconditional love" she receives and performs it to show that there is enough love to share with others, that love costs something, love is worth paying a price to be had, and it can be sweet, but it can also be nutritious. She has witnessed her mother apply and benefit from these values. By example, Jhaire's mother is teaching her practical lessons that are "learned values and responsibilities" for Black girls (Swauger 2010, 9). Jhaire, in turn, uses SWP as pedagogy to teach those lessons to us.

"*Of Water and the Spirit*": Girls, Mommas, and Spiritual Beliefs

Spiritual and religious practices add another layer to what we can surmise about Jhaire's mother. Her enrollment at a Christian school likely indicates her mother's religious beliefs. However, it would be a mistake to assume that all children enrolled in Catholic schools practice this religion. During my time with the girls in Soweto, I spent a few hours interviewing the regional director of the Catholic school that hosted me. He said the school incorporates religious curriculum and some of the girls' families are Catholic, but most send their children there because of the other support services, quality of education, reliability, and safety they offer, rather than faith or beliefs. He shared that most families participate in a combination of Christian faith and indigenous religious practices, of which there is an interesting overlap (fieldnotes, 2020). The same might be said of the girls' families enrolled in the school in NOLA. There is a sense of respect for the beliefs outlined in the curriculum and a basic grasp of those principles, but not necessarily a commitment to the Catholic church or religion. What are the other promises of a Catholic education in New Orleans?

When natural disasters have ravaged the political landscape, which was already grossly under-resourced for equitable public education, private school becomes a necessity (Cook and Dixson 2010; Dixson 2011; Dixson et al. 2015; Henry and Dixson 2016). The changes in leadership, the influx of charter schools, and privatization of public education for primarily Black and Brown students continues to have dire consequences, and Adrienne Dixson (2003) has long argued that Black teachers and students of color politicize educational spaces and challenge existing power structures in public education. Postdisaster reconstitution of public education and distribution of funding presents parents in New Orleans with limited choices for their children's education. Private Catholic schools like the one Jhaire attends offer consistent curriculum and local teachers and staff who either experienced Katrina or have roots in south Louisiana. The long-standing respectability attached to the Catholic Church in Louisiana likely adds another element of comfort for parents like Jhaire's mother. The fact that the school admits only girls and has a college acceptance rate of 99 percent for graduating seniors guarantees that students will receive personal attention from teachers and staff who are dedicated to their educational achievement. Success, social mobility, and respectability continue to make complicated arrangements for girls of color in NOLA, and their mothers' decisions are infused with desires for their protection, well-being, and self-sufficiency (Nyachae and Ohito 2019; Walkerdine 1997). The NOLA mommas enrolled their daughters at the school with every intention of bettering their chances of happiness. The reverberations to Simmons's archival work are deep here, too. In NOLA specifically, Simmons (2015) reminds that a Catholic education equates to "messages of sexual purity and moral wholesomeness" (111). Evelyn Brooks Higginbotham (1993) developed the concept of "respectability" in the context of social reform efforts conducted by middle-class Black women involved in the Baptist Church who worked to change individual moral behavior as a means of shifting social perceptions and influencing public policy. There continues to be evidence of the ineffectiveness of this moral religious approach to "humanize" Black people, thus rendering them as subjects worth saving or protecting. We continue to see in current times how respectability performances persist as wasted exercises for an unjust system that perpetuates police brutality and misogyny, yet the girls' SWP celebrates the strategic moves of their mothers even when those moves mimic the aims of respectability.

Every day NOLA girls' mothers make tactical decisions to position them on pathways aimed at traditional success through academic achievement, college education, and social mobility. Private tuition likely seems a worthy cost for those who can pay it. Despite the frailty and falsity of the narrative that respectability will protect Black girls from harm, school remains an entry point for the average Black mothers to thrust their daughters toward financial stability and peaceful, prosperous lives. So, the NOLA girls are trained there in social etiquette and the refined manners of the South while also receiving home training—lessons around the kitchen table about discernment and social navigation and subversion through the examples of their mothers. Deliberately ambiguous, these calculated decisions occur in spaces where knowledge of self is fine-tuned based on knowledge of the world (Endsley 2020). The NOLA girls point to the crossroads of their mothers' pasts as they recast their future from the ever present and work to discern one from the other. Their decision to perform respectability does not diminish them as mothers; on the contrary, these endeavors are manifestations of the capacity for love and care that they have for their daughters and the knowledge that failure to adhere to mainstream productions of womanhood will assuredly make them targets. Nyachae and Ohito (2019) remind, "Both the judicial courts and the courts of public opinion may see fit to judge and vilify the Black girl whose being is beyond what is normalized as good with regard to girlhood and womanhood," and, I add to this list, motherhood (23). NOLA girls' SWP conjures representations of their mothers to both honor and critique them and their methods of survival and pleasure, expressing a desire to replicate and simultaneously reimagine the lives their mothers have led. In an unexpected quantum justice leap, they slice through the complicated layers of mother-daughter relationships and expectations that both reinforce respectability and expose a deep desire to groom agentic decision-making practices to subvert those performances. Jhaire has already positioned her mother as an entrepreneur who earns her own money, and she continues her poem by admiring her mother's faith in God.

Fluent in Faith and Fear

Jhaire's SWP describes her mother's faith and fear as a practice that provides her with agency. She is "God fearing" but also fearless when it comes time "to worship the Lord" or "speak her mind." The last two lyrics read together like a sermon, and I find myself waving my hand in the air and bearing witness with Jhaire's testimony. The variety of ways "fear" is used in these two lines connects the practice of faith with the practice of "speaking her mind." Jhaire's mother takes up the embodied performance of "worship" that is a physical and often public emotional out-loud expression of gratitude and submission to God. Simultaneously, Jhaire repeats that her mother is "sassy" and can be relied upon to "speak her mind." Both actions accentuate her mother's agency as a speaking subject. Jhaire equates being active spiritually to the earlier poetic echo of Backtalk. First, she describes her mother's position of selective submissiveness, but only in relationship with God, and situates her mother as choosing to take up a position of surrender and admiration toward "the Lord." "God-fearing" is another way of saying she reveres God, and that steers her conduct in public. Her "worship" implies a dialogic relationship with "the Lord." Jhaire observes a mutual exchange between her mother and her mother's God and describes a relationship with God that is two-way, beneficial, and communicative. This illuminates how Jhaire may conceive of power and her own spirituality. According to her mother's example, to "show . . . unconditional love," and to "always do what is right," requires a connected relationship inscribed with "worship" of "the Lord." To enjoy the financial fruits of her labor, like her mother, Jhaire understands that these actions must be taken, and she must be vocal about "her mind." Second, Jhaire situates her mother as both "sassy" and a "lady," and the two terms seem to contradict. Historically, the voices of Black girls and women are ignored or silenced (Pough 2004). When heard, their voices are misunderstood or misperceived (Brown 2013). Regardless of the words being spoken or the meaning within their message, hearing and understanding Black girls' and women's voices is possible only through the affect of their "controlling image" counterpart (Collins 1990). This contingency circulates the popular image of the "sassy Black girl" as either disrespectful and deserving of punishment if the sass targets a (usually White) authority figure, or smart and competent if the sass is directed toward a peer or friend (Stevens 2002; White 2017). The respectability performed by Black women features here again as responses to pressures of these roles. Although embedded within activist aims, respectability works toward distancing Black women from the cultural caricatures of the Mammy and her homegirls and edging them closer to an ideal "White lady" that is equally impossible to attain, undesirable, and exaggerated based on White supremacist imaginations that project illusory purity onto White women (Collins 1990). What if we push beyond a reactionary take on respectability? What if this is a literacy move? Melissa Harris-Perry (2011) reminds us that to understand "the political strategies" within Black women's public performances and actions, we must interrogate the soundness of the structures that work to constrain them (29). One such structure specific to this analysis is school, which requires a process that Lauren Leigh Kelly (2013) records as the "shed[ding] of true selves to be successful academically" (52). Different contexts require different maneuvers for Black girls to succeed and stay safe. The challenges to a Black girl's respectability in New Orleans could upend her label as a "nice" girl to a "bad" girl, and such factors fall beyond the control of the girls, so their efforts at safety and success demand deft tactics (Simmons 2015, 112). What if Jhaire's momma is using spirituality as a pedagogy of faith for her daughter to become socially and geographically literate and mobile?

Adaptive literacies like these sometimes sound like speaking out and sometimes sound like silence. Quantum justice allows us to inquire into both of these action strategies. Jhaire's mother enjoys the freedom of a cathartic, public, emotional response to her spiritual practice and flexes her authority when "speaking her mind." The adjective "sassy" prefacing "lady" positions her mother as a subject in the making, who is located somewhere between the acceptable social discourse for Black mothers while summoning these historical rhetorical assertions as maneuvers only to dispel them. She is a contradiction, and her daughter knows that. More importantly, she finds freedom in the contradictions. Jhaire's momma has modeled a way to live a full life within these binding contradictions even as she acknowledges their overbearing persistence. Jhaire's SWP interfaces with her mother on an intimate level, privately "show[ing] her love" and publicly as she "worship[s]" and then "speak[s]." Jhaire admires her mother's ability to successfully adapt in each environment while creating herself a life between them. Quantum justice hovers here and urges us again to observe the usefulness of the in-between spaces of Time and position. Jhaire's SWP openly admires that her mother's example is a sustainable one, and her practice demonstrates a form of Hip-hop feminist pedagogy, defined as "life-sustaining work of self-affirmation and determination [that] creates relationships to practice love, and works collectively to do culture, politics and education" (Brown 2009, 191). To teach and learn via Hip-hop feminism assumes that love relationships require rehearsal—even those relationships we take for granted as natural or inherent, like mother-daughter. Jhaire investigates her mother's praxis and uses SWP as a tool to excavate the lessons she finds most applicable and useful for her in the present moment. This practice reminds me of how Vajra Watson (2017) uses SWP as a tool for creating spaces for deep learning, which she asserts as powerful enough to transform a traditional classroom setting into "sanctuary," where "something sacred" is taking place (15). This sacredness is an essential characteristic of most SWP performance spaces, where building sustainable community is a founding principle (Fisher 2003; Keith 2019; Weinstein 2018). The mutability of these lessons does not diminish their value. On the contrary, Hip-hop values the remix as both a flex of inventiveness and a nod to the original artist. NOLA girls are grounded in strength as they watch their mothers work to keep together their families and communities while balancing work outside the home (Shorter-Gooden and Washington 1996). Self-actualization, self-determination, and the ability to make decisions remain critical to the survival of Black girls in the Global North (Collins 1990, 185; Wade-Gales 1984). Jhaire may or may not replicate her mother's model but pays undeniable tribute to her example through SWP by already rehearsing the mode of talking back that her mother taught her. This is exactly how a "Black girl sound" is developed and echoed back poetically to her momma and to her girl audience: Jhaire doesn't seek anyone else's validation or approval for her performance—she has already gotten that from her momma.

What Happened to That Boy? The Absence of Men

I don't want to linger on this topic, simply because the NOLA girls did not. Writing poetry is not a new avenue of expression for girls of color in New Orleans. Simmons records and analyzes romantic love poems written in the 1930s as proof of joy and creativity employed in the pursuit of pleasure (2015, 182). The historic poetry complicates and adds depth to the backdrop for present-day NOLA girls who choose to write about everything, except, it seems, romantic love.

The rates of domestic violence reported by women tripled across the southern regions where women from Louisiana were forced to relocate in the first year following Hurricane Katrina (http://www.iwpr.org/publications). Unfortunately, this is a global trend after natural disasters occur. Even worse, there never seem to be ample institutional resources to support those victimized. Vague references to "abuse" or "pain" were raised in many of the NOLA girls' poetry, but there were no clear links between these themes and men. When Black mothers are conjured in broader popular culture, the only consistency is the controversy that follows in the wake of a disrupted discourse.

More recently, in what the media reported as controversial, rapper Cardi B filmed her 2018 music video *Money*, featuring her partially nude body busy at work in a variety of ways: stripping, dancing in a sexually suggestive way, and breastfeeding her newborn daughter, Kulture. Not long after, rapper Remy Ma's widely publicized pregnancy centered her on the television show *Love and Hip-Hop* NY, where on January 6, 2020, in an episode featuring her in the studio holding her baby daughter, she read lyrics off her phone that state "real mothers don't twerk / she a nurse / laundry cooks dinner and dessert." From Lauryn Hill, who sang about being nearly persuaded to have an abortion to preserve her career when she learned she was pregnant out of wedlock, to the divine symbolism referencing spiritual ritual and ceremony in Beyoncé's performances during her 2017 pregnancy with twins, intricacies about contemporary Black motherhood in the Global North continue to diverge over time. In her development of a "black maternal aesthetic," Jennifer C. Nash (2019) expounds that pregnancies and births like Beyoncé's (she also explores elite athlete superstar Serena Williams) revise a Black motherhood "that emphasizes abundance, visibility, and even spirituality as black maternal ethics" (533). How do such aesthetics translate to the daughters who inherit them? These performances of Black motherhood are expansively explored through association with Hip-hop culture and oriented toward creativity even as they encompass grief. They are rich with multiple representations of different sorts of mothering work that is still operating in the margins yet showcases glamorous appeal to mainstream notions of the universality of motherhood previously only marginally accessible by certain types of White women. Navigating the political terrain of Black motherhood to the benefit of their interests is made more possible by the financial security enjoyed by these celebrities.

It is no coincidence that childbirth and child-rearing are still approached from an economic perspective. The historical capitalist exploitation positions motherhood as equal to security, safety, and guaranteed privileges not afforded to women's bodies who do not or cannot reproduce. Children continue to be a symbol of wealth, status, and desirability, but only as long as they are attached to a version of the Black mother who is "strong enough to bear the children / then get back to business" or return to earning income and to sexual attractiveness and availability (Beyoncé 2011). If Black girls are born into poverty or to mothers who cannot participate in this way, then they are positioned as a drain on society's resources and tax dollars and thus are mistreated. Jhaire's momma is a "sassy lady who speaks her mind," and I wonder to what degree her freedom to do so is related to her financial independence. While we love to see the successful entrepreneurship of Black beauties who can "do it all," have we considered why we are taught to take pleasure in this iteration of mommas? There remain very real gaps in maternal healthcare in the Global North for women of color (Barlow and Dill 2018; Owens and Feit 2019; Siefert and Martin 1988). The iconic expressions of pleasure, sexuality post-childbirth, and attractiveness that are sold via mainstream culture are titillating, never mind that they occur at the nexus of an incredibly challenging time in women's lives, where they are often overwhelmed and undersupported in their workplaces and homes. But what happens to the everyday mommas who don't have the money or the bodies of Cardi B and Beyoncé?

What agency do they experience rooted in the reality that maternal mortality rates for Black women in the Global North mark them as vulnerable?

Even now Black mothers have significantly higher rates of infant mortality from all major recorded causes than any other race category (CDC 1999; MacDorman and Mathews 2011). Black mothers in the Global North also continue to die at higher rates than other women during childbirth (Tsigas et al. 2017). In addition to possible death, there are other arduous stakes for Black mothers and their babies shared via the personal narratives of women who have survived to tell horrific tales of maltreatment at the hands of medical professionals in the prenatal wards of hospitals, clinics, and doctors' offices (Cleeton 2003). Many of these stories are circulated via networks formed on social media, which allows Black mothers and loved ones to offer informal support to one another by establishing virtual communities around a shared social experience (Abebe et al. 2020). Dorothy Roberts (1988) catalogs the historic, legal, and social conditions that have long endangered Black mothers in her groundbreaking work *Killing the Black Body*.

Firsthand experiences combined with statistics-based medical reports provide ample evidence to shatter Global North/Global South discourses of empowerment that suggest girls and mothers hailing from the Global North are exempt from challenges related to childbirth assumed to be faced by those in the Global South. Contemporary funding sources for research remain heavily invested in the "health" or "well-being" of adolescent girls' bodies and centralize the external indicators of a girl's life in place of centering girls themselves. Although the complications and particularities of the difficulties they face are unique to each location throughout GGG, the effects are painful. These frightening truths about motherhood hark back to Sophia's statement at Girls Speak Out on behalf of Indigenous girls on our first quantum justice leap in chapter 1. Indigenous communities are reliant upon their connection to the Earth, and to women and girls as caretakers and future mothers of the land and waters. How does their connection reckon with dominant "settler state views [of] Indigenous women as what could be—and must be—conquered and controlled as a way to secure and maintain Indigenous dispossession" (Rule 2018, 243)? Sophia incorporates future generations to assert her self-determination through SWP as a blatant rejection of assimilation, and her uplifting of Indigenous culture. Sophia's intentional gestures to the futures of Indigenous communities are embedded in her performance through the critical role mothers play in the "transmission of Indigenous lifeway[s] to children" (752). During an epidemic of violence against Indigenous women as well as the history of sterilization of these women, motherhood to Sophia is representative not only of her culture but of her sovereignty. She performs motherhood as desire and a call to revolutionary activism, and she expects to hear global girls respond (Deer 2015; Kline 1993; Lucchesi and Echo-Hawk 2018). Poetic prophecy functions to rewrite the past and uses the present to speak the future into existence. Global girls are writing and performing within and against the theme of motherhood to deconstruct and rebuild their collective futures. Structural forces are bolstered by oppression, and yet Black girls in NOLA have long resisted and subverted them in complex ways. Together, stories and scientific quantitative reports are devastating tangible examples of how and why access to healthcare, financial stability, and political economy are enmeshed across Indigenous, Black, and mixed-race, multi-ethnic, mother-daughter relationships and thus shape how girls approach and understand motherhood.

How do the NOLA girls negotiate the comparison of popular culture mothers as they model their subjectivity from their mommas? None of the NOLA girls referred to themselves as potential mothers the way that Sophia did in her performance, or Marjani and Tegnane in Hawassa did, but they express respect for their mommas. Could it be that they are able to envision themselves as accomplishing all that they have witnessed their mothers accomplish outside of motherhood? Jhaire's SWP has drawn an in-depth portrait of a Black momma who is a complex emotional, spiritual, and intellectual being. The power that objectifies and inscribes meaning, importance, and certain characteristics of humanity to one person and not to another is embodied most powerfully in performative spaces (Endsley 2014). Because Jhaire identifies as "com[ing] from" her mother, she claims all those things through her performance, too. The daughter of a lion is a lion also.

Stop Acting Like My Mama! Performance and Mothering

For girls of color, the act of rewriting defies reality without denying the material consequences they are subjected to, and according to Weinstein and West, "the space of performance creates a forum for negotiating the tensions between safety and risk" (2012, 289). Immaterial tensions occur when our critiques of the narratives scripting our relationships are made tangible through performance. Indeed, "performers present critical representations of social realities, [and] the dominant culture's interpretations of those realities are renegotiated by audiences and performers who explore the discursive tensions" (289). Maisha Fisher (2003) defines the performance space of an open mic as upheld by the belief that "everyone has something to say and everyone deserves active listening" (365). The reciprocal process of support that occurs during a live performance embodies "active listening" and holds space on the stage and in the crowd for the ambiguities and contradictions that crowd our interactions to be explored. Critical performance and literacy are tied to a strong sense of self-esteem for girls in New Orleans (Zambo 2011). In concert, the NOLA girls' SWP exudes examples of "how the normalizing influences of the dominant society have been challenged, or at least countered, often by those most visible as its targets'" (Cohen 2004, 30). Performance makes such ambiguities inhabitable and proves that subversion is always possible.

The NOLA girls uplift their mothers by renegotiating and reimagining the flat stereotypes made available to them by society. They amplify the agency their mommas exercise and praise their resistance and backtalk as well as their sacrificial decisions to position their daughters beyond where they were able to reach. The mommas they depict are not threatened by the success of their daughters, but they are written such that their lives have been lived, freeing their daughters to chart their own courses with confidence. The duality of "successful girls" or "at-risk" and "can do" girls that pervades the racial binary of the Global North is not specifically in play throughout these poems, although it is undoubtedly part of the reality the girls must navigate (Harris 2004, 9). The NOLA girls' SWP seems to invert what Ridolfo et al. (2013) determine, which is that mother-daughter relationships must encourage "independence," and instead emphasize linkages, connections with others and relationship as the key to their "problem solving ability" and "self-esteem" (507). Kinship and collaboration are threaded through the strategies their mothers model. The girls' SWP performance also serves as a rehearsal of their own remixes of "embodied resistance," which asserts the right for their poetic echoes to receive a response (Hobson 2012, 144).

A quantum justice leap always requires radical care and courage. The girls' SWP in Hawassa and NOLA exercises their futurity and rewrites the mothers they have or wish to become. Their reassurance is based on the global collaboration they create together; the only sure thing is the uncertainty of where such an exploration will propel them next. This soft whisper of a poetic echo, the intangibility of feelings, the conflicting ideals of freedom are wrapped up in a figure that must be exercised, practiced, invited—poetry. If fulfillment can be found "where they did not need to consider others' views of them, worry about their safety, or worry if they belonged," then the inverse is true: a sense of belonging and release of external pressures creates safe spaces and permits love in relationships (Simmons 2015, 178). SWP is quantum justice in action, cultivating and rewriting a new past, reciting and processing their feelings toward a yet-to-happen future. We *do* poetry, it becomes real, and the worlds and truths it contains become real when we *do* it. The girls pick up and put down courage as if they are trying on clothes in a dressing room. They try on poetry, and use each other as mirrors to check their reflections, mixing and matching outfits, rehearsing whom they may want to transform into, contemplating evolution. Poetry is troubling, because those of us who were not birthed by Black mothers but are nurtured by them must tangle with what it means to have benefited from their care. Those of us with White mothers must reconcile what it means if they have also whispered to us in our dreams about poetry. I must examine and reexamine who has whispered to me as I sleep, who has taught me what freedom is, that I am more than my thoughts, that my spirit translates the language of liberation. Poetry does that. My spirit in communion with the Holy Spirit does that through poetry—it's how we conversate. How and where do I enter to teach the girls about the night whispers? I, who am not a mother, who am racially ambiguous, who am US-born undertaking transnational work, I who am perpetual Outsider and Other, what do I know of "mothering"? Poetry has been my radical care, lifting me to stages and drowning me in my own darkness. In this endeavor the only useful assessment of my work, of the mothering, of the poetry, must ask, "Does it improve on use?" (Brown 2013, 159) This is at least one question that White Western feminists from the Global North need to pose in any endeavor to teach Black girls in schools or through nonprofit agencies: does your contribution "improve on use?" If so, how do you know? And so, this is the final question that I ask of the SWP written by the GGG girls in Hawassa and NOLA about their mommas, about how they reconfigure themselves and deconstruct ideas around motherhood. This is the question that natural-disaster policy makers and national legislators need answered the most. This is the inquiry that infuses familial and romantic relationships with a new approach to the effects of uneven power. How do girls' knowledges about mothers produced through SWP improve upon use?

My Momma Said: Inheritance and Prophesying the Past

This was not a chapter I wanted to write. What does it mean to be a daughter in a world where femicide is common? Where fathers often breathe a sigh of relief and pride simultaneously when they learn their unborn child is to be a boy? What are we inheriting from our mothers? What do we do when mothers reject, deny, sell, or abuse us? How do we learn to become girls or what it means to be a girl? Our mothers are also implicated here, and they have sacrificed and resented and bragged on and neglected us. What prepares a girl to become a mother? The tunnels between mothers and daughters run deep and dark. Even when they are safe to traverse, memories, triggers, generational trauma, subconscious actions make the process about relationship, always responding to another, never singular. Who are the judging subjects in this case? An audience of global girls, each risking a peep into the caverns of their hearts. Each sending us down, but with a flashlight of their words.

Global girls use SWP to work through the categories of mother and daughter and to worry the management and maintenance of them. Their lyrics piece together a composite and then pick the mosaic apart again, shard by shard. I learn that to be a daughter, to be a mother, to be both or recognized as neither is a puzzle that will never be completed. When I first introduced the Bronx girls to some of the poetry from the NOLA girls, they immediately latched onto the similarities they could relate to.

>   LUNA: Oh, they go to Catholic school too!
>   SIERRA: Look. We match. We even have the same school colors.
>   ATHENA: Did you—do you know them, Crystal?
>   CRYSTAL: What do you mean?
>   ATHENA: Like, are they family?—Like that—
>   CRYSTAL: No, not related at all. Not like that. I just have a friend at the school.
>   IVY: You could be, though.
>   *I laugh, I shrug.*
>   CRYSTAL: We could be.
>   AMY: Yeah, we could all be.

CHAPTER 7

Girls Making a Way

Girls are always thinking about the future. Their forward tilt underscores one of the major reasons that I anchor my efforts in work with youth—hope. Whether the poetic echo is on motherhood in the future or in the past, girls are cultivating disruption of easy assumptions about their present lives. Even during the most harrowing circumstances, global girls exercise the ability to crank the future wide open through their creativity and imagination. However, any effort to create change inevitably encounters resistance. Girls Making a Way means finding out what works and what doesn't, what helps and what hurts, and offering advice on how to get imaginative with what is available. Making a way means innovation and limitlessness. Relying on each other and taking chances. This is a constant movement, it fluctuates, it is where fluidity is possible. The final chapter of this book holds space for the poetic echoes of the girls and their photovoice projects. Making a way comes at the end of this text because it is the furthest quantum justice leap that pushes us as far as we dare to be in the future. And it means that global girls have found utility in SWP, have pursued pathways, gotten lost, turned around at crossroads, camped out, returned, and set out again, and that they are always actively creating who and where they are and will be.

When Girls Are Seen and Not Heard:
Photovoice in Zanzibar and Trenton

This was our third time through the poem, and with each rehearsal, the girls' comfort and physicality were pumping up, taking a deep breath, swelling with energy. We were on Pemba Island, Zanzibar, on the Swahili coast of

Tanzania, at an all-girl, all-Muslim high school. Tucked in the square-shaped grassy courtyard, we were hidden from the sight of the other students and staff. There was plenty of space for us to spread out into a circle between the white-painted walls that bordered us like a picture frame. The rain stopped the night before, and the sun was high during our performance session. We were glad to be outdoors. The same Pemba girls who were so shy at the start of our time together, and even at the start of this rehearsal, couldn't help but laugh as they recited their community poem, first for each other and then for the video camera. The breeze would whip up unexpectedly, and every time it did, it flung their long robes and headscarves around so that the girl reciting her lines burst into giggles and we had to start the poem over. The school uniforms the girls wore were standard: white headscarves draping their shoulders, closely framing their faces, and loose, long-sleeved black robes swinging to the ground. We were supposed to be going around the circle, each girl reciting her lines in the community poem in Swahili. Each day we split the workshop three ways. First, poetry writing. Second, lessons about the solar suitcase, energy, and the city of Trenton, New Jersey, the hometown of the girls who sent poetry and built the solar suitcases we were installing together. Third, performance techniques that included moving our physical bodies. Earlier that day I shared the photovoice projects sent to Pemba from the Trenton girls. Photovoice combines poetry or creative writing with images to convey a message (Mitchell and Moletsane 2018). The Pemba girls had just completed their community poem that they wanted to send back to the girls in Trenton, and the intensity of being recorded for total strangers was sending us all into a tizzy.

By our third time through the poem, what started out as a circle became an elongated shape with a few of the girls holding hands in pairs or standing separately. The girls began to get more dramatic, moving their bodies and boldly making eye contact with Bentrice Jusu, the videographer of the project and my friend. Bentrice was in the center of the circle, moving in and out between the girls with her handheld camera as we rehearsed. The girls started to relax, loosening up between laughter and their struggle to remember their poem. Bentrice took her eye from the camera screen, laughing, and said, "Nah, Crys, we gotta start over again." The girls started laughing out loud then, and I said, "Let's take a break from the poem. Let's just release our bodies a little. You do what I do." We had annoyed our translator enough to send her back to the main classroom where the other students were working on different aspects of the project. I began to do some basic stretches and shake-outs of my extremities. We got loud, deep-breathing and doing vocal warm-ups. I noticed when suddenly the girls directly across from me in the

Chicago

circle dropped their arms to their sides and looked down. I turned around and saw three boys looking around the edge of the cement wall, watching quietly. One of the girls, Miriam, held up her hand. "Eh eh!" she said loudly. "Not for you!" She watched them as they ducked back on the other side of the wall before she turned back to the circle. During our time together, Miriam emerged as a slightly older girl who was confident and more outspoken than her peers. Again, Bentrice met my eyes, nodding her approval at Miriam's quick work of the voyeurs. Our eyebrows raised in silent communication, as if to say, all right then, honey! Miriam caught Bentrice's and my exchange, and one corner of her lips curved up in a knowing smile. "This is just for us," she said. Miriam pointed to Bentrice's camera, "And them." "Them who?" asked Bentrice, looking down at her camera. "Those other girls," said Miriam.

I am beautiful
I am Intelligent
I am brave
I am Talented in acting
I am proud of who
I am

Trenton

Previous page: Soweto

Hawassa

New York

Advocacy and activist work invested in facilitating opportunities for global girls to meet in politically affirming ways is difficult, yet the arts offer a unique starting point for centering girls' experiences while connecting them across borders, time, and space. The exchange of creative cultural productions of girls of color living in Trenton, New Jersey, and Pemba Island, Zanzibar, Tanzania, were made possible because they participated in Girls Do STEAM (GDS): a series of science, technology, engineering, arts + design, math (STEAM) workshops, which featured the building of solar suitcases by girls in Trenton and their installation by girls in Pemba Island. The solar suitcases and installation process served as a vehicle for the girls to forge new networks with each other and exchange their artwork. First, the girls were led in a series of instructive workshops focused on SWP and photovoice techniques to construct personal narratives culminating in the production and exchange of *khanga* designs. This workshop specifically used khanga design as part of the curriculum, since khangas originate in East Africa: they are printed fabric commonly designed and worn by women and girls with written messages of advice or observations. Khangas are pieces of cloth printed with visual images or patterns in the center and bordered with designs. This specific project enabled Black girls in Trenton and African girls in Pemba Island to link up with each other, scaffolded by the STEAM project and their artwork. Their

Pemba

communication offers a fresh take on making a way by occupying the space of community through cultivating disruption. In his work on Hip-hop and spirituality, Daniel W. Hodge (2017) argues, "Hip-Hop creates . . . a voice to pushback. . . . It is a vehicle in which those who are questioning authority, challenging dominant narratives of normality, the disenfranchised and the voiceless can still find solace in a community of like-minded people" (3). SWP and photovoice combine as such a vehicle to incorporate the messages that girls want to share with each other. Quantum justice invites a reading of their artwork that deepens the variation of poetic echoes responding to the question, What do girls want?

SWP and photovoice incorporated in a STEAM curriculum interrupts constrictive narratives about global girlhoods as two-dimensional monologues. Implementing participatory action and arts-based projects makes useful connections and locates similarities across geopolitical borders of presumed difference (Khoja-Moolji 2015). Girls' self-representations and conversations with each other must be understood within localized contexts as well as transnational frameworks. For us, using khangas and SWP as integral parts of the photovoice project centered something familiar from both communities.

This exchange was unusual for several reasons. My GGG work typically involved only me, traveling solo or meeting up with cofacilitators on site in the community where we would be working. Although I have always relied on collaboration with partners living in the communities I work with, GGG allows me a great deal of autonomy and flexibility, because I am responsible only to the local community-based organization, and for myself. For this exchange, there were additional components. First, I was working under the auspices of my college, and I was scheduled to lead a study abroad program to Zanzibar with a group of undergraduate students. Second, I worked closely with two collaborators, Dr. Marla Jaksch and Bentrice Jusu, to design workshops for our project that used technology and the arts as activism with high school girls. Third, this workshop was unique in that it also included the building and installation of solar suitcases. This experience was both enriched and complicated. This program was atypical for me and my colleagues, but it was thrilling. Thus, Girls Do STEAM was formed.

STEAM prioritizes spoken word poetry, photography, and writing as pedagogical tools central to the installation of solar-related technologies because they function as catalysts for personal empowerment and community change. My students and the girls in each location underwent training with photography, khanga design, poetry, STEAM curriculum, and lessons including historical information about each other's community. Collaborating with girls in transnational activist projects demands collectivity, paying tribute to the community that makes such a project possible, thus "refut[ing] the ideology of individualism and isolation" (Endsley 2018, 65). STEAM contends with power in stratified and dynamic relationships for girls living in globalized communities through the devices of Time, space, and concepts of collective memory, histories, and futures as tools that are essential for liberatory transnational relationships.

We began each set of workshops by asking, "What is the most important thing for the other girls to know about where you live? What is the most important thing they should know about you?" The exchange of SWP pushes us to consider the stories that the girls told each other through their khangas, emphasizing their "relationality [as a new] framework for analyzing girls' lived experiences as differentially embodied, varied and disparate" (Bent and Switzer 2016, 3). SWP and photovoice equip girls to coconstruct new futures by forging connections to each other (Bent 2013). The workshop further disrupts this divide because only Black girls were featured as participants: whether located in the Global North or Global South, the experiences of Black girls as represented by their artworks challenge local and global conventions. We must reconsider their local racialized experiences and expand assumed understandings about each demographic of girls and their capacity for empowerment. The girls' SWP resists this tension and complicates what kinds of girls are allowed to experience vulnerability and empowerment.

On both ends of the workshops were "Black girls . . . whose life stories will never cohere in a society that chooses to see and react to them as dichotomous tropes: victim or perpetrator, perpetual failure or incomprehensible success" (Cox 2015, 150). Through their creative dialogue, we can better understand the nuanced ambiguous ways these girls make sense of the stories circulated about them, and how they reinterpret or reimagine themselves in closer accordance with their lived experiences. What does it take to form a new and informal network of girls who are interested in addressing the injustices they face? How are global girls making a way through SWP to translate their desires?

Rather than give in to the temptation of easy assumptions that somehow the girls from Trenton are knowable and therefore that their precarity is more understandable, simply because they are familiar and geographically accessible, cultivating disruption requires an examination of the ways power shapes subjectivities. Practicing collective recollection, using photovoice and poetry to re-member the girls to one another, and their efforts at new forms of self-representation are key parts of what positions this analysis as potentially transformative and transnationally justice oriented. Re-membering produces "reflexive, embodied, and engaged conversation about the researcher/ed relationship with media, with living memories" (Durham 2014, 126). Their poems and works of visual art grow once they are out in the world. Considerations of the power of culture are critical for thinking about social justice work with global girls. As Aimee Cox reminds, the adult that works with a girl network carries a sense of entitlement and access to power that situates girls of color always at a point of reflection and deflection of that same power and access. Girls are always asking how this will also impact my community or those I am accountable to, and responsible for. Cox (2015) further describes "Black girl entitlement," which "takes it for granted that individual actions always have larger consequences for the community," thus connecting Black girls to contextualized space and place (71). Girls in Pemba and Trenton express acute awareness that the aspects of their communities they select to introduce and represent through their khangas may be taken in ways they do not intend, and that their choices will impact others. Quantum justice assumes that girls in each location can be only partially glimpsed through their artworks, and as soon as one aspect of their lives is understood, it changes. The girls already understand the notion of partially grasped knowledge with the unfair assignation of full responsibility. Their texts encourage as much connection as possible through self-expression. This representation must be one where girls are both seen *and* heard, and read, here, too.

Mixing Methods: STEAM, Khanga, and Photovoice

In each location girls were asked to represent themselves and their community through a series of photographs and poems, and they created a khanga portrait at the end of each workshop, which was exchanged between the two communities. Khangas are commonplace for the Pemba girls and can be used as powerful forms of subversive connection and global networking to communicate disruptive messages in spaces where the girls live under constant threat of "embodied vulnerability" (Grear 2004, 3). The sayings printed on khangas are meaningful, and women and girls use them to communicate in often subversive and discreet ways. According to Elinami Swai (2010), "Sayings in khanga are fashions and texts with powerful messages to change one's perspective about the people and the world in which they live" and "function as important inventories of knowledge" (81). Khangas serve two purposes: first, they are representations of localized knowledge about Pemban girls' home communities. Second, they reference the generational knowledge inherited and used by girls as "the act of wearing a khanga and writings on khangas and related text can be regarded as a form of literary genre, where knowledge is produced, used, and disseminated mostly by women" (Swai 82). The girls designed photovoice khanga portraits using photographs and creative artwork to border their photos and the poetry that accompanied the images. These khanga portraits challenge the viewers to "look and respond with love," holding outsiders accountable for how and why they engage with the images and texts presented by the girls (Brown 2013, 115). Viewers must reflect on their preconceived perceptions about the girls and begin with inquiry: How are their relationships with those girls constructed? The imagination of the viewer is invoked, and these methods coalesce "to categorically reject the passivity (and therefore dehumanizing) of the one being seen" and instead require the viewer to become vulnerable through "a wholehearted and embodied engagement of multiple senses that promotes an embrace of humanity and living" (115). Durham (2014) reminds that the reflexive process occurs only "by placing [the] self in relation to other bodies" (126). Reflexivity is essential in building transnational relationships between girls and is a primary aspect of their transformative dialogues. These methods are useful to girls whose localized experiences could not trust language alone, especially when they aren't the ones delivering the messages. Exchanging khangas ensured that the girls in Trenton were taught a practice that was familiar to Pemban girls, disrupting power dynamics of the Global North and Global South by positioning each group of girls as both learners and teachers of an artistic practice. Another artistic practice that all the girls enjoyed was photography. Worldwide, the selfie reigns supreme. As a methodology and means of connection, photovoice incorporates image and language in effective ways.

For these reasons photovoice and SWP are complementary methods. In this instance the solar suitcase served as a vehicle to carry these cultural productions of photography, SWP, and visual art between the two communities and allowed the girls to learn more about the environments they lived in. Pedagogically, photovoice demonstrates a Hip-hop feminist philosophy about creating and remixing knowledge by incorporating process deliberately in the co-learning process. Since this technique was new to me, and because I was out of my depth in new surroundings, although I was a facilitator, I was constantly co-learning alongside the global girls from each community (Wang 2006, 156). The incorporation of photovoice into GGG's curricular focus encouraged the girls "to advocate their concerns using their language and experiences" and "concurrently promote meaningful inter-generational partnerships and infuse youth perspectives into the process of policy and program design" (Wang 2006, 159). The program and partnership between Trenton and Pemba Island is unique in that it includes a solar suitcase installation and build; however, even in my GGG workshops without this technology, photovoice ensured an opportunity to connect girls of color to a variety of ways of thinking through advocacy, social issues, and understanding global injustices against other girls. The photographs allowed girls who preferred to use their primary language to tell their stories in multiple formats. They were not restricted to reliance on only one mode of representation or interpretation. They did not require any interpreter or translator beyond what they were already expecting from their girl audience.

Merging khangas with poetry and photovoice "illuminate[s] the various forms of resistance that the girls use in challenging power relations perpetuating their marginalization" (Shah 2015, 55). Taken together, SWP and photovoice engaged the girls as competent social actors, capable of making meaning and transforming their worlds by linking them together. A close examination of how the girls use their khangas reveals a contention with personal agency and stratified power dynamics present in normative empowerment discourse (Moeller 2014). Their experiences reject this oversimplified individualized construction (Collins 1990). Instead, the girls' art is connective, using memory work in the Hip-hop feminist tradition Durham outlines to link with other girls, "to make a member again, to bring that member back into the community of imagination, re-awakening past trajectories and giving new momentum along new paths of the present" (Mwangi 2013). Although a major objective of each exchange was to connect girls through commonalities across time and place, the girls' cultural productions provided complicated instances of familiarity and singularity among them. Quantum justice allows for this act of Recognition and also instantly diffuses any commonality among each group of girls. For example, the contradictory desires of the Trenton girls to find connection while articulating clear distinctions between themselves and the Pemban girls showed up in their work in several ways.

Learning from Girls' Khangas

Shamika, a girl who calls Trenton home, offers a departure from the other Trenton girls' designs, as she does not use text on the border framing her photograph. Instead, Shamika is pictured holding a piece of white paper with the words "You never know how strong you are until being strong is the only choice you have" written in black marker. Shamika's face is neutral, reflecting visually what her sign describes as "strong." She is standing elevated on stairs; the camera tilts up to frame her figure. Her image is the only one from Trenton that doesn't feature a colorful graffiti background. Shamika wants the viewer's entire focus to center on her body within the portrait, placing a demand on us, insisting that we acknowledge the ways in which "unequally distributed effects of power act on and through bodies" and how additional complex systems of oppression magnify inequalities (Butler 2014, 112). Her choice to position her Black girl body as the most central figure in the image insists that bodies like hers deserve recognition and simultaneously withstand the worst of local and global injustices. Her portrait makes tangible her memory work, visualizing a circumstance when her "only choice" was to be "strong," and becomes a moment from which she draws strength. This act of simultaneous artistic conjuring and projection contextualizes the ways that girls of color enact disruption in relationally disparate locations (Endsley 2018, 66). Shamika does not offer details surrounding the situation that permitted her only to be strong, but she has survived it. Shamika has built momentum; she seems to have gained a sense of her own determination and the depth of her fortitude because of this personal struggle.

As with the khanga Shamika designed, girls in Pemba and in Trenton relate to one another across deeply vulnerable and autonomously articulated creative work. The act of combining visual art with SWP pushed girls in Trenton to think beyond how they are perceived within their home communities and "to see that [they are] . . . *both* a member of multiple dominant groups *and* a member of multiple subordinate groups" (Collins 1990, 221). The interplay of past, present, and future, fact, and imagination, in Shamika's photovoice represents one way that the girls in both locations call up ancient wisdom and simultaneously imagine new ways of fashioning their lives, because "both look back as a way of moving forward" (Durham 2014, 104). Her interpretation of what girlhood can be is mobilized by her subjective experiences and imaginations of the girls in other communities.

Chriki, from Pemba, imagines how she can relate to the girls in Trenton and utilizes her campus environment in her khanga portrait invoking a sense of pride. The large sign marking the school entrance is centered directly above her head, and her gaze is aimed straight into the camera lens. Her hands hold a stack of books that are easily assumed to be textbooks. Encased in red and yellow colors, the words "study like a slave to become a king or queen" boldly frame her photograph, accompanied by a complex design of leaves, flowers, and vines. All at once, Chriki invokes the painful and complicated parallel national histories of enslavement that occurred in the US and across the Zanzibar Islands while simultaneously representing herself to the girls in Trenton by another shared experience they can relate to—attending school. Like Shamika, Chriki insists that her viewer acknowledge her embodied experience, except that for Chriki the experience is one of a Muslim girl enrolled in a school she is proud to attend. Chriki's khanga poetry offers advice infused with a robust hope for social mobility through education. She calls up the history of the global slave trade and local Zanzibari conflict as a colonial tool to underscore her position as enslaved to her own education; she must sacrifice and work for no reward, all while planning for her eventual liberation. Chriki suggests "to become a king or queen" is a possibility even for someone who begins life in the position of a slave with no agency or choice in service except studying. She relies on this mutual experience, knowing the girls in Trenton are also secondary school students who are pressured to pursue an education if they want to access a life beyond their current material limitations. Although the specifics of her schooling experience are unique to her location and Pemban culture, Chriki seeks common ground by prioritizing this representation in her exchange with the girls in Trenton.

Together, these khangas from distinct communities "illustrat[e] ways poetic transcription can be constitutive of multiple histories, subject positions, and experiences that overlap, intersect, and diverge" (Durham 2014, 105). Chriki and Shamika employ this opportunity to communicate to edify the girls in the other community *and* to claim their individual agency. Their khanga poetry provides an example of how global girls of color exercise "the ability to construct a vision for [their] life and to act even in some small way to move toward that goal affirm[ing] humanity in the face of continual dehumanization" (Cox 2015, 52). The acknowledgment of mutual struggle does not diminish the creative or artistic ways these two girls visualize their lives and abilities to support others. Despite "the realities of their socioeconomic status and the multiple exclusionary practices that challenge their mobility and personal efficacy," Chriki and Shamika recognize one another's right to grow and affirm that they both have worthy contributions to make in the world while also sustaining themselves emotionally (67). This quantum justice leap makes such similarities apparent and calls them forth systemically and personally. Their design choices exemplify a girl in the act of "replacing a view of agency as an individual process" with that of communal participation (Hesford 2011, 156). Establishing new transnational relationships invokes a search for relatability and an understanding of ways that larger systems of girls who form community might confront and change society.

Shamika's khanga creatively distills a common struggle, one in which she is not the exception but the rule. She desires not only to have the burden of responsibility for her limited choices but to also enjoy the rights therein, thus making it possible for other girls to rehearse a similar script. Surviving becomes an event worth celebrating. Through her efforts to encourage other girls to do what she has done, and in claiming her own abilities, Shamika accesses "entitled ownership of one's self"; a space where we might make life rise up to meet us in ways that do not obey social confinements (Cox 2015, 7). Similarly, Chriki distills a common hope, a message of encouragement in her khanga. She shares the necessary dream of pursuing an education with the optimism of one day being recognized in a position of autonomy and authority in her own life. Survival and forecasting coexist, and quantum justice synchronizes these moves and translates them in a tangible way through photovoice. Shamika and Chriki use their khangas to remind us that girlhood remains a highly contested discursive space, constructed and impacted by competing demands, and asks how these girlhoods and subjectivities are generated, and how they are producing each other, historically and contingently. Exercising self-determination in relationships echoes as an important theme for Pemban girls as well. Sharifa writes "peace and love is the link to unity and cooperation" in colorful words on her khanga portrait. The photograph stages two girls clasping hands in a common Pemban greeting, standing close together but facing the camera. Their school uniforms are identical. The handshake symbolizes the link that Sharifa's poetry references, as if one girl in her photograph represents "peace" and the other "love." Her message emphasizes unity and cooperation as necessary components for collaborative work. Although I don't think Sharifa included the elements to represent Hip-hop culture, I want to note that peace, love, and unity are also core principles of Hip-hop according to the Zulu Nation (Chang and Watkins 2007). Sharifa's desires for peace and love function as quantum justice theory frequencies resonating unexpectedly with Hip-hop. Amina Issa (2016) positions the khanga as a political intervention, one that Sharifa enacts in her representation and her reliance on the Trenton girls' ability to discern her meaning and recognize their reflection in her khanga. She counts on their desire to commit to cultivating the "unity" and "cooperation" that made this collaborative work possible, because it will be demanded of them in the future. Transnational girls engaging with each other as an exploration into activism depends heavily on links that Sharifa describes, and she does not assume the Trenton girls' automatic agreement. Instead, Sharifa issues an invitation to the girls in Trenton with the transparent admission that teamwork will require each of the girls to contribute.

While such contributions may seem small, their SWP offers a way to interrupt discursive practices that obscure power relations between these two groups of girls, who are rendered powerless in broader discourse. Because of their localized social positions and the general lack of access to power that global girls of color experience, the khangas offer an opportunity for counter-representation by girls. Quantum justice with transnational girls to understand how they interface with activism requires focus on the small, because "sometimes all you get is a sentence . . . a turn of phrase. Something specific. A small work. A question" (Brown 2013, 44). The girls' poetics are unequivocally deserving of attention: the girls chose these lines deliberately, with care and intention. Each group presented their khangas to their own communities before the exchange occurred, taking care to explain their choices and inferences. They demand that we, in the role of their audience, interpreters, caretakers, "put in conversation with other girls' singular truths using imagination," placing the onus on us to act, while the agency of articulating only what they wish to share still rests with them. The girls' SWP prompts us again to recall that "creative work is foundational to collective social-justice efforts and to our individual well-being" (Brown 2013, 45). Quantum justice theory acknowledges the ways that small eruptions of social change can charge into multiple directions at varying speeds. Unpredictability and a refusal to be controlled are to be expected and encouraged when girls conduct social change efforts. For our individual sake, and for the sake of the past and the future, imaginative and energetic artistic endeavors must become embedded in all aspects of our work in all fields. We are reminded to release the illusion of control, and to pursue the prophecies that have been spoken over social justice work.

Contextualizing Community

Although socially and politically constructed as hypervisible, the girls from Trenton and Pemba are not unilaterally treated as agents of social change by others in their home communities for the same reasons they are put on display: their Blackness, their social position, and the rules governing their social interactions.

It was no surprise, then, when the Trenton girls raised issues about "giving" and "donating to help the girls in Africa," although none of the girls in Trenton donated anything or raised any funds as part of their participation in GDS (fieldnotes, 2015). In fact, the solar suitcases were donated to *them* as part of our program. Throughout our workshops the Trenton girls disclosed that their perceptions of girls receiving the solar suitcases were based on the idea that they were poor and African. The initial perceptions of girls in Trenton simply regurgitated the collapsed narratives of Global South and Global North girl "into oversimplified categories of hero and victim," which had subtly invaded their consciousness and self-definition even as it penalized them (Bent and Switzer 2016, 3). Within this script, Trenton girls sought to locate themselves as power-holding subjects within the hierarchical dichotomy of the Global North and Global South without first reflecting on their own highly contested access to citizenship and protection at home. After all, "experience and memory are open to contradictory interpretations governed by social interest and prevailing discourses" (Richardson and St. Pierre 2005, 961–962). Keisha, one of the girls representing Trenton, seemed especially aware of this when she wrote, "My home is my first teacher," on her khanga.

Keisha acknowledges her sense of space and location, her concepts of "home" and the pedagogical transactions that occur there. What does it mean for a Black girl enrolled in Trenton's public high school to correlate her home with her teacher(s)? How does Keisha's home operate as an educational space given her experiences in a failing school district? What are the lessons her home teaches her? Keisha compels us to reconsider how we understand her daily experiences in the domestic sphere. Keisha overlaps her subjectivities as a daughter and a student, calling up both identity categories as equally important and constitutive of how she views herself.

Keisha's khanga tangles with the lack of recognition and in/visibility for her girlhood by positioning herself as a student, implying that she is one of many in a class, and she is temporarily in a less powerful position but enjoys agency and access to the resource of education. Hip-hop feminist Aisha Durham (2014) posits, "Writing about home, then, has meant reconfiguring my body (of knowledges) in spaces where I might be overlooked, misperceived, or unrecognized" (125). As her "first teacher," Keisha's home is assigned deep value that coincides with being the "first," the longest lasting, the most enduring, the most recalled. Keisha has reconfigured her "body of knowledges" to produce subjectivities that immediately put us in remembrance of her "embodied vulnerability" (Grear 2014, 3). Her instincts for self-defense are logical, given recent research on excessive discipline of Black girls in schools (Crenshaw 2015; Epstein et al. 2017; Evans-Winters and Esposito 2010; Morris 2016). Yet she juxtaposes her words with a photograph of her body in a position that does not portray defenselessness. Instead, Keisha's image honors herself, and thus her home, as her "first teacher": her home helps her in becoming, and she challenges the perceived limitations of social scripts that constrain her.

Keisha's image incorporates the graffiti in her neighborhood, and there are several legible words in the background. "Faith," "respect," and "hope" figure prominently in the image, with Keisha posed alongside of them, turning her body toward them, framing the words with her arms. There are clearly visible faces in the graffiti as well, the largest one boasting a smile. These three words contradict the story communicated by the statistics about

Trenton's public education system and her probable experience within that system. Keisha faces the camera, with a slight smile that seems to mirror the one painted on the face in the graffiti, one arm straight up against the wall, one resting firmly by her side—she is comfortable in her body and with her body's location in her home.

Landscape plays a key role for Marlinda too, who wrote, "a shaded tree won't grow," an apt metaphor applied to herself, as well as to the community of Trenton. Marlinda's photograph shows her entire body leaning against a wall colorful with graffiti. There are two readable words tagged in the graffiti: "anger" and "fear." Marlinda has positioned herself standing up, yet leaning her back against the wall, making it possible that she understands "anger" and "fear" as forces casting metaphysical "shade" over her tree, yet she persists in standing tall. Marlinda might conceive of herself as a tree, understanding the potential she must develop into a self that is miraculous in size and reach compared to its seed. Marlinda's khanga calls up a past state of being, the seed, and the possibility of her future state of being, the tree. This multiple subjectivity is an example of Afrofuturist renderings of Time, because Marlinda makes herself legible by positioning herself as in-between or ambiguous.

While Marlinda's graffiti words highlight the negative emotions "fear" and "anger," Keisha's image points the viewer toward positive practices such as "faith" and "hope." The artistic choices of these two girls, who hail from the same community, offer multiple readings of their socially constructed experiences. To a degree, Marlinda's and Keisha's "shared relational experiences as intersectional subjects" are obvious because they live in the same community and share some identity categories (Bent and Switzer 2016, 13). However, a broad generality cannot and should not be assumed by outsiders or applied to the girls, even within their own communities.

In much smaller and less embellished script in the bottom right corner of Keisha's photograph are the words "the seed you plant . . . ," which implies two things. First, nature features as a common theme, referencing seeds and agriculture in the graffiti in Keisha's chosen image and Marlinda's statement that "a shaded tree won't grow." These phrases and this theme might first appear misleading, as their neighborhood is urban, with city landscapes of concrete. Yet both girls incorporate something that is not necessarily a large part of their lives, as neither spends a great deal of time in wooded outdoor environments, but they seem to understand and appreciate the systems and biological laws of nature. For example, trees must have certain nourishment to grow to their full potential, and seeds must be planted. If Keisha's "home is [her] first teacher," then where and how did she learn the lessons about seeds, harvesting, planting, and growth, which do not seem to match up with the master narratives about her urban Black girl life? These questions provoke her viewers to reflexively interrogate "how [she] can 'represent' experience and how [she] might imagine deploying the poetic to make meaningful interventions in those places we call home" (Durham 2014, 106). How do we repay the soil after the harvest?

At this crossroads of the girls' lives, I imagine overlaps between the art of henna and the Hip-hop element of self-representation through the mark-making of graffiti. The graffiti tag establishes the artist's performance of an identity and their desire to be seen and acknowledged (Pabón-Colón 2018). The Trenton girls were not the graffiti artists whose work is in their photographs, but graffiti sends clear messages via the physical blueprint of their communities. The Trenton girls count on this familiarity with Hip-hop's script and work the global discourse it offers, convinced that graffiti functions to locate and represent them at least aesthetically. Likewise, the Pemban girls' incorporation of specific leaves and flowers in their khanga designs are a way of shouting out their region based on the assumption that the Trenton girls might appreciate the henna influences in their artwork. Both groups of girls presumed a level of geographical literacy about their homes from the others, which they leveraged. After all, the audience is responsible for how we read other girls (Durham 2014). The unique visual markers they selected to connect those firsthand experiences to larger discourses is another indicator that these girls desired to be legibly comprehended by their counterparts, and so they called up every possible relatable means of facilitating connection. The girls' desires for intimacy in their networks is clear when, at the risk of overgeneralization but for the sake of connection to their peers, they insert these familiar cultural signifiers. Larger discourses are put to work not to parrot dominant narratives but to utilize the specifics of their locale in service of connection with the other group of girls.

Flexibility in the Future

The girls were motivated to choose their words and images carefully; they are accustomed to being misunderstood. They exercise artistic choice while understanding clearly that their work is impermanent and changeable (Richardson and St. Pierre 2005, 960). While they allotted themselves the flexibility to change their minds about their identity performances given how their own memories might shift their views, they were under no pretense that outsiders, even other girls, would interpret their experiences with clarity. The girls' utility of language reminds us of our culpability as we work with and research girls. Their artwork insists on subjective instability. Girls of color employ multiple subjectivities and take up various recapitulations and remakings of themselves in response to, and as a means of reckoning with, the dominant discourses that exclude or diminish their experiences. The enforcement of Global North/South binaries is countered through an application of African girls' and women's knowledge systems and cultural production. GID discourse unravels when we are reminded that "much of the ideas that associate lack of modern education with ignorance or education with freedom and empowerment seldom consider the knowledge systems that African women have developed for many centuries and that have sustained their lives and communities for generations" (Swai 2010, 6). We must tune into the poetic echoes resounding via the stories that Black girls across the Global North and South are transmitting to one another. If Hip-hop feminism is going to challenge "the very rupture and unspeakable process of socialization that all women must undergo, and that scholars and social elites are either unable or unwilling to acknowledge," then we need to pursue new and creative ways to address the incapacities of the academy and the community and transform powerful political spaces into welcoming platforms where girls are safe to countermove against the mainstream (6). Often we resist tuning in to what cultivating disruption asks of us, a praxis of deep listening, because on some level we know we will have to acknowledge the ways we have actively benefited from the silence and censure of global girls of color. Swai continues, "The stories of women illustrate the process of dislocating them and underplaying the value of their agency while undermining their potential as human beings" (7). The girls represent aspects of themselves only partially, simply because they choose to, and because it is only incompletion that is possible. Girls and girl advocates can learn from their willingness to revise and rehearse subject positions in the interest of social justice and as an exercise of their own agency. Girls have sustained their communities even as they undergo the devastating and dehumanizing process of socialization. The SWP and photovoice in this example of STEAM curriculum produce unexpected overlaps and emergences of these processes as they occur through quantum justice between global girls. Using these tools, the girls have issued and responded to the poetic echoes of making a way with choruses that declare how producing and expressing desire aids them in cultivating disruption.

"Cristo, come!" Hilima grabbed hold of my wrist to pull me up from my seat on the ground where I was organizing the papers I needed to copy and making notes of what was left to do. With my other hand, I dusted off my bottom and put the papers under my bag so they wouldn't blow away. I smiled to myself. Even though we knew one another's names after our time together,

Chicago

the Pemba girls thought my name, Crystal, was pronounced Chris-toe. I blame my Louisiana roots for the confusion about pronunciation. Besides, I was relieved I wasn't the only one struggling with pronunciation. Nothing will humble a poet like trying to learn a new language, and although Swahili is beautiful to hear and read, I became flustered when I tried to speak it. I cleared my head with a quick shake. Looking up, I saw the girls all crammed into the narrow room where the shiny plastic of the new light switch was affixed to the wall. I had to force myself to walk slowly. Even in emergencies, Zanzibari women do not run, and every time my New York City feet would begin to speed up, the Madame Director put her hand gingerly on my forearm: "Walk, please." I was so excited I wanted to run at a full sprint to see the lights. The girls were about to flip the light switch for the first time on the solar suitcases we had just installed through their campus and dorm. The rain had finally petered out so that we could climb on the roof and safely install the wiring. The Pemba girls had designated where each light should go and hotly debated their placement. Emotions among my students were volatile as the days passed, which is not uncommon for experiences like this, but I was tired of soothing them. After uncooperative rainy weather, Ramadan fasting, and hardware issues that are typical with installation, we were all ready for some good news. "Cristo, come. Look!" Hilima pulled me into the crowded room,

Pemba

Soweto

Hawassa

New York

warm with the number of bodies shifting to fit inside. I took her hand from my wrist and put it on the switch. I glanced around the room, sweeping the smiling faces of everyone present, talking happily. I looked Hilima in her eyes. "You ready?" She nodded excitedly and flipped the switch. The lightbulbs came on, and the girls and students crammed in the room erupted into shouts of cheer. My students slung their arms around each other and high-fived. I laughed and clapped my hands, tears in my eyes. Hilima was hollering with the rest of them, bouncing on the balls of her feet, arms stretched to the roof, palms wide open. She looked at me. "We did it! We did it!"

Forecasting the Future

The crossroads poem that began this journey is symbolic of the decisions, desires, and determination that are being cultivated within me during the experiences I lay before you, so that I could disrupt where I was while co-charting the courses of girls who worked with me. The poetic echo of girls who are making a way encompasses the past and builds the future through quantum justice in images, performing bodies, and written texts. To join global girls in an effort to make a way, we are pushed back to the inception of GGG and the framing of cultivating disruption, and we are pulled for-

Pemba

ward into a crossroads of problem-solving, sustainable energy, and the fifth element. Cultivating disruption operationalizes SWP as its main source of inquiry, and quantum justice offers new readings of the poetic echoes and calls and responses (Endsley 2018). As I sat with all the poetry, photographs, and recordings of girls' performances I have collected, I was faced with the ethical and feminist question of which poems to analyze and which themes to include in this text. Organizing the manuscript itself is a practice of power and I considered how this work might best serve the girls. I turned to poetry as I always do when I am working to process a situation. Poetry distills experience, and as I scratched out lines that would hopefully form a poem, this methodology—Cultivating Disruption—is what I found (Lorde 1984). Cultivating disruption centers SWP because it does not exclude experiences that emerge beyond normalized local, social boundaries based on gender: rather, it delves into complex expressions of love, desire, pain, and contradiction of daily lived experiences (Endsley 2018). SWP lends itself as a method to cultivating disruption by providing clear steps for analyzing creative works written by global girls oriented toward social justice because SWP is a praxis that invites our time and attention to the ambiguity in-between and messy areas of overlap in these undeniable expressions. SWP traces the ebb and flow of power and provides a grounding place, reliable roots to audition wild and feral ideas, and accountability laced with grace for unpredictable outcomes. Poems are unwieldy and performances never provide guarantees; they are always changing and fluctuating. Establishing disciplined artistic practices for qualitative poetic research provides a trellis these poems can cling to or uproot as they grow (Dill 2015). SWP is afforded the room to be unruly when the research framework is stable, and the framework provides concrete keys for collaboratively using SWP and performance in the interest of social justice.

This conclusion is not a tidy ending at all but another rupture, an invitation, a threshold, an opening for you to cross through with us.

The analysis via quantum justice theory responds to the call issued by the research design. Quantum justice theory allows for laser sharp focus on the specific, localized experience and performances of global girls with and for one another. The small, everyday shifts that are crucial for small every day social change occur within interactions that cannot be predicted but can be prepared for and invited. *Mic checking, connecting with the community, call and response*, and finally *remixing and reflection* offer clear procedures to understand our encounters with the intangible. The stages of cultivating disruption offer a point of contact for glimpses into what matters most to girls and quantum justice theory supports us in working through our transnational relationships with each other in more immediate ways (Hobson 2012). Janell Hobson points toward the need for a global appreciation and respect of these relationships, and the "demand for sustainable praxis" that makes transnational scholarship global. I implement quantum justice theory as a way to understand how global girls are forming a web to span Time and distance, and then to apply their prophetic techniques I observe to my artistic and scholarly praxis. I've learned this—we need each other to sustain this work and pleasure. Once their network is acknowledged, quantum justice leaps provide a way to understand the movements and synergies girls are making through the vehicle of SWP and performance to cultivate disruption to the ties that bind them. In the instances amplified through this text, global girls have made clear that there is so much more at stake than a common physical anatomy, race, and national identity. Although those categories and hierarchies link them to each other, they are divergent and specifically informed by the immediate context for each girl. Quantum justice theory provides a lens to zoom in close to those immediacies made evident through SWP without losing sight of the macro-scale systems that construct and manage power. This is a theory for the fifth element.

The poetic echoes that manifest through their SWP and performance highlight their abilities and desires through their futurity and prophetic praxis. Together, they employ imaginative conjuring through performances of Backtalk and resistance to dominant narratives. They project new ways to be in community and activate their networks despite Contradicting Conditions. Global girls assert their autonomy and acknowledge their flexible subjectivity through Making Decisions. Their poetry cultivated disruption of this very text with Blackout Poetic Transcription and shake loose the possibility of an easy, tidy reading or generalization about What Girls Want. Motherhood refracts into unique echoes, calling, and responding from inevitable outcomes of their future at times. For some girls, poetic responses were hearkening to the past histories of their own mothers and revising them. Finally, global girls continue to Make A Way, shining through their photovoice projects and khangas, reminding us that mic checking is where we always start and finish. The crossroads are intersections busy with movement and shadowed with danger, but global girls are always already charting the way to liberation, leaving a quantum justice trail, a beam of light, a gesture for us to follow.

We won't always follow the light, but we can't hide from it (Keith 2019). So, in case you are ever in a space where you look carefully and find you do not like the kind of girl you are, or that you want to change. There may be times when you feel insignificant, like nothing you do matters. Like you don't

Community poem circle. Artwork by Bentrice Jusu.

matter. When I have those times I return and re-member the poem of my SC girls who wrote these powerful words for the world to hear in 2018:

> when you feel like you are nothing to the world
> remember, you are everything
> you are the past, present, future
> love the person you are becoming and who you already are

AFTERWORD

Looking Back to Look Ahead

My work with GGG reminds me once again exactly how much my life purpose is that of a bridge: I exist as one medium of many connecting the girls from different parts of the world, and the world to them. In a similar way, quantum justice theory functions somewhere between science and spirituality. I began this work over a decade ago, first with college students and then with any community member who was willing to center the lives of girls. In each instance some iteration of poetry and performance continues to prove the most disruptive yet productive experience for the youth I worked with and for achieving a sense of progress. The driving question that shapes this project asks: how might global girls on the margins utilize SWP to engage with one another and political power? The leaps of quantum justice have emerged from my analysis. Audre Lorde (1984) reminds us that "without community there is no liberation"; and to affirm what I know and the power of creativity that hums any time girls gather, I share the girls' freedom work with you.

Moving between different locations and the Times of past, present, and future makes different demands; one is that I home in on my listening skills. I realized that I urgently needed to take the time to unpack what had been happening foundationally between the girls in the same places as well as across workshops. I want to be transparent about my privilege without crowding out the point of it all—the girls' poetry and liberatory actions that are happening whether I am there to document them or not. I wanted answers for the little girl I used to be and for the girls that hold me accountable today, as a grown woman. I have been unsatisfied with the sluggish nature of the systems of public policy and academia. We cry out for change and then wait until it trickles down, and this takes so long that the folks with the least access to power see no difference in their daily lives. My goal here is to be more than reactionary and to clarify this process. Like other scholars who are committed to justice in the community beyond the academy, I have tried to start with the girls, to foster their connections, and to cultivate what they are *already* doing. So often academic publications are used like the high beams of a car shining light onto some inky darkness while any eyeball daring to look back into those lights is blinded. The members of a community being researched and receiving the glaring attention from the academy not only don't benefit, they risk immobility or death if they look back. If theoretical interventions are doled out from a top-down approach rather than being cocreated with the communities they are intended for, then the research causes harm. The vulnerability for girls of color is increasing, which is why girls, especially Black and Indigenous girls, are experts on what the academy needs to do better. When the girls talk back, literally, through their poetic performances, to political and educational systems peopled by adults who disregard their experiences, then they position themselves as experts on the stage and as available for connection with other girls. Connecting with other girls provides support, collaboration, and collectivity, breeding new forms of creative responses to detrimental circumstances or environments maintained by dysfunctional systems. The girls' talking back through SWP is liberatory praxis—it is the fifth element. My project strives to honor, record, archive, and remix that which is already occurring so that hopefully, even more of us can get free. Foregrounded in this analysis are the experiences of girls who dare to do more than look, girls who talk back and who shared during these workshops. Beware that this publication is intended to be dialectic. The academy needs saving, and to recalibrate, and it would behoove them to listen up to what these girls know.

To be clear, this book was not written with the intention of drawing a fixed map. I do not intend to imply that you can simply turn here, go here, and then end up with girls knowing what they want and understanding them. I *do* intend to make a quantum justice connection in the deep valley, to point to the endless ocean of re-membering, toward the peaks of mountains that we who are no longer girls can only remember. I do intend to bathe you, reader, in the girls' messages to one another, and in my love for you and especially for them, and to deliver each one as the precious treasure that it is. There is hope here and we need each other to survive. I do not intend to offer a formulaic recipe for "how to work with girls." I do not imply that this is a finished flawless study, because purpose and progress are my only goals. I want you to travel Time, because to read this collection is to be in motion, on a quantum justice leap. I want you to feel the contradiction of pleasure and anguish that is at the center of becoming for all of us, but especially and

AFTERWORD

uniquely for global girls of color. There is joy in these poems, and there are questions. Maybe there is an answer, and maybe there is always and only another question.

A Note on Format and Cultivating Disruption as a Method

I used the stages outlined below to design the research method and methodology for GGG. Each step guides the poet researcher through an exploration of the fifth element. These steps describe my own process and are intended as a blueprint. Read them as a guide with instructions on how to undertake each part with the intention of inviting participation.

STAGE 1. MIC CHECK: REFLECTION AND ROUGH DRAFTS

This step is about writing, generating questions, and developing the plan for research. When a venue is set up to host an open mic event that will feature performances by poets, there is always a mic check. The mic check determines whether the poet will be heard clearly, and confirms whether the venue is arranged appropriately for all audience members to engage with the show before they arrive. Mic checking is mostly about preparation and provides time for adjustments behind the scenes, technical issues, and reconsiderations to make the live show the best it can be. In the same way, the first stage of this research invites a private time of self-reflection and testing out ideas is a space where they can be prematurely tested.

The first draft of a poem takes shape in a notebook or on a phone or laptop, often using a singular prompt or question, or in response to a circumstance or situation that provokes a strong reaction. Similarly, mic checking initializes with the technique of a stream of consciousness, an internal monologue that returns to a particular question. Think of this first step as the brainstorming phase of a new piece of poetry—do not hold back. Write down everything with reckless abandon. This is not the version of the poem that gets performed in front of an audience; rather, this stage invites total intimacy and provides privacy as a delicate idea takes shape. Mic checking is messy and should generate energy. Writing a poetic first draft includes getting all the emotionally charged responses into words and down on paper, and then reviewing the writing over again from different starting points to find the central focus. Some poems never leave this stage of writing, because they are not meant to, but they help clarify the core ideas. Consider the following prompts:

- How is my heart?
- How is my project?
- What do I still want to know?
- Have things shifted? How have I changed?
- What is it that I hope to learn, from whom, and why?

Begin by documenting every single question about the topic or project. It is especially important to record the setting, environment, event, or situation that prompted interest in the research topic. There will come a time when the poet researcher is called upon to discuss the "beginnings" of their creative-scholarly work, and the archive that mic checking requires as a step of the research process will prove useful to trace that origin story. Recording a pathway of interest is critical because it reveals the epistemological lenses that focus a theoretical approach. I realized the importance of a personal archive after a conversation with Tony Keith who urged me to "add to the archives of self" so that I could "document my history" (2019, personal communication). Poet researchers write only about what they care about. Mic checking offers a first step toward accountability, because this stage invites internal reflection on what motivates an inquiry. Do not rush through this stage, and take the time to return to it often during the project. Because it is fluid and rewritable, mic checking invites an outpouring of questions or ideas and then asks the poet researcher to return to this outpouring repeatedly to test the strength of each idea recorded. With every review, the central thesis, question, or idea seed reveals itself, so this is a good way to check in and check on the self, state of mind, relationships with collaborators, the project, and the goals.

STAGE 2. CONNECTING WITH THE COMMUNITY: REVISION AND REHEARSAL

Think of connecting with the community as the rehearsal process of a spoken word poem. The poem is written and needs to be auditioned, perhaps revised, rehearsed, and shared with a trusted cypher of friends or a small audience. This step asks for an intentional physical embodiment of the written words and requires communion with others. Connecting with the community brings the ideas and questions brainstormed in your mic check forward and into fruition. This step initiates the process of rehearsal, which centers and anticipates an audience. Additionally, this step begins to plan and anticipate logistical needs for a performance. Taking the time to thoughtfully consider how connections are forged demonstrates a level of care and commitment to the community that the poet researcher is partnering with. Consider the following questions:

- Who is the audience?
- How is the poet a part of this community, or not?
- What considerations need to be taken for arriving to the venue?
- How long will they have onstage to perform?
- Who is hosting the event?
- What relationships are in place or need to be developed to form a connection with them?
- What do you have to offer to the community? How does the project serve them?
- How will the community be impacted after the research process is over?
- How are you implementing the action plan with the emerging artists or girls you are writing with?

These are just a few sample questions that need answers. This step calls for a clear plan of action and expected costs—materially and energetically. Time and attention must be devoted to the community the poet researcher hopes to connect with, and there is no shortcut for this step, even if you are researching your home community. Sometimes learning about your home community is the most difficult, because it is easier to assume that you know what there is to know about a place and a people who raised you. Familiarity does not preclude care and attention to how the poet researcher connects with the community; in fact, when working with girls from the same communities where I live, this stage of cultivating disruption required extra care to ensure that my access to girls was not mistaken as knowing them. There is a temptation for poet researchers who operate based in the Global North to assume that somehow the girls from the Global North can be known in ways the girls from the Global South cannot, and therefore to assume I could understand their precarity, simply because they are familiar to me. I rely instead on Durham's (2014) "Hip-Hop feminist fundamentals." To cultivate disruption to this easy yet dangerous assumption, I employ what she calls "the Three R's: recall, re-member, and represent" (125), to examine the ways our subjectivities as researchers and researched are interconnected, how we write about experiences and memories. These acts are foundational tools necessary for a Hip-hop feminist analysis. Practicing collective recollection through the arts to re-member the girls to one another, and our efforts at alternative forms of representation contribute to what positions this analysis as potentially transformative and justice oriented. Through their participation in the various phases of this project, girls express acute awareness that the aspects of their communities they select to introduce and represent through their art may be taken in ways they do not intend. The girls were motivated to choose their words and images carefully; they were accustomed to being misunderstood, "overlooked, mis-perceived, or unrecognized" (Durham 2014, 125). They were under no illusion that outsiders, even other girls, would interpret their artwork with clarity. Girls are so accustomed to being misread and therefore perform as if they are going to be interacted with based on the assumptions others have of them. This precaution influenced their artistic choices and demonstrated the glaring shortcomings of the "global sisterhood" narrative.

Connecting with the community requires organizational skills and the discipline to prioritize values, time, and resources. Adaptability and discipline are not dichotomous opposites; rather, they are an interdependent system. This is often the most rushed and overlooked step in the process. There are logistical demands on planning any sort of program or event that require attention, and often the time it takes to get those pieces organized leaves almost nothing for the people themselves. Paying attention to detail is critical for planning, but the most important aspect of any project, poetic or academic, is the people. Connection requires relationship building. Our current systems do not prioritize or reward the time it takes to build authentic exchanges between people, and this connection is critical and delicate. All the planning in the world cannot force forthrightness or vulnerability. However, preparing for these events, the outreach and setup for each workshop, and the demand they will place on you as poet researcher will help to carve out realistic expectations for what this sort of deep work requires.

STAGE 3. CALL-AND-RESPONSE: DEEP LISTENING, RE-MEMBERING, AND RESPONSE-ABILITY

Call-and-response is a phrase most often used in reference to the oral traditions rooted in Black performance practices where the orator says a statement and the audience replies with another statement. From Hip-hop music to live concerts, to the Black church, to poetry slams, oral traditions all make use of this form of engagement with the audience (Hodge 2017; Labov 1969; Van Hofwegen and Wolfram 2010).

Cultivating disruption uses stage three, call-and-response, as an approach to discourse and literary analysis. When the girls issue and respond to poetic echoes they represent aspects of themselves only partially. Quantum justice theory helps us engage with the echoes and partial representation by acknowledging our position as audience and outsiders who are not entitled to any part of the girls' lives. Global girls do not owe the world anything. Instead, girls are in control and represent what they want to for their own satisfaction, because they choose to, and because only incomplete understanding is possible for us. The girls' use of language to formulate a call and their subsequent choices about what, who, and how they respond remind us that "subjectivity is shifting and—contradictory—not stable, fixed, and rigid" (Richardson and St. Pierre 2005, 962). Girls of color employ various recapitulations and remakings of themselves in response to, and as a means of reckoning with the dominant discourses and structures that exclude or diminish their experiences. Marnina Gonick (2003) describes how "social meanings and practices" determine available ways for "girls [to] become girls" (5), thus allowing for meaningful re-viewings of the girls' artworks. After all, we "ha[ve] to live with the consequences of how [we] read another" girl (Durham 2014, 126). The girls did not need to claim an inauthentic sisterhood to respond or call to one another or to add to or subtract from the stories they want told. There was no need for fiction or forced familiarity. In some cases, there are literally oceans between the girls. All they need to connect or respond is to engage in an authentic SWP practice. Each community of girls seemed to enjoy certain commonalities and draw pleasure and strength from finding those moments in common, "even if they did not share the same politics of location" (Bent and Switzer 2016, 13). Whatever connections they share are not falsely construed; they simply exist or do not, and I am able to locate, identify, and represent such connections through poetic echoes. These stories are always under revision, and their performances are never identical even if the script remains the same. Within the cultivated disruption framework, the poet researcher must ask:

- Who is answering when I call?
- When the poems are performed, what is echoed?
- Which frequencies resonate across the poetry?
- What is being called out and from where, and who can hear?
- Of equal importance, we must ask, who is *able* to respond?

Multiple listening sessions, readings, and viewings are essential to the call-and-response stage of the cultivated disruption analysis process. Sit with the works. Consult the girls. Consult the heart. Revisit the mic checking stage. Calling out what is being named by the girls' poetry and discovering who will respond is the job of the poet researcher.

Where the themes resonate is best understood as poetic echoes. Echoes are never identical to the original callout; instead they resemble or are related to it and yet feature clear nuances that reflect the localized environment of the girls who either created or responded to the performed poetry. The expansiveness of echoes refuses two-dimensional representation. The poetic echoes are composed of what is returned to the poet researcher in the analysis of call-and-response between the poems. Holding space for these echoes, listening deeply to them, and exploring what they reveal even when they don't consistently harmonize is critical.

STAGE 4. THE REMIX: SHOWCASE AND SPOTLIGHT

The final stage in cultivating disruption invokes creativity and offers the poet researcher a fresh start, a clean canvas of the imagination, to multiply engagement with the data. Remixing promises a chance for innovation, for renderings that insist on hybridity and adaptability. This is evolution. Gwendolyn Pough (2007) effectively situates Hip-hop feminism as driven by what she describes as "a Hip-hop state of mind—one that freely samples, mixes and remixes," rendering old narratives and tropes through new strategies and visions, "while always keeping in mind . . . there won't be *one* truth, but multiple ones" (79). This editorial power invites retellings and remixes of the girls' poetry, each sample resulting in something fresh to appreciate; each location where the cypher continued provided new tools for listening and participating in restaging what global girlhood might be. Durham's (2014) Hip-hop fundamentals leave us with the third component of "representation" to consider the form that research takes; in the methodology of cultivating disruption the poet researcher considers how stage four, the remix, situates each iteration of the research as a reminder that "writing in multiple forms [has] the potential to reach multiple audiences" (127). This stage of the research process opens up the data to many different interpretations and possibilities and makes it accessible. Questions to consider for this stage include:

- How many ways and from how many angles can girls' SWP and performances be explored?
- How does remixing the formats and methods of sharing outcomes of the analysis provide new information and insights?
- How do creating and presenting mixed modalities of data findings support the girls and mobilize social change?
- Who needs to hear the analysis differently?
- How creative can the poet researcher be in coming up with new ways to present and examine and best honor the girls who wrote the poems?
- What do the new formats and audiences teach you?

Acknowledgments

Deep gratitude to the many girls and women, named and unnamed, known and unknown.

This book is made possible by the enduring enthusiasm and commitment of Dawn Durante—across state lines and through a pandemic. My thanks to Mia I. Uribe Kozlovsky for diving in with such joy, and to the whole University of Texas Press team.

Funding for this research was made possible by the Office for the Advancement of Research at John Jay College and through generous grant funding from the Research Foundation City University New York. Special thanks to the CUNY Black, Race, and Ethnic Studies Initiative (BRESI) for the grant supporting the development of this manuscript.

To the countless community collaborators, friends, and helpers, much love and thanks to you for all you do.

Erika Ospina Awad, Anne Canter, LeTrez Myer Cole, Dawn LaFargue-Armelin, Harriet Huell Lampkin, Mr. Joseph Lyttle, Dr. Toby Jenkins, Dr. Marnina Gonick, Dr. Anthony Keith Jr., Dr. Erin Wyble Newcomb, Dr. Caty Taborda: I would not have made it without you!

To the audience, past, present, and future: thank you for seeing us, hearing us, and believing us.

Bruce Wayne, I love you. Thank you for holding space for my calling.

All power to the people, and all glory to God. May this word accomplish everything it was sent to do. So be it. And so it is. Amen.

References

Abebe, Rediet, Salvatore Giorgi, Anna Tedijanto, Anneke Buffone, and H. Andrew A. Schwartz. 2020. "Quantifying Community Characteristics of Maternal Mortality Using Social Media." In *Proceedings of the Web Conference 2020*, 2976–2983. New York: Association for Computing Machinery.

Adekeye, Lara. 2019. "To Be a Child without the Protections of Innocence: The Repercussions of the Adultification of Black Youth by School Teachers in the United States Education System." PhD diss., Boston University.

Agarwal, Bina. 1994. "Gender, Resistance and Land: Interlinked Struggles over Resources and Meanings in South Asia. *Journal of Peasant Studies* 22 (1): 81–125.

Alexander, M. Jacqui. 2007. "Danger and Desire: Crossings Are Never Undertaken All at Once or Once and for All." *Small Axe* 11 (3): 154–166.

Ampofo, Akosua, Josephine Beoku-Betts, Wairimu Njambi, and Mary Osirim. 2004. "Women's and Gender Studies in English-Speaking Sub-Saharan Africa." *Gender and Society* 18 (6): 685–714.

Anzaldúa, Gloria. 1987. *Borderlands/La Frontera: The New Mestiza*. 1st ed. Spinsters/Aunt Lute.

Anzaldúa, Gloria. 1996. "To Live in the Borderlands Means You." *Frontiers* 17 (3): 4.

Appadurai, Arjun. 2004. "The Capacity to Aspire: Culture and the Terms of Recognition." In *Culture and Public Action*, edited by V. Rao and M. Walton, 59–84. Stanford University Press.

Associated Press. 2005. "Looters Take Advantage of New Orleans Mess." NBC News, August 30, https://www.nbcnews.com/id/wbna9131493#.XxYDWihKhyw.

Barlow, J. Nicole, and LeConté J. Dill. 2018. "Speaking for Ourselves: Reclaiming, Redesigning, and Reimagining Research on Black Women's Health." *Meridians* 16 (2): 219–229.

Bates, Lisa K., Sharita A. Towne, Christopher Paul Jordan, Kitso Lynn Lelliott, Monique S. Johnson, Bev Wilson, Tanja Winkler, et al. 2018. "Race and Spatial Imaginary: Planning Otherwise." *Planning Theory & Practice* 19 (2): 254–288.

REFERENCES

Becker, Carol. 1994. *The Subversive Imagination: Artists, Society, and Social Responsibility*. London: Routledge.

Beckmann Nadine. 2010. "Pleasure and Danger: Muslim Views on Sex and Gender in Zanzibar." *Culture, Health and Sexuality* 12 (6): 619–632.

Belle, Crystal. 2016. "Don't Believe the Hype: Hip-hop Literacies and English Education." *Journal of Adolescent and Adult Literacy* 60 (3): 287–294.

Bent, Emily. 2013a. "A Different Girl Effect: Producing Political Girlhoods in the 'Invest in Girls' Climate." In *Youth Engagement: The Civic-Political Lives of Children and Youth*, edited by S. K. Nenga and J. K. Taft, 3–20. United Kingdom: Emerald Group.

Bent, Emily. 2013b. "The Boundaries of Girls' Political Participation: A Critical Exploration of Girls' Experiences as Delegates to the Commission on the Status of Women." *Global Studies of Childhood* 3 (2): 173–182.

Bent, Emily. 2016. "Making It Up: Intergenerational Activism and the Ethics of Empowering Girls. *Girlhood Studies* 9 (3): 105–121.

Bent, Emily, and Heather Switzer. 2016. "Oppositional Girlhoods and the Challenge of Relational Politics." *Gender Issues* 33 (2): 122–147.

Berents, Helen. 2016. "Hashtagging Girlhood: #IAmMalala, #BringBackOurGirls and Gendering Representations of Global Politics." *International Feminist Journal of Politics* 18 (4): 513–527.

Berhan, Yifru, and Asres Berhan. 2015. "Is Higher Risk Sex Common among Male or Female Youths?" *SAHARA-J: Journal of Social Aspects of HIV/AIDS* 12 (1): 106–115.

Bernstein, Robin. 2011. *Racial Innocence: Performing American Childhood from Slavery to Civil Rights*. NYU Press.

Beyoncé. 2011. "Who Run the World?" (song). Parkwood Entertainment.

Bhana, Deevia. 1999. "Education, Race and Human Rights in South Africa." *Perspectives in Education* 18 (2): 19–30.

Biseswar, Indrawatie. 2008a. "Problems of Feminist Leadership among Educated Women in Ethiopia: Taking Stock in the Third Millennium." *Journal of Developing Societies* 24: 125–158.

Biseswar, Indrawatie. 2008b. "A New Discourse on 'Gender' in Ethiopia." *African Identities* 6 (4): 405–429.

Boswell, Rosabelle. 2008. "Sexual Practices and Sensual Selves in Zanzibar." *Anthropology Southern Africa* 31 (1–2): 70–83.

Biggs-El, Cynthia. 2012. "Spreading the Indigenous Gospel of Rap Music and Spoken Word Poetry: Critical Pedagogy in the Public Sphere as a Stratagem of Empowerment and Critique." *Western Journal of Black Studies* 36 (2): 161–168.

Boal, Augusto. 1979. *Theater of the Oppressed*. New York: Urizen Books.

Boyden, Jo, Alula Pankhurst, and Yisak Tafere. 2012. "Child Protection and Harmful Traditional Practices: Female Early Marriage and Genital Modification in Ethiopia." *Development in Practice* 22 (4): 510–522.

Bradshaw, Sarah. 2002. "Gendered Poverties and Power Relations: Looking Inside Communities and Households." Draft document, Puntos Encuentro, Managua. Available at http://eprints.mdx.ac.uk/4031/1/genderedpoverties.pdf.

REFERENCES

Brewer, Robert Lee. 2014. "Erasure and Blackout Poems: Poetic Forms." *Writer's Digest*, November 20. https://www.writersdigest.com/write-better-poetry/erasure-and-blackout-poems-poetic-forms.

Britzman, Deborah P. 1998. *Lost Subjects, Contested Objects: Toward a Psychoanalytic Inquiry of Learning.* Albany: SUNY Press.

brown, adrienne maree. 2017. *Emergent Strategy: Shaping Change, Changing Worlds.* Chico, CA: AK Press.

Brown, Duncan. 2001. "National Belonging and Cultural Difference: South Africa and the Global Imaginary." *Journal of South African Studies* 27 (4): 751–757.

Brown, Kathleen M., George B. Schreiber, Robert P. McMahon, Patricia Crawford, and Kenneth. L. Ghee. 1995. "Maternal Influences on Body Satisfaction in Black and White Girls Aged 9 and 10: The NHLBI Growth and Health Study (NGHS)." *Annals of Behavioral Medicine* 17 (3): 213.

Brown, Ruth N. 2009. *Black Girlhood Celebration: Toward a Hip-hop Feminist Pedagogy.* New York: Peter Lang.

Brown, Ruth N. 2013. *Hear Our Truths: The Creative Potential of Black Girlhood.* Champaign: University of Illinois Press.

Burman, Erica. 1995. "The Abnormal Distribution of Development: Policies for Southern Women and Children." *Gender, Place and Culture* 2: 21–36.

Butler, Judith. 1993. *Bodies That Matter: On the Discursive Limits of "Sex."* New York: Routledge.

Butler, Judith. 2013. *Excitable Speech: A Politics of the Performative.* London: Routledge.

Butler, Judith. 2014. "Bodily Vulnerability, Coalitions, and Street Politics." In *Differences in Common*, edited by J. Sabadell-Nieto and M. Segarra, 97–119. Leiden, the Netherlands: Brill.

Butler, Octavia. 1993. *Parable of the Sower.* New York: Four Walls Eight Windows.

Bynum, Shalanda A., Marcie Wright, Heather Brandt, Judith Burgis, and Janice Bacon. 2009. "Knowledge, Beliefs, and Attitudes Related to Human Papillomavirus Infection and Vaccination, Pap Tests, and Cervical Intraepithelial Neoplasia among Adolescent Girls and Young Women." *Journal of the South Carolina Medical Association* 105 (7): 267–272.

Byrne, Gillian. 2017. "Narrative Inquiry and the Problem of Representation: 'Giving Voice,' Making Meaning." *International Journal of Research and Method in Education* 40 (1): 36–52.

Centers for Disease Control and Prevention (CDC). 1999. "State-Specific Maternal Mortality among Black and White Women in the United States, 1987–1996." *Morbidity and Mortality Weekly Report* 48 (23): 492.

Chang, Jeff, and S. Craig Watkins. 2007. "It's a Hip-hop World." *Foreign Policy* 163: 58.

Chesney-Lind, Meda, and Alida V. Merlo. 2015. "Global War on Girls? Policing Girls' Sexuality and Criminalizing Their Victimization." *Women and Criminal Justice: Is There a War on Women or Are Females Fine?* 25 (1–2): 71–82.

Civil, Gabrielle, and Zetta Elliott. 2017. "Opening Up Space for Global Black Girls: A

REFERENCES

Dialogue between Gabrielle Civil and Zetta Elliott." *Departures in Critical Qualitative Research* 6 (3): 11–33.

Clark, Natalie. 2016. "Red Intersectionality and Violence-Informed Witnessing Praxis with Indigenous Girls." *Girlhood Studies* 9 (2): 46–64.

Cleage, Pearl. 2014. *Things I Should Have Told My Daughter: Lies, Lessons, and Love Affairs*. New York: Atria Books.

Cleaver, Molly. 2020. "What's the Difference between Cajun and Creole—or Is There One?" Historic New Orleans. https://www.hnoc.org/publications/first-draft/whats-difference-between-cajun-and-creole-or-there-one.

Cleeton, Elaine R. 2003. "'Are You Beginning to See a Pattern Here?' Family and Medical Discourses Shape the Story of Black Infant Mortality." *Journal of Sociology and Social Welfare* 30 (1): 41–64.

Coalition for Adolescent Girls. 2012. *Missing the Emergency: Shifting the Paradigm for Relief to Adolescent Girls*. Coalition for Adolescent Girls. http://www.coalitionforadolescentgirls.org/wp-content/uploads/2012/05/2012-05-23-Missing-the-Emergency-FINAL1.pdf.

Cohen, Cathy J. 2004. Deviance as Resistance: A New Research Agenda for the Study of Black Politics. *Du Bois Review: Social Science Research on Race* 1 (1): 27–45.

Cohen, Deborah A., J. Scott Ashwood, Molly M. Scott, Adrian Overton, Kelly R. Evanson, Lisa K. Staten, Dwayne Porter, Thomas L. McKenzie, Diane Catellier. 2006. "Public Parks and Physical Activity among Adolescent Girls." *Pediatrics* 118 (5): e1381–e1389.

Collins, Patricia H. 1990. *Black Feminist Thought: Knowledge, Consciousness, and the Politics of Empowerment*. London: Routledge.

Collins, Patricia H. 2004. *Black Sexual Politics: African Americans, Gender, and the New Racism*. London: Routledge.

Conquergood, Dwight. 2002. "Performance Studies: Interventions and Radical Research." *Drama Review* 46 (2): 145–156.

Cook, Daniella A., and Adrienne D. Dixson. 2013. "Writing Critical Race Theory and Method: A Composite Counterstory on the Experiences of Black Teachers in New Orleans Post-Katrina." *International Journal of Qualitative Studies in Education* 26 (10): 1238–1258.

Cornwall, Andrea, and Karen Brock. 2005. "What Do Fuzzwords Do for Development Policy? A Critical Look at 'Empowerment,' 'Participation' and 'Poverty Reduction.'" *Third World Quarterly* 26, 1043–60.

Cox, Aimee M. 2015. *Shapeshifters: Black Girls and the Choreography of Citizenship*. Durham, NC: Duke University Press.

Crenshaw, Kimberlé, Priscilla Ocen, and Jyoti Nanda. 2015. *Black Girls Matter: Pushed Out, Overpoliced and Underprotected*. New York: African American Policy Forum and Center for Intersectionality and Social Policy Studies. https://www.atlanticphilanthropies.org/wp- content/uploads/2015/09/BlackGirlsMatter_Report.pdf.

Croll, Elisabeth. 2007. "From the Girl Child to Girls' Rights." *Third World Quarterly* 27: 1285–1297.

REFERENCES

Davies, Bronwyn. 2000. *A Body of Writing, 1990–1999*. Lanham, MD: Rowman & Littlefield.

Davies, Bronwyn, Jenny Browne, Susanne Gannon, Eileen Honan, Cath Laws, Babette Mueller-Rockstroh, and Eva Petersen. 2004. "The Ambivalent Practices of Reflexivity." *Qualitative Inquiry* 10 (3): 360–389.

Davis, Angela. 1981. "Reflections on the Black Woman's Role in the Community of Slaves." *Black Scholar* 12 (6): 2–15.

Decker, Carol. 2007. *Investing in Ideas: Girls' Education in Colonial Zanzibar*. Berkeley: University of California Press.

Decker, Carol. 2014a. "Biology, Islam, and the Science of Sex Education. *Past and Present* 222: 215–247.

Decker, Carol. 2014b. *Mobilizing Zanzibar Women: The Struggle for Respectability and Self-Reliance in Colonial East Africa*. London: Palgrave Macmillan.

Decker, Carol. 2015a. "The Elusive Power of Colonial Prey: Sexualizing the Schoolgirl in the Zanzibar Protectorate." *Africa Today* 61 (4): 43–60.

Decker, Carol. 2015b. "Love and Sex in Islamic Africa: Introduction." *Africa Today* 61 (4): 1–10.

Deer, Sarah. 2015. *The Beginning and End of Rape: Confronting Sexual Violence in Native America*. Minneapolis: University of Minnesota Press.

Denzin, Norman K. 2003. *Performance Ethnography: Critical Pedagogy and the Politics of Culture*. Thousand Oaks, CA: Sage.

Dereje, Nebiyu, Sabit Abazinab, and Abiot Girma. 2014. "Prevalence and Predictors of Cigarette Smoking among Adolescdents of Ethiopia: School Based Cross Sectional Survey." *Journal of Child and Adolescent Behaviour* 3 : 182–190.

Dery, Mark. 1993. "Black to the Future: Interviews with Samuel R. Delany, Greg Tate, and Tricia Rose. From the book *Flame Wars: The Discourse of Cyberculture*, edited by Mark Dery." *South Atlantic Quarterly* 94 (4): 735–778.

Desai, Shiv Raj, and Tyson Marsh. 2005. "Weaving Multiple Dialects in the Classroom Discourse: Poetry and Spoken Word as a Critical Teaching Tool." *Taboo: Journal of Culture and Education* 9 (2): 71–90.

Dill, LeConté J. 2015. "Poetic Justice: Engaging in Participatory Narrative Analysis to Find Solace in the 'Killer Corridor.'" *American Journal of Community Psychology* 55 (1–2): 128–135.

Dillard, Cynthia. 2012. *Learning to (Re)member the Things We've Learned to Forget: Endarkened Feminisms, Spirituality, and the Sacred Nature of Research and Teaching*. New York: Peter Lang.

Dillon, Grace L. 2016. "Indigenous Futurisms, Bimaashi Biidaas Mose, Flying and Walking towards You." *Extrapolation* 57 (1/2): 1.

Dishman, Rod K., Derek Hales, Karin Pfeiffer, Gwen Felton, Ruth Saunders, Dianne Ward, Marsha Dowda, and Russell Pate. 2006. "Physical Self-Concept and Self-Esteem Mediate Cross-Sectional Relations of Physical Activity and Sport Participation with Depression Symptoms among Adolescent Girls." *Health Psychology* 25 (3): 396–407.

Dixson, Adrienne D. 2003. "'Let's Do This!' Black Women Teachers' Politics and Pedagogy." *Urban Education* 38 (2): 217–235.

Dixson, Adrienne D. 2011. "Whose Choice? A Critical Race Perspective on Charter Schools." In *The Neoliberal Deluge: Hurricane Katrina, Late Capitalism, and the Remaking of New Orleans*, edited by C. Johnson, 130–151. Minneapolis: University of Minnesota Press.

Dixson, Adrienne D., Kristen L. Buras, and Elizabeth K. Jeffers. 2015. "The Color of Reform: Race, Education Reform, and Charter Schools in Post-Katrina New Orleans." *Qualitative Inquiry* 21 (3): 288–299.

Dumas, Michael J., and Joseph D. Nelson. 2016. "(Re)imagining Black Boyhood: Toward a Critical Framework for Educational Research." *Harvard Educational Review* 86 (1): 27–47.

Durham, Aisha. 2010. "Hip-hop Feminist Media Studies." *International Journal of Africana Studies* 16 (1): 117.

Durham, Aisha. 2014. *Home with Hip-hop Feminism: Performances in Communication and Culture*. New York: Peter Lang.

Durham, Aisha, B. C. Cooper, and S. M. Morris. 2013. "The Stage Hip-hop Feminism Built: A New Directions Essay." *Signs: Journal of Women in Culture and Society* 38 (3): 721–737.

Elliott, Sinikka, Rachel Powell, and Joslyn Brenton. 2015. "Being a Good Mom: Low-Income, Black Single Mothers Negotiate Intensive Mothering." *Journal of Family Issues* 36 (3): 351–370.

Ellis, B. Heidi, Helen Z. MacDonald, Julie Klunk-Gillis, Alisa Lincoln, Lee Strunin, and Howard J. Cabral. 2010. "Discrimination and Mental Health among Somali Refugee Adolescents: The Role of Acculturation and Gender." *American Journal of Orthopsychiatry* 80 (4): 564.

Ellsworth, Elizabeth. 2005. *Places of Learning: Media, Architecture, Pedagogy*. London: Routledge.

Emdin, Christopher. 2017. "On Innervisions and Becoming in Urban Education: Pentecostal Hip-hop Pedagogies in the Key of Life." *Review of Education, Pedagogy, and Cultural Studies* 39 (1): 106–119.

Endsley, Crystal L. 2016. *The Fifth Element: Social Justice Pedagogy through Spoken Word Poetry*. Albany: SUNY Press.

Endsley, Crystal L. 2017. "Poetry Is My Politics: Linking Spoken Word and Social Activism." In *Open Mic Night: Campus Programs That Champion College Student Voice and Engagement*, edited by T. S. Jenkins et al., 37–48. Sterling, VA: Stylus.

Endsley, Crystal L. 2018. "Something Good Distracts Us from the Bad: Girls Cultivating Disruption." *Girlhood Studies* 11 (2): 63–78.

Endsley, Crystal L. 2020. "I Am Both, Yet I Am Neither: Exploring the Fifth Element of Hip-hop as Spiritual Social Justice Praxis through Spoken Word Poetry." In *HipHopEd: The Compilation on Hip-hop Education: Hip-hop as Praxis and Social Justice*, edited by E. Adjapong and I. Levy, 11–24. New York: Peter Lang.

Epstein, Rebecca, Jamilia J. Blake, and Thalia González. 2017. "Girlhood Interrupted: The Erasure of Black Girls' Childhood." Center on Poverty and Inequality at

REFERENCES

Georgetown Law. Available at SSRN 3000695. https://www.blendedandblack.com/wp-content/uploads/2017/08/girlhood-interrupted.pdf.

Eshun, Kodwo. 2003. "Further Considerations of Afrofuturism." *New Centennial Review* 3 (2): 287–302.

Essof, Shereen, and Ronald Wesso. 2011. Introduction to *My Dream Is to Be Bold: Our Work to End Patriarchy*. Oxon, UK: Fahamu Books & Pambazuka Press.

Evans-Winters, Venus E., and Jennifer Esposito. 2010. "Other People's Daughters: Critical Race Feminism and Black Girls' Education." *Educational Foundations* 24: 11–24.

Evans-Winters, Venus E., and Girls for Gender Equity. 2017. "Flipping the Script: The Dangerous Bodies of Girls of Color." *Cultural Studies—Critical Methodologies* 17 (5): 415–423.

Everatt, David, and Sifiso Zulu. 2001. "Analysing Rural Development Programmes in South Africa 1994–2000." *Development Update* 3 (4): 1–38.

Falcón, Sylvanna M., and Jennifer C. Nash. 2015. "Shifting Analytics and Linking Theories: A Conversation about the 'Meaning-Making' of Intersectionality and Transnational Feminism." *Women's Studies International Forum* 50: 1–10.

Felton, Gwen M., and Monina Bartoces. 2002. "Predictors of Initiation of Early Sex in Black and White Adolescent Females." *Public Health Nursing* 19 (1): 59–67.

Fennell, Shailaja, and Madeleine Arnot. 2008. "Decentering Hegemonic Gender Theory: The Implications for Educational Research." *Compare: A Journal of Comparative and International Education* 38 (5): 525–538.

Ferns, Ilse, and Dorothea P. Thom. 2001. "Moral Development of Black and White South African Adolescents: Evidence against Cultural Universality in Kohlberg's Theory." *South African Journal of Psychology* 31 (4): 38–47.

Ferrie, Chris. 2018. *Quantum Physics for Babies*. Naperville, IL: Sourcebooks.

Fisher, Maisha. 2003. "Open Mics and Open Minds: Spoken Word Poetry in African Diaspora Participatory Literacy Communities." *Harvard Educational Review* 73 (3): 362–389.

Fisher, Maisha T. 2007. *Writing in Rhythm: Spoken Word Poetry in Urban Classrooms*. New York: Teachers College Press.

Ford, Kenneth W. 2004. *The Quantum World: Quantum Physics for Everyone*. Cambridge: Harvard University Press.

Fox, Kathleen A., and Crista Johnson-Agbakwu. 2020. "Crime Victimization, Health, and Female Genital Mutilation or Cutting among Somali Women and Adolescent Girls in the United States, 2017." *American Journal of Public Health* 110 (1): 112-118.

Fraser, Nancy. 2000. "Why Overcoming Prejudice Is Not Enough: A Rejoinder to Richard Rorty." *Critical Horizons* 1 (1): 21–28.

Freire, Paulo. 2000. *Pedagogy of Freedom: Ethics, Democracy, and Civic Courage*. Lanham, MD: Rowman & Littlefield.

Freire, Paulo, and D. Macedo. 1993. *Pedagogy of the City*. London: Continuum International.

REFERENCES

Gaganakis, Margie. 2003. "Gender and Future Role Choice: A Study of Black Adolescent Girls." *South African Journal of Education* 23 (4): 281–286.

Gaganakis, Margie. 2004. "Imposed Identities: Adolescent Girls' Perceptions of Being Black and Being White." *Perspectives in Education* 22 (1): 59–70.

Gaganakis, Margie. 2006. "Identity Construction in Adolescent Girls: The Context Dependency of Racial and Gendered Perceptions." *Gender and Education* 18 (4): 361–379.

Garrett, H. James, and Sara Matthews. 2014. "Containing Pedagogical Complexity through the Assignment of Photography: Two Case Presentations." *Curriculum Inquiry* 44 (3): 332–357.

George, Nelson. 1998. *Hip-hop America*. New York: Viking Press.

Gholson, Maisie, and Danny B. Martin. 2014. "Smart Girls, Black Girls, Mean Girls, and Bullies: At the Intersection of Identities and the Mediating Role of Young Girls' Social Network in Mathematical Communities of Practice." *Journal of Education* 194 (1): 19–33.

Gilmore, Leigh, and Elizabeth Marshall. 2010. "Girls in Crisis: Rescue and Transnational Feminist Autobiographical Resistance." *Feminist Studies* 36 (3): 667–690.

Ginwright, Shawn A. 2010. "Peace Out to Revolution! Activism among African American Youth: An Argument for Radical Healing." *Young* 18 (1): 77–96.

Giroux, Henry A., and Peter McLaren. 1992. "Writing from the Margins: Geographies of Identity, Pedagogy, and Power." *Journal of Education* 174 (1): 7–30.

Gladstone, David, and Jolie Préau. 2008. "Gentrification in Tourist Cities: Evidence from New Orleans before and after Hurricane Katrina." *Housing Policy Debate* 19 (1): 137–175.

Glesne, Corrine. 1997. "That Rare Feeling: Re-presenting Research through Poetic Transcription." *Qualitative Inquiry* 3 (2): 202–221.

Gonick, Marnina. 2003. *Between Femininities: Ambivalence, Identity, and the Education of Girls*. Albany: SUNY Press.

Gonick, Marnina, Emma Renold, Jessica Ringrose, and Lisa Weems. 2009. "Rethinking Agency and Resistance: What Comes after Girl Power?" *Girlhood Studies* 2 (2): 1–9.

Gonsamo, Dagim D. 2019. "Challenges and Coping Strategies of Rural Girls to the New Industrial Working Culture: The Case of Female Workers in Hawassa Industrial Park." *Journal of Humanities and Social Science* 24 (9): 26–39.

González, Thalia. 2018. *From the Classroom to the Courtroom: The Adultification of Black Girls*. New York: Fordham University Press.

Gotham, Kevin F. 2005. "Tourism Gentrification: The Case of New Orleans' Vieux Carré." *Urban Studies* 42 (7): 1099–1121.

Grear, Anna. 2014. "Vulnerability, Advanced Global Capitalism, and Co-symptomatic Injustice: Locating the Vulnerable Subject." In *Vulnerability: Reflections on a New Ethical Foundation for Law and Politics*, edited by M. A. Fineman and A. Grear, 41–60. Farnham, UK: Ashgate.

Halliday, Aria. 2019. *The Black Girlhood Studies Collection*. Toronto: Women's Press.

Hansberry, Lorraine. "An Author's Reflections: Willy Loman, Walter Younger, and He Who Must Live." *Village Voice*, August 12, 1959.

REFERENCES

Haraway, Donna. 1988. "Situated Knowledges: The Science Question in Feminism and the Privilege of Partial Perspective." *Feminist Studies* 14 (3): 575–599.

Harris-Perry, Melissa V. 2011. *Sister Citizen: Shame, Stereotypes, and Black Women in America*. New Haven: Yale University Press.

Hayhurst, Lyndsay MC. 2011. "Corporatising Sport, Gender, and Development: Postcolonial IR Feminisms, Transnational Private Governance and Global Corporate Social Engagement." *Third World Quarterly* 32 (3): 531-549.

Henry, Annette. 1998. "Invisible and Womanish: Black Girls Negotiating Their Lives in an African-Centered School in the USA." *Race Ethnicity and Education* 1 (2): 151–170.

Henry, Kevin Lawrence, Jr., and Adrienne D. Dixson. 2016. "Locking the Door before We Got the Keys: Racial Realities of the Charter School Authorization Process in Post-Katrina New Orleans." *Educational Policy* 30 (1): 218–240.

Herz, Barbara, and Gene B. Sperling. 2004. *What Works in Girls' Education: Evidence and Policies from the Developing World*. New York: Council on Foreign Relations.

Hesford, Wendy. 2011. *Spectacular Rhetorics: Human Rights Visions, Recognitions, Feminisms*. Charlotte, NC: Duke University Press.

Higginbotham, Evelyn B. 1994. *Righteous Discontent: The Women's Movement in the Black Baptist Church, 1880–1920*. Cambridge: Harvard University Press.

Hill, Dominique C. 2014. "A Vulnerable Disclosure: Dangerous Negotiations of Race and Identity in the Classroom." *Journal of Pedagogy* 5 (2): 161.

Hobson, Janell. 2012. *Body as Evidence: Mediating Race, Globalizing Gender*. Albany: SUNY Press.

Hodge, Daniel. W. 2017. *Hip-hop's Hostile Gospel: A Post-Soul Theological Exploration*. Leiden, the Netherlands: Brill Academic.

Holzmann, Robert, and Valerie Kozel. 2007. "The Role of Social Risk Management in Development: A World Bank View." *IDS Bulletin* 38 (3): 8–13.

hooks, bell. 1989. *Talking Back: Thinking Feminist, Thinking Black*. Boston: South End Press.

hooks, bell. 1992. "The Oppositional Gaze: Black Female Spectators." In *Black American Cinema*, edited by M. Diawara, 288–302. London: Routledge.

hooks, bell. 1994. *Teaching to Transgress*. London: Routledge.

Hoque, Anna S. 2017. "Speculative Design/Indigenous Futurisms." Visions for Canada 2042: Imagining a Future Canada. Conference Proceedings. June 15. https://core.ac.uk/download/pdf/217613578.pdf.

Hsieh, Betina. 2021. "Learning to Trust: The Life and Times of an Evolving Academic." www.professorhsieh.edublogs.org. March 30.

Ibrahim, Abdurahman H., Degwale G. Belay, Asfaw Z. Tiruneh, and Tsegaye T. Kia. 2018. "Social and Health Risks of Female Genital Mutilation for Medication and Braveness." *International Journal of Risk and Contingency Management* 7 (1): 20–36.

Inness, Sherrie A., ed. 1998. *Delinquents and Debutantes: Twentieth-Century American Girls' Cultures*. New York: NYU Press.

Institute for Women's Policy Research. 2010. "Women, Disasters, and Hurricane Katrina, Factsheet." http://www.iwpr.org/publications. August.

REFERENCES

Issa, Amina A. 2016. "Women, Kanga and Political Movements in Zanzibar, 1958–1964." Special issue, "Muslim Women in Africa & the Diaspora." *JENdA: A Journal of Culture and African Women Studies* 28: 23–37.

Ivashkevich, Olga, DeAnne K. Hilfinger Messias, Suzan N. Soltani, and Ebru Cayir. 2018. "Mapping Social and Gender Inequalities: An Analysis of Art and New Media Work Created by Adolescent Girls in a Juvenile Arbitration Program." In *Creating Social Change through Creativity*, edited by M. Capous-Desyllas and K. Morgaine, 151–170. London: Palgrave Macmillan.

Jackson, Cecile. 2003. "Gender Analysis of Land: Beyond Land Rights for Women?" *Journal of Agrarian Change* 3 (4): 453–480.

Jacobs, Harriet A., and John S. Jacobs. 2009. *Incidents in the Life of a Slave Girl: Written by Herself*. Harvard Library, vol. 119. Cambridge: Harvard University Press.

Jamila, Shani. 2002. "Can I Get a Witness? Testimony from a Hip-hop Feminist." In *Colonize This! Young Women of Color on Today's Feminism*, edited by D. Hernandez and B. Rehman, 382–394. New York: Seal Press.

Jenkins, Toby. S. 2017. "Talking Back and Mouthing Off: The Importance of Privileging Student Voice in Student Affairs Programming." In *Open Mic Night: Campus Programs That Champion College Student Voice and Engagement*, edited by T. S. Jenkins, C. L. Endsley, M. L. Jaksch, and A. R. Keith, 53–63. Sterling, VA: Stylus.

Jocson, Korina M. 2005. "Taking It to the Mic: Pedagogy of June Jordan's Poetry for the People and Partnership with an Urban High School." *English Education* 37 (2): 132–148.

Jocson, Korina M. 2006. "Bob Dylan and Hip-hop: Intersecting Literacy Practices in Youth Poetry Communities." *Written Communication* 23 (3): 231–259.

Jocson, Korina M. 2008. *Youth Poets: Empowering Literacies In and Out of Schools*. New York: Peter Lang.

Johnson, Yvonne. 1993. "The Voices of African-American Women: The Use of Narrative and Authorial Voice in the Works of Harriet Jacobs, Zora Neale Hurston, and Alice Walker." PhD. diss., University of Texas at Austin. ProQuest.

Jones, Alison. 1993. "Becoming a 'Girl': Post-Structuralist Suggestions for Educational Research." *Gender and Education* 5 (2): 157–166.

Jones, Nicola, Elizabeth Presler-Marshall, Bekele Tefera, and Bethelihem G. Alwab. 2018. "The Politics of Policy and Programme Implementation to Advance Adolescent Girls' Well-Being in Ethiopia." In *Empowering Adolescent Girls in Developing Countries*, edited by C. Harper et al., 62–80. London: Routledge.

Jones, Nicola, Bekele Tefera, Guday Emirie, and Elizabeth Presler-Marshall. 2018. "Sticky Gendered Norms: Change and Stasis in the Patterning of Child Marriage in Amhara, Ethiopia." In *Empowering Adolescent Girls in Developing Countries*, edited by C. Harper et al., 49–70. London: Routledge.

Juvenile. 2001. "From Her Mama" (song). On *Project English*. CashMoney Records.

Kalipeni, Ezekiel, Joseph Oppong, and Assata Zerai. 2007. "HIV/AIDS, Gender, Agency and Empowerment Issues in Africa." *Social Science and Medicine* 64 (5): 1015–1018.

REFERENCES

Kamper, Gerrit, and Jo Badenhorst. 2010. "Facing the Future: The Perceptions of Black Adolescents on Their Prospects in South Africa." *Journal of Asian and African Studies* 45 (3): 243–257.

Katshunga, Jen. 2019. "Contesting Black Girlhood(s) beyond Northern Borders: Exploring a Black African Girl Approach." In *The Black Girlhood Studies Collection*, edited by A. Halliday, 45–80. Toronto: Women's Press.

Keith, Anthony R., Jr. 2019. "Educational Emcees: Mastering Conditions in Education through Hip-hop and Spoken Words." PhD Diss., George Mason University.

Keith, Anthony R., Jr., and Crystal Leigh Endsley. 2020. "Knowledge of Self: Possibilities for Spoken Word Poetry, Hip-hop Pedagogy, 'Blackout Poetic Transcription' in Critical Qualitative Research." *International Journal of Critical Media Literacy* 2: 58–82.

Kelley, Michelle L., Thomas G. Power, and Dawn D. Wimbush. 1992. "Determinants of Disciplinary Practices in Low-Income Black Mothers." *Child Development* 63 (3): 573–582.

Kellner, Douglas. 1983. "Critical Theory, Commodities and the Consumer Society." *Theory, Culture and Society* 1 (3): 66–83.

Kelly, Lauren L. 2013. "Hip-hop Literature: The Politics, Poetics, and Power of Hip-hop in the English Classroom." *English Journal* 102 (5): 51–56.

Khoja-Moolji, Shenila. 2015. "Suturing Together Girls and Education: An Investigation into the Social (Re)production of Girls' Education as a Hegemonic Ideology." *Diaspora, Indigenous, and Minority Education* 9 (2): 87–107.

Khoja-Moolji, Shenila. 2018. *Forging the Ideal Educated Girl: The Production of Desirable Subjects in Muslim South Asia*. Berkeley: University of California Press.

Kieran, Caitlin, Kathryn Sproule, Cheryl Doss, Agnes Quisumbing, and Sung Mi Kim. 2015. "Examining Gender Inequalities in Land Rights Indicators in Asia." *Agricultural Economics* 46 (S1): 119–138.

Kim, Jung, and Isaura Pulido. 2015. "Examining Hip-hop as Culturally Relevant Pedagogy." *Journal of Curriculum and Pedagogy* 12 (1): 17–35.

Kinloch, Valerie F. 2005. "Poetry, Literacy, and Creativity: Fostering Effective Learning Strategies in an Urban Classroom." *English Education* 37 (2): 96–114.

Kirk, Jackie, and Stephanie Garrow. 2003. "Girls in Policy: Challenges for the Education Sector." *Agenda* 17 (56): 4–15.

Kleon, Austin. 2010. *Newspaper Blackout*. 1st ed. New York: Harper Perennial.

Kline, Marlee. 1993. "Complicating the Ideology of Motherhood: Child Welfare Law and First Nation Women." *Queen's Law Journal* 18: 306.

Knowles, J. Gary, and Ardra L. Cole. 2007. *Handbook of the Arts in Qualitative Research: Perspectives, Methodologies, Examples, and Issues*. Thousand Oaks, CA: Sage.

Koffman, Ofra, and Rosalind Gill. 2013. "The Revolution Will Be Led by a 12-Year-Old Girl: Girl Power and Global Biopolitics." *Feminist Review* 105 (1): 83–102.

Krieg, Brigette. 2016. "Understanding the Role of Cultural Continuity in Reclaiming the Identity of Young Indigenous Women." *Girlhood Studies* 9 (2): 28–45.

KRS-One. 2002. "Know Thyself." (song). On *Spiritual Minded*. Koch Records.

Kynard, Carmen. 2015. "Teaching While Black: Witnessing and Countering Disci-

REFERENCES

plinary Whiteness, Racial Violence, and University Race-Management." *Literacy in Composition Studies* 3 (1): 1–20. https://doi.org/10.21623/1.3.1.2.

Labov, William. 1969. "A Study of Non-standard English." Educational Resources Information Center Clearinghouse for Linguistics. US Department of Education. https://eric.ed.gov/?id=ED024053.

Ladner, Joyce A. 1971. *Tomorrow's Tomorrow: The Black Woman.* New York: Doubleday.

Langellier, Kristin. 1998. "Voiceless Bodies, Bodiless Voices: The Future of Personal Narrative Performance." In *The Future of Performance Studies: Visions and Revisions,* edited by S. J. Dailey, 207–213. Washington, DC: National Communication Association.

Langer, Carol L., and Rich Furman. 2004. "Exploring Identity and Assimilation: Research and Interpretive Poems." *Forum: Qualitative Social Research* 5 (2). https://doi.org/10.17169/fqs-5.2.609.

Lempert, William. 2014. "Decolonizing Encounters of the Third Kind: Alternative Futuring in Native Science Fiction Film. *Visual Anthropology Review* 30 (2): 164–176.

Lempert, William. 2018. "Indigenous Media Futures: An Introduction." *Cultural Anthropology* 33 (2): 173–179.

Lesko, Nancy. 1996. "Denaturalizing Adolescence: The Politics of Contemporary Representations." *Youth and Society* 28 (2): 139–161.

Levy, Ian, Christopher Emdin, and Edmund S. Adjapong. "Hip-hop Cypher in Group Work." *Social Work with Groups* 41 (1–2): 103–110.

Lewis, Janaka B. 2018. "Building the Worlds of Our Dreams: Black Girlhood and Queer Narratives in African American Literature." *South: A Scholarly Journal* 51 (1): 96–114.

Lidchi, Henrietta, and Suzanne N. Fricke. 2019. "Future History: Indigenous Futurisms in North American Visual Arts." *World Art* 9 (2): 99–102.

Lindsey, Treva B. 2015. "Let Me Blow Your Mind: Hip-hop Feminist Futures in Theory and Praxis." *Urban Education* 50 (1): 52–77.

Lock, S. E., and Vincent L. Murray. 1995. "Sexual Decision-Making among Rural Adolescent Females." *Health Values: The Journal of Health Behavior, Education and Promotion* 19 (1): 47–58.

Lomax, Tamura. 2011. "In Search of Our Daughters' Gardens: Hip-hop as Womanist Prose." *Bulletin for the Study of Religion* 40 (3): 15–20.

Long, Carolyn M. 2007. *A New Orleans Voudou Priestess: The Legend and Reality of Marie Laveau.* Gainesville: University Press of Florida.

Lorde, Audre. 1984. *Sister Outsider.* Berkeley, CA: Ten Speed Press.

Love, Bettina L. 2016. "Complex Personhood of Hip-hop and the Sensibilities of the Culture That Fosters Knowledge of Self and Self-Determination." *Equity and Excellence in Education* 49 (4): 414–427.

Löw, Christine. 2020. "Gender and Indigenous Concepts of Climate Protection: A Critical Revision of REDD+ Projects." *Current Opinion in Environmental Sustainability* 43: 91–98.

REFERENCES

Lucchesi, Annita, and Abigail Echo-Hawk. 2018. "Missing and Murdered Indigenous Women and Girls: A Snapshot of Data from 71 Urban Cities in the United States." Seattle Indian Health Board: Urban Indian Health Institute. https://www.uihi.org/wp-content/uploads/2018/11/Missing-and-Murdered-Indigenous-Women-and-Girls-Report.pdf.

MacDorman, Marian F., and T. J. Mathews. 2011. "Understanding Racial and Ethnic Disparities in US Infant Mortality Rates. *NCHS Data Brief* 74: 1–8.

Madison, D. Soyini. "Co-performative Witnessing." *Cultural Studies* 21 (6): 826–831.

Mafe, Diana. 2010. "Knowing Your Place." In *African Women Writing Resistance: Contemporary Voices*, edited by Jennifer Browdy de Hernandez, Pauline Dongala, and Omotayo Jolaosho. 281–284. Madison: University of Wisconsin Press.

Mama, Amina. 1996. *Women's Studies and Studies of Women in Africa during the 1990s*. Dakar: CODESRIA.

Mama, Amina. 2001. "Challenging Subjects: Gender and Power in African Contexts." *African Sociological Review/Revue Africaine de Sociologie* 5 (2): 63–73.

Mama, Amina. 2004. "Demythologising Gender in Development: Feminist Studies in African Contexts." *IDS Bulletin* 35 (4): 121–124.

Mama, Amina. 2011. "What Does It Mean to Do Feminist Research in African Contexts?" *Feminist Review* 98 (1): e4–e20.

Mama, Amina. 2015. "Beyond the Frontiers: Feminist Activism in the 'Global' Academy." *Caribbean Review of Gender Studies* 9: 35–48.

Matters, Samantha. 2019. "Strategic Foresight in Metis Communities: Lessons from Indigenous Futurism." MA thesis, OCAD University. https://creativecommons.org/licenses/by-nc-sa/4.0/legalcode.

Mbilinyi, Marjorie. 2015. "Transformative Feminism in Tanzania: Animation and Grassroots Women's Struggles for Land and Livelihoods." In *Oxford Handbook of Transnational Feminist Movements: Knowledge, Power and Social Change*, edited by B. Rawwida and W. Harcourt, 507–527. Oxford: Oxford University Press.

McBrien, J. Lynn. 2009. "Beyond Survival: School-Related Experiences of Adolescent Refugee Girls in the United States and Their Relationship to Motivation and Academic Success." *Global Issues in Education: Pedagogy, Policy, Practices, and the Minority Experience*, edited by Greg A. Wiggan and Charles B. Hutchison, 199–217. Lanham, MD: Rowman & Littlefield Education.

McFadden, Patricia. 1993. "Being a Woman in a Racist, Gendered World." *Southern Africa Political and Economic Monthly* 7: 50–52.

McFadden, Patricia. 2010. "Challenging Empowerment." *Development* 53 (2): 161–164.

McLaughlin, Colleen, Sharlene Swartz, Susan Kiragu, Shelina Walli, and Mussa Mohamed. 2012. *Old Enough to Know: Consulting Children about Sex and AIDS Education in Africa*. Cape Town: HSRC Press.

McRobbie, Angela, and Mica Nava. 1984. *Gender and Generation*. New York: Macmillan International Higher Education.

Medak-Saltzman, Danika. 2017. "Coming to You from the Indigenous Future: Native

REFERENCES

Women, Speculative Film Shorts, and the Art of the Possible." *Studies in American Indian Literatures* 29 (1): 139–171.

Mitchell, Claudia. 2008. "Getting the Picture and Changing the Picture: Visual Methodologies and Educational Research in South Africa." *South African Journal of Education* 28 (3): 365–383.

Mitchell, Claudia, and Marni Sommer. 2016. "Participatory Visual Methodologies in Global Public Health." *Global Public Health* 11 (5–6): 521–527.

Mitchell, Claudia, and Relebohile Moletsane. 2018. "Disrupting Shameful Legacies: Girls and Young Women Speak Back through the Arts to Address Sexual Violence." In *Disrupting Shameful Legacies*, edited by Claudia Mitchell and Relebohile Moletsane, 1–17. Leiden, the Netherlands: Brill.

Mitiku, Liyuwork. 2011. "Transactional Sex with 'Sugar Daddies' among Female Preparatory Students: HIV Risk Assessment in Hawassa Town, SNNPR, Ethiopia." MA thesis, Addis Ababa University.

Moeller, Kathryn. 2014. "Searching for Adolescent Girls in Brazil: The Transnational Politics of Poverty in 'The Girl Effect.'" *Feminist Studies* 40 (3): 575–601.

Moletsane, Relebohile, Claudia Mitchell, Ann Smith, and Linda Chisholm. 2008. *Methodologies for Mapping a Southern African Girlhood in the Age of AIDS*. Leiden, the Netherlands: Brill.

Moosa, Fathima, Gary Moonsamy, and P. Fridjhon. 1997. "Identification Patterns among Young Black Students at a Predominantly White University." *South African Journal of Psychology* 27 (4): 256–260.

Moraga, Cherríe. 1981. "La Güera." In *This Bridge Called My Back: Writings by Radical Women of Color*, edited by Gloria Anzaldúa and Cherríe Moraga, 27–34. New York: Kitchen Table Press.

Morgan, Joan. 1999. *When Chickenheads Come Home to Roost: My Life as a Hip-hop Feminist*. New York: Simon and Schuster.

Morrell, Ernest. 2005. "Critical English Education." *English Education* 37 (4): 312–321.

Morris, Monique W. 2016. *Pushout: The Criminalization of Black Girls in Schools*. New York: New Press.

Morris, Susana M. 2013. "Black Girls Are from the Future: Afrofuturist Feminism in Octavia E. Butler's *Fledgling*." *Women's Studies Quarterly* 40 (3): 146–166.

Morris, Susana M. 2016. "More than Human: Black Feminisms of the Future in Jewelle Gomez's *The Gilda Stories*." *Black Scholar* 46 (2): 33–45.

Morrison, Toni 1975. Black Studies Center Public Dialogue, Part 2. Portland State University. May 30.

Morrison, Toni. 2004. *Beloved*. Vintage Edition. New York: Knopf.

Morrison, Toni. 2019. *The Source of Self-Regard: Selected Essays, Speeches, and Meditations*. New York: Knopf.

Mosselson, Jacqueline. 2006. "Roots and Routes: A Re-imagining of Refugee Identity Constructions and the Implications for Schooling." *Current Issues in Comparative Education* 9 (1): 20.

Mtshali, Oswald M. 1988. *Give Us a Break: Diaries of a Group of Soweto Children: A*

REFERENCES

Collection of Anecdotes, Episodes, Incidents, Events and Experiences of a Group of School Children from Pace College, Soweto. Johannesburg: Skotaville.

Muller, Lauren, and June Jordan, eds. 1995. *June Jordan's Poetry for the People: A Revolutionary Blueprint.* Oxford: Taylor and Francis.

Mullings, Leith. 2000. "African-American Women Making Themselves: Notes on the Role of Black Feminist Research." *Souls: A Critical Journal of Black Politics, Culture, and Society* 2 (4): 18–29.

Mulugeta, A. 2004. "The Potential and Limitations of Legal Reforms in Ensuring Gender Equality in Ethiopia." *Reflections* 10: 49–60.

Mulvey, Laura. 1975. "A/The Cinema Offers a Number of Possible Pleasures." *Screen* 16 (3): 1-7.

Mwangi, Wambui. 2013. "Silence Is a Woman." The New Inquiry, June 4. https://thenewinquiry.com/silence-is-a-woman/.

Narayan, Uma. 2003. "The Project of Feminist Epistemology: Perspectives from a Non-Western Feminist." In *Feminist Theory Readers: Local and Global Perspectives*, edited by C. R. McCann and K. Seung-kyung, 308–318. New York: Routledge.

Nash, Jennifer. C. 2019. "Black Maternal Aesthetics." *Theory and Event* 22 (3): 551–575.

Nelson, Alondra. 2000. "Afrofuturism: Past Future Visions." *Colorlines* (Spring): 34–37.

Nelson, Alondra. 2002. "Introduction: Future Texts." *Social Text* 20 (2): 1–15.

Ngutuku, Elizabeth, and Auma Okwany. 2017. "Youth as Researchers: Navigating Generational Power Issues in Adolescent Sexuality and Reproductive Health Research." *Childhood in Africa* 4 (1): 70–82.

Nnaemeka, Obioma. 2003. "Nego-Feminism: Theorizing, Practicing, and Pruning Africa's Way." *Signs* (29): 357–385.

Ntombela, Sithabile, and Nontokozo Mashiya. 2009. "In My Time, Girls . . .: Reflections of African Adolescent Girl Identities and Realities across Two Generations." *Agenda: Empowering Women for Gender Equity* 79: 94–106.

Nunn, Nia M. 2018. "Super-Girl: Strength and Sadness in Black Girlhood." *Gender and Education* 30 (2): 239–258.

Nyachae, Tiffany M., and Esther O. Ohito. 2019. "No Disrespect: A Womanist Critique of Respectability Discourses in Extracurricular Programming for Black Girls." *Urban Education.* https://journals.sagepub.com/doi/abs/10.1177/0042085919893733.

Nyanzi, Stella, Robert Pool, and John Kinsman. 2001. "The Negotiation of Sexual Relationships among School Pupils in Southwestern Uganda." *AIDS Care* 13 (1): 83–98.

Ogola, Margaret. 1995. *The River and the Source.* Nairobi: Focus.

Okwany, Auma. 2016. "Gendered Norms and Girls' Education in Kenya and Uganda: A Social Norms Perspective." In *Changing Social Norms to Universalize Girls' Education in East Africa: Lessons from a Pilot Project*, edited by R. Wazir, 12–28. Chicago: Garant.

Okwany, Auma, and Hasina B. Ebrahim. 2015. "Rethinking Epistemology and Methodology in Early Childhood Research in Africa." In *The SAGE Handbook of Early Childhood Research*, edited by A. Farrell et al., 432–448. Thousand Oaks, CA: Sage.

REFERENCES

Orner, Mimi. 1992. "Interrupting the Calls for Student Voice in 'Liberatory' Education: A Feminist Poststructural Perspective." In *Feminism and Critical Pedagogy*, edited by Carmen Luke and Jennifer Gore, 74–89. New York: Routledge.

Overton, Lisa. R. 2014. "From Vulnerability to Resilience: An Exploration of Gender Performance Art and How It Has Enabled Young Women's Empowerment in Post-Hurricane New Orleans." *Procedia Economics and Finance* 18: 214–221.

Owens, Tammy C., Durrell M. Callier, Jessica L. Robinson, and Porshé R. Garner. 2017. "Towards an Interdisciplinary Field of Black Girlhood Studies." *Departures in Critical Qualitative Research* 6 (3): 116–132.

Owens, Deirdre C., and Sharla M. Fett. 2019. "Black Maternal and Infant Health: Historical Legacies of Slavery." *American Journal of Public Health* 109 (10): 1342–1345.

Oyěwùmí, Oyeronke. 1997. *The Invention of Women: Making an African Sense of Western Gender Discourses*. Minneapolis: University of Minnesota Press.

Oyěwùmí, Oyeronke. 1998. "De-confounding Gender: Feminist Theorizing and Western Culture, a Comment on Hawkesworth's 'Confounding Gender.'" *Signs* 23 (4): 1049–1062.

Oyowe, Oritsegbubemi A. 2014. "An African Conception of Human Rights? Comments on the Challenges of Relativism." *Human Rights Review* 15 (3): 329–347.

Pabón-Colón, Jessica. 2018. *Graffiti Grrlz: Performing Feminism in the Hip-hop Diaspora*. New York: NYU Press.

Pankhurst, Alula, Agazi Tiumelissan, and Nardos Chuta. 2016. "The Interplay between Community, Household and Child Level Influences on Trajectories to Early Marriage in Ethiopia: Evidence from Young Lives." Working Paper 162. www.younglives.org.uk.

Parekh, Trushna. 2015. "They Want to Live in the Tremé, but They Want It for Their Ways of Living: Gentrification and Neighborhood Practice in Tremé, New Orleans." *Urban Geography* 36 (2): 201–220.

Paris, Django, and H. Samy Alim, eds. 2017. *Culturally Sustaining Pedagogies: Teaching and Learning for Justice in a Changing World*. New York: Teachers College Press.

Pate, Russell, Dianne Ward, Jennifer O'Neill, and Marsha Dowda. 2007. "Enrollment in Physical Education Is Associated with Overall Physical Activity in Adolescent Girls." *Research Quarterly for Exercise and Sport* 78 (4): 265–270.

Pellegrini, Anthony D., Jane C. Perlmutter, Lee Galda, and Gene H. Brody. 1990. "Joint Reading between Black Head Start Children and Their Mothers." *Child Development* 61 (2): 443–453.

Peoples, Whitney. 2008. "Under Construction: Identifying Foundations of Hip-hop Feminism and Exploring Bridges between Black Second-Wave and Hip-hop Feminisms." *Meridians* 8 (1): 19–52.

Perry, Brea L., Erin L. Pullen, and Carrie B. Oser. 2012. "Too Much of a Good Thing? Psychosocial Resources, Gendered Racism, and Suicidal Ideation among Low Socioeconomic Status African American Women." *Social Psychology Quarterly* 75 (4): 334–359.

REFERENCES

Petchauer, Emery. 2012. "Sampling Memories: Using Hip-hop Aesthetics to Learn from Urban Schooling Experiences." *Educational Studies* 48 (2): 137–155.

Phillip, Abby. 2015. "White People in New Orleans Say They're Better Off after Katrina. Black People Don't. *Washington Post*, August 24.

Pierre, Jemima 2012. *The Predicament of Blackness: Postcolonial Ghana and the Politics of Race*. Chicago: University of Chicago Press.

Popkewitz, Thomas S. 1998. *Struggling for the Soul: The Politics of Schooling and the Construction of the Teacher*. New York: Teachers College Press.

Potter, Russell. 1995. *Spectacular Vernaculars: Hip-hop and the Politics of Postmodernism*. New York: SUNY Press.

Pough, Gwendolyn D. 2003. "Do the Ladies Run This . . . ? Some Thoughts on Hip-hop Feminism." In *Catching a Wave: Reclaiming Feminism for the 21st Century*, edited by R. Dicker and A. Piepmeier, 232–243. Boston: Northeastern University Press.

Pough, Gwendolyn D. 2004. *Check It While I Wreck It: Black Womanhood, Hip-hop Culture and the Public Sphere*. Boston: Northeastern University Press.

Pough, Gwendolyn D. 2007. "What It Do, Shorty? Women, Hip-hop, and a Feminist Agenda." *Black Women, Gender, and Families* 1 (2): 78–99.

Pough, Gwendolyn D., Rachel Raimist, Elaine B. Richardson, and Aisha. S. Durham. 2007. *Home Girls Make Some Noise: Hip-hop Feminism Anthology*. West Nyack, NY: Parker.

Presler-Marshall, Elizabeth, Minna Lyytikainen, Nicola Jones, Andrew Montes, Paola Pereznieto, and Bekele Tefera. "Child Marriage in Ethiopia: A Review of the Evidence and an Analysis of the Prevalence of Child Marriage in Hotspot Districts." March 2016. https://www.unicef.org/ethiopia/media/1516/file/Child%20marriage%20in%20Ethiopia%20.pdf.

Price-Styles, Alice. 2015. "MC Origins: Rap and Spoken Word Poetry." In *The Cambridge Companion to Hip-hop*, edited by J. A. Williams, 11–21. Cambridge: Cambridge University Press.

Projansky, Sarah. 2014. *Spectacular Girls: Media Fascination and Celebrity Culture*. New York: NYU Press.

Ramsby, Howard II. 2013. "American Studies." *Lawrence* 52 (4): 205–216.

Renold, Emma, and Jessica. Ringrose. 2011. "Schizoid Subjectivities? Re-theorizing Teen Girls' Sexual Cultures in an Era of 'Sexualization.'" *Journal of Sociology* 47 (4): 389–409.

Ricardo, Christine, Gary Barker, Julie Pulerwitz, and Valeria Rocha. 2006. "Gender, Sexual Behaviour and Vulnerability among Young People." In *Promoting Young People's Sexual Health*, edited by Roger Ingham and Peter Aggleton, 61–78. New York: Routledge.

Rich, Adrienne. 1994. *Blood, Bread, and Poetry: Selected Prose, 1979–1985*. New York: W. W. Norton.

Richardson, Elaine. 2003. *African American Literacies*. New York: Routledge.

Richardson, Elaine. 2006. *Hiphop Literacies*. New York: Routledge.

REFERENCES

Richardson, Elaine. 2007. "'She Was Workin Like Foreal': Critical Literacy and Discourse Practices of African American Females in the Age of Hip-hop." *Discourse and Society* 18 (6): 789–809.

Richardson, Elaine. 2009. "My 'Ill' Literacy Narrative: Growing Up Black, Po and a Girl in the Hood." *Gender and Education* 21 (6): 753–767.

Richardson, Elaine. 2013. "Developing Critical Hip-hop Feminist Literacies: Centrality and Subversion of Sexuality in the Lives of Black Girls." *Equity and Excellence in Education* 46 (3): 327–341.

Richardson, Laurel, and Elizabeth. A. St. Pierre. 2005. "Writing: A Method of Inquiry." In *The SAGE Handbook of Qualitative Research*, edited by Norman K. Denzin and Yvonna S. Lincoln, 959–1026. Thousand Oaks, CA: Sage.

Ridolfo, Heather, Valerie Chepp, and Melissa Milkie. 2013. "Race and Girls' Self-Evaluations: How Mothering Matters." *Sex Roles* 68 (7–8): 496–509.

Rifkin, Mark. 2017. *Beyond Settler Time: Temporal Sovereignty and Indigenous Self-Determination*. Charlotte, NC: Duke University Press.

Ringrose, Jessica. 2007. "Successful Girls? Complicating Post-feminist, Neoliberal Discourses of Educational Achievement and Gender Equality." *Gender and Education* 19 (4): 471–489.

Roba, Alemzewed C., Kebebush Gabriel-Micheal, Gordon A. Zello, Joann Jaffe, Susan J. Whiting, and Carol J. Henry. 2015. "A Low Pulse Food Intake May Contribute to the Poor Nutritional Status and Low Dietary Intakes of Adolescent Girls in Rural Southern Ethiopia." *Ecology of Food and Nutrition* 54 (3): 240–254.

Roberts, Dorothy. 1998. *Killing the Black Body: Race, Reproduction, and the Meaning of Liberty, Twentieth Anniversary Edition*. New York: Pantheon Books.

Rose, Tricia. 1994. *Black Noise: Rap Music and Black Culture in Contemporary America*. Lebanon, NH: University Press of New England.

Rule, Elizabeth. 2018. "Seals, Selfies, and the Settler State: Indigenous Motherhood and Gendered Violence in Canada." *American Quarterly* 70 (4): 741–754.

Schinke, Steven, Jennifer Di Noia, Traci Schwinn, and Kristin Cole. 2006. "Drug Abuse Risk and Protective Factors among Black Urban Adolescent Girls: A Group-Randomized Trial of Computer-Delivered Mother-Daughter Intervention." *Psychology of Addictive Behaviors* 20 (4): 496.

Semela, Tesfaye, Hirut Bekele, and Rahel Abraham. 2019. "Women and Development in Ethiopia: A Sociohistorical Analysis." *Journal of Developing Societies* 35 (2): 230–255.

Sensoy, Özlem, and Elizabeth Marshall. 2010. "Missionary Girl Power: Saving the 'Third World' One Girl at a Time." *Gender and Education* 22 (3): 295–311.

Shah, Payal. "Spaces to Speak: Photovoice and the Reimagination of Girls' Education in India." *Comparative Education Review* 59, no. 1 (2015): 50–74.

Sharpe, Christina. 2016. *In the Wake: On Blackness and Being*. Charlotte, NC: Duke University Press.

Shor, Ira, and Paulo Freire. 1987. *A Pedagogy for Liberation: Dialogues on Transforming Education*. Westport, CT: Greenwood.

REFERENCES

Shorter-Gooden, Kumea, and N. Chanell Washington. 1996. "Young, Black, and Female: The Challenge of Weaving an Identity." *Journal of Adolescence* 19 (5): 465–475.

Siefert, Kristine, and Louise D. Martin. 1988. "Preventing Black Maternal Mortality: A Challenge for the 90s." *Journal of Primary Prevention* 9 (1–2): 57–65.

Simmons, LaKisha M. 2015. *Crescent City Girls: The Lives of Young Black Women in Segregated New Orleans*. Chapel Hill: University of North Carolina Press.

Skalli, Loubna Hanna, and Randolph B. Persaud. 2015. "The Girl Factor and the (In)Security of Coloniality: A View from the Middle East." *Alternatives* 40 (2): 174–187.

Smith, Linda T. 1999. *Decolonizing Methodologies: Research and Indigenous Peoples*. London: Zed Books.

Sommer, Marni. 2010. "The Changing Nature of Girlhood in Tanzania: Influences from Global Imagery and Globalization." *Girlhood Studies: An Interdisciplinary Journal* 3 (1): 116+.

Stark, Lindsay, Khudejha Asghar, Ilana Seff, Gary Yu, Teame T. Gessesse, Leora Ward, Asham A. Baysa, Amy Neima, and Kathryn L. Falb. 2018. "Preventing Violence against Refugee Adolescent Girls: Findings from a Cluster Randomised Controlled Trial in Ethiopia." *BMJ Global Health* 3 (5): e000825.

Stevens, Joyce W. 2002. *Smart and Sassy: The Strengths of Inner-City Black Girls*. Oxford: Oxford University Press.

Stevenson, Harold W., Chuansheng Chen, and David H. Uttal. 1990. "Beliefs and Achievement: A Study of Black, White, and Hispanic Children." *Child Development* 61 (2): 508–523.

Stovall, David. 2006. "Forging Community in Race and Class: Critical Race Theory and the Quest for Social Justice in Education." *Race Ethnicity and Education* 9 (3): 243–259.

Strzepek, Katy. 2015. "Stop Saving the Girl? Pedagogical Considerations for Transforming Girls' Studies." In *Difficult Dialogues about Twenty-First-Century Girls*, edited by D. M. Johnson and Alice E. Ginsberg, 123–143. Albany: SUNY Press.

Sublette, Ned. 2009. *The Year before the Flood: A Story of New Orleans*. Chicago Review Press.

Swai, Elinami 2010. *Beyond Women's Empowerment in Africa: Exploring Dislocation and Agency*. New York: Macmillan.

Swauger, Melissa. 2010. "Do (Not) Follow in My Footsteps: How Mothers Influence Working-Class Girls' Aspirations." *Girlhood Studies: An Interdisciplinary Journal* 3 (2): 49+.

Switzer, Heather D. 2009. "Making the Maasai Schoolgirl: Developing Modernities on the Margins." PhD. diss., Virginia Tech University.

Switzer, Heather D. 2018. *When the Light Is Fire: Maasai Schoolgirls in Contemporary Kenya*. Champaign: University of Illinois Press.

Switzer, Heather D., Emily Bent, and Crystal Leigh Endsley. 2016. "Precarious Politics and Girl Effects: Exploring the Limits of the Girl Gone Global." *Feminist Formations* 28 (1), 33–59.

REFERENCES

Tal, Kali. "The Unbearable Whiteness of Being: African American Critical Theory and Cyberculture." www.kalital.com/the-unbearable-whiteness-of-being-african-american-critical-theory-and-cybercultur/.

Tal, Mary. 2011. "The Whole World Women's Association." In *My Dream Is To Be Bold: Our Work to End Patriarchy*, edited by Feminist Alternatives, 24–34. Cape-Town, ZA: Pambazuka Press.

Taylor, Julie J. 2007. "Assisting or Compromising Interventions? The Concept of 'Culture' in Biomedical and Social Research on HIV/AIDS." *Social Science and Medicine* 64: 965–975.

Temin, Meriam, Ruth Levine, and Sandy Stonesifer. 2009. "Start with a Girl: A New Agenda for Global Health: A Girls Count Report on Adolescent Girls." Center for Global Development. https://search.issuelab.org/resources/11195/11195.pdf.

Teshome, Tesfalem, Pragya Singh, and Debebe Moges. 2013. "Prevalence and Associated Factors of Overweight and Obesity among High School Adolescents in Urban Communities of Hawassa, Southern Ethiopia." *Current Research in Nutrition and Food Science Journal* 1 (1): 23–36.

Thomas, Anita J., and Constance T. King. 2007. "Gendered Racial Socialization of African American Mothers and Daughters." *Family Journal* 15 (2): 137–142.

Thompson, Katrina D. 2011. "Zanzibari Women's Discursive and Sexual Agency: Violating Gendered Speech Prohibitions through Talk about Supernatural Sex." *Discourse and Society* 22 (1): 3–20.

Tiger, Yvonne N. 2019. "Indigenizing the (Final) Frontier: The Art of Indigenous Storytelling through Graphic Novels." *World Art* 9 (2): 145–160.

Tilley, Elspeth. 2018. "Feminist Discourse Analysis." In *The Blackwell Encyclopedia of Sociology*, edited by G. Ritzer. doi:10.1002/9781405165518.wbeos1098.

Toliver, Stephanie R. 2018. "Alterity and Innocence: The Hunger Games, Rue, and Black Girl Adultification." *Journal of Children's Literature* 44 (2): 4–15.

Toliver, Stephanie R. 2019. "Breaking Binaries: #BlackGirlMagic and the Black Ratchet Imagination." *Journal of Language and Literacy Education* 15 (1): n1.

Toliver, Stephanie R. 2020. "Afrocarnival: Celebrating Black Bodies and Critiquing Oppressive Bodies in Afrofuturist Literature." *Children's Literature in Education* 52 (3), 1–17.

Treffry-Goatley, Astrid, Lisa Wiebesiek, Naydene D. Lange, and Relebohile Moletsane. 2017. "Technologies of Nonviolence. *Girlhood Studies* 10 (2): 45–61.

Troester, Rosalie R. 1984. "Turbulence and Tenderness: Mothers, Daughters, and 'Othermothers' in Paule Marshall's 'Brown Girl, Brownstones.'" *Sage* 1 (2): 13–16.

Treuth, Margarita S., Chris D. Baggett, Charlotte A. Pratt, Scott. B. Going, John P. Elder, Eileen Y. Charneco, and Larry S. Webber. 2009. "A Longitudinal Study of Sedentary Behavior and Overweight in Adolescent Girls." *Obesity* 17 (5): 1003–1008.

Tsigas, Eleni Z., William M. Callaghan, Lisa M. Hollier, Mary-Ann Etiebet, John K. Iskander, Phoebe Thorpe, and Susan Laird. "Meeting the Challenges of Measuring and Preventing Maternal Mortality in the United States." Center for Disease Control and Prevention. November 14, 2017.

REFERENCES

Tuck, Eve, and Rubén A. Gaztambide-Fernández. 2013. "Curriculum, Replacement, and Settler Futurity." *Journal of Curriculum Theorizing* 29 (1).

Turki, Benyan S. 1987. "British Policy and Education in Zanzibar, 1890–1945." PhD diss., University of Exeter.

Van Hofwegen, Janneke, and Walt Wolfram. 2010. "Coming of Age in African American English: A Longitudinal Study." *Journal of Sociolinguistics* 14 (4): 427–455.

Van Holm, Eric J., and Christopher K. Wyczalkowski. 2019. "Gentrification in the Wake of a Hurricane: New Orleans after Katrina." *Urban Studies* 56 (13): 2763–2778.

Vanner, Catherine. 2019. "Toward a Definition of Transnational Girlhood." *Girlhood Studies* 12 (2): 115–132.

Vavrus, Frances. 2002. "Uncoupling the Articulation between Girls' Education and Tradition in Tanzania." *Gender and Education* 14 (4): 367–389.

Voorhees, Carolyn C., David Murray, Greg Welk, Amanda Birnbaum, Kurt M. Ribisl, Carolyn C. Johnson, Karin Allor Pfeiffer, Brit Saksvig, and Jared B. Jobe. 2005. "The Role of Peer Social Network Factors and Physical Activity in Adolescent Girls." *American Journal of Health Behavior* 29 (2): 183–190. https://doi.org/10.5993/ajhb.29.2.

Wade-Gayles, Gloria. 1984. "The Truths of Our Mothers' Lives: Mother-Daughter Relationships in Black Women's Fiction." *Sage* 1 (2): 8–12.

Walker, Cheryle. 2003. "Piety in the Sky? Gender Policy and Land Reform in South Africa. *Journal of Agrarian Change* 3 (1–2): 113–148.

Walker, Felicia R., and Voice Kuykendall. 2005. "Manifestations of Nommo in Def Poetry." *Journal of Black Studies* 36 (2): 229–247.

Walkerdine, Valerie. 1997. "Postmodernity, Subjectivity and the Media." In *Critical Social Psychology*, ed. Tomás Ibáñez and Lucinid Íñiguez, 169–177. Thousand Oaks, CA: Sage.

Walters, A. L. 1992. *Talking Indian: Reflections on Survival and Writing*. Ann Arbor, MI: Firebrand Books.

Walters, Rosie. 2017. "This Is My Story: The Reclaiming of Girls' Education Discourses in Malala Yousafzai's Autobiography." *Girlhood Studies* 10 (3): 23–38.

Wang, Caroline. C., and Mary Anne Burris. 1994. "Empowerment through Photo Novella: Portraits of Participation." *Health Education Quarterly* 21 (2): 171–186.

Wang, Caroline C. 1999. "Photovoice: A Participatory Action Research Strategy Applied to Women's Health." *Journal of Women's Health* 8 (2): 185–192.

Wang, Caroline C. 2006. "Youth Participation in Photovoice as a Strategy for Community Change." *Journal of Community Practice* 14 (1–2): 147–161.

Wang, Caroline C., Wu Ken Yi, Zhan Wen Tao, and Kathryn Carovano. 1998. "Photovoice as a Participatory Health Promotion Strategy. *Health Promotion International* 13 (1): 75–86.

Watson, Vajra. 2017. "Life as Primary Text: English Classrooms as Sites for Soulful Learning." *Journal of the Assembly for Expanded Perspectives on Learning* 22 (1): 6–18.

REFERENCES

Weedon, Chris. 1997. *Feminist Practice and Poststructuralist Theory*. Oxford: Oxford University Press.

Weinstein, Susan. 2009. *Feel These Words: Writing in the Lives of Urban Youth*. Albany: SUNY Press.

Weinstein, Susan. 2010. "A Unified Poet Alliance: The Personal and Social Outcomes of Youth Spoken Word Poetry Programming." *International Journal of Education and the Arts* 11 (2): 1–25.

Weinstein, Susan. 2018. *The Room Is on Fire: The History, Pedagogy, and Practice of Youth Spoken Word Poetry*. Albany: SUNY Press.

Weinstein, Susan, and Anna West. 2012. "Call and Responsibility: Critical Questions for Youth Spoken Word Poetry." *Harvard Educational Review* 82 (2): 282–302.

West, Candace, and Don H. Zimmerman. 1987. "Doing Gender." *Gender and Society* 1 (2): 125–151.

West, Carolyn M. 1995. "Mammy, Sapphire, and Jezebel: Historical Images of Black Women and Their Implications for Psychotherapy." *Psychotherapy: Theory, Research, Practice, Training* 32 (3): 458.

West, Carolyn M. 2008. "Mammy, Sapphire, Jezebel, and the Bad Girls of Reality Television: Media Representations of Black Women." In *Lectures on the Psychology of Women*, edited by Joan C. Chrisler, Carla Golden, and Patricia Rozee, 139-160. New York: McGraw Hill.

White, Aaronette M. 2011. "Unpacking Black Feminist Pedagogy in Ethiopia." *Feminist Teacher* 21 (3): 195–211.

White, Bianca A. 2017. "The Invisible Victims of the School-to-Prison Pipeline: Understanding Black Girls, School Push-Out, and the Impact of the Every Student Succeeds Act." *William & Mary Journal of Women and the Law* 24 (3): 641.

Williams, Brit. 2021. "There's an Amanda Gorman at Every HS You Call Underperforming, Inner City, and/or the G Word. Honor. Black. Students. Art." Twitter, @DrBritWilliams. https://twitter.com/DrBritWilliams/status/1351947029535141894?t=mduLoO1EIZLzRN4cEgyie w&s=19. January 21.

Winnicott, Donald W. 1989. "Basis for Self in Body. In *Psycho-analytic Explorations*, edited by C. Winnicott et al., 261–271. Cambridge: Harvard University Press.

Wolfe, Patrick. 2006. "Settler Colonialism and the Elimination of the Native." *Journal of Genocide Research* 8 (4): 387–409.

Womack, Ytasha. L. 2013. *Afrofuturism: The World of Black Sci-Fi and Fantasy Culture*. Chicago Review Press.

Wright, Nazera S. 2016. *Black Girlhood in the Nineteenth Century*. Champaign: University of Illinois Press.

Wun, Connie. 2016. "Against Captivity: Black Girls and School Discipline Policies in the Afterlife of Slavery. *Educational Policy* 30 (1): 171–196.

Zambo, Debby. 2011. "Young Girls Discovering Their Voice with Literacy and Readers Theater." *Young Children* 66 (2): 28–35.

Index

Act of Recognition, 18–20, 32, 58, 62, 126, 215
Adamson, Beth, 6
adultification, 124
Africana feminisms, 14, 36, 151–152
Afrofuturism, 41–42, 52, 55, 58–59, 62, 77
Aidoo, Adwoa, 6, 43
Aisha (girl), 69–70
Alem (girl), 134–135
Almaz (girl), 148
Amina (girl), 69–70
Amy (girl), 27–28, 31, 78, 95, 201
Anderson, Vivian, 87
Anzaldúa, Gloria, 19, 36, 60
apartheid, 96–97, 99
Athena (girl), 31, 46, 95, 201
Aynalm (girl), 83

backtalk, 42–43, 48, 55–56, 62, 234
Bent, Emily, 6, 15, 43, 45, 101
Beyoncé, 196
Black feminism, 10
Blackout Poetic Transcription method (BPT), 28–29, 132–136, 230
brown, adrienne maree, 77
Brown, Ruth Nicole, 8, 18, 37, 60

Butler, Octavia, 41, 77

Call-and-Response, 2, 24, 94, 229, 238–240
Canada, 43–44, 46, 49, 52
Cardi B, 195–196
Caroline (girl), 95
"Chains That Bind" (poem), 136, 140–143
Chriki (girl), 216–218
Claudia (girl), 104–113, 115, 117–121, 123–124, 126, 128–129, 147
Clark, Natalie, 7, 48
Clarsey (girl), 124–125, 173–179, 181, 187
Collins, Patricia Hill, 174
community poems, 69, 71, 84, 90
Connecting with the Community, 2, 24, 229, 236–238
Conquergood, Dwight, 36
Cox, Aimee Meredith, 118, 213
Crenshaw, Kimberlé, 7
critical pedagogy, 7
"Crossroads" (poem), 26–28, 31, 94
cultivating disruption, 15–16, 18, 23, 113, 229; four stages of, 2, 24; Spoken Word Poetry (SWP) and, 3–4, 11, 13, 21, 57, 61

INDEX

"Data Poem" (poem), 134–136
Davionne (girl), 173, 178, 183–187
Dillon, Grace, 48

Esther (girl), 104–106, 110, 113, 115, 117, 119, 121–124, 126
Evans-Winters, Venus, 117
Every Black Girl, 87

"Feeling Afraid" (poem), 136, 139–140
"Feeling Myself" (poem), 136–139

Gaganakis, Margie, 97
"The Game of Life" (poem), 144–145
gaze, 91–92
"Girl Effect" (Nike campaign), 81
GirlForward, 103–104, 117, 120
girlhood: agency and, 13; Black, 17, 124–126, 128, 151, 155, 157, 169–170, 181–182, 184, 188, 212–213, 219; as cultural producers, 5; defining, 104, 107, 113–114, 120, 124; as exceptional, 1; as global, xi–xii, 17, 57, 114; marginalization of, xi, 34; success and, 6, 50, 56, 71, 96, 120; as transnational 2, 6, 8, 12, 15–17, 20, 24, 53, 75–76, 78, 128–129, 218
Girls Do STEAM (GDS), 209, 211–212, 219
Girls Gone Global (GGG): x–xii, 1, 4, 34–5, 172, 214; Global North, 5, 9, 11, 15, 17, 80–82, 85, 87, 92, 94, 98, 196–197, 214, 219–220, 223; Global South, 5, 11, 14–15, 80–82, 85, 98, 115, 117, 167, 180, 197, 214, 219–220, 223; participants in, and racial identity, 9, 16, 175
girls in development (GID), 13–14, 28, 71, 80–81, 104, 151–152, 157, 163, 167, 223
Girls Speak Out, xi, 6, 26–27, 35, 43, 46–48, 85, 94, 144

Gonick, Marnina, 56, 239
Gorman, Amanda, 1

Halliday, Aria, 17
Harris, Anita, 189
Higginbotham, Evelyn Brooks, 191
Hilima (girl), 223–224, 227
Hilina (girl), 79
Hill, Lauryn, 195–196
Hip-hop: cypher, 2, 9; feminism and, 10–11, 23, 38–39, 95, 59–60, 115, 194, 237; fifth element, 2, 21–2, 38; the five elements of, 23; Spoken Word Poetry (SWP) and, 9–10, 23
Hobson, Janell, 42, 230
hooks, bell, 74, 91
Hoque, Anna Shah, 49–50, 55
Hurricane Katrina, 171–172, 195
"Hurting Girls" (poem), 136, 143–144

Imani (girl), 126–127
Indigenous futurism, 42, 48–50, 52–53, 55, 62
Ivy (girl), 27–28, 31, 46, 95, 201

Jamila, Shani, 10
Jenkins, Toby, 56, 85
Jhaire (girl), 178, 187, 189–196, 198
Jordan, June, 17, 155

Katshunga, Jen, 5, 11
Keisha (girl), 220–221
Keith, Anthony (Tony), 28, 132, 134
Khadija (girl), 69–70
khanga, 209, 212–222
Khoja-Moolji, Shenila, 68
Knowledge of Self, 21–22
Krieg, Bridgett, 8, 49–50

Ladner, Joyce, 114–115

266

INDEX

Lelliott, Kisto Synn, 32
Lesogo (girl), 83
Lily (girl), 83
Lorde, Audre, 76
Luna (girl), 27–28, 94, 201

Mama, Amina, 14, 82
Mammy, 180–181, 186
Mariana (girl), 105–106
Marjani (girl), 79–80, 83, 156–158, 161–167, 173, 198
Marlinda (girl), 221
Mbilinyi, Marjorie, 81
Medak-Saltzman, Danika, 48
Mic Checking, 2, 24, 229, 235–236
Milan (girl), 83
Miriam (girl), 205
Moraga, Cherrie, 93
Morgan, Joan, 10
Morris, Susana, 58–60
Morrison, Toni, 16, 60–61
motherhood, 29, 147, 157, 162–169, 171, 174, 179–180, 183, 185–186, 195–200; work and, 188, 195–196
Mulvey, Laura, 91

nature, 78–79
Nike, 81
Nondumiso (girl), ix–x
Nunn, Nia, 125–127

Overton, Lisa 172
Oyěwùmí, Oyeronke, 14, 114, 117

Penelope, 66–67
performance pedagogy, 93
photovoice, 11–13, 204, 214
poetic echoes, 3, 8, 12, 16–17, 24–25, 27–28, 39, 42, 63, 82, 93
Pough, Gwendolyn, 10

Projansky, Sarah 189
prophecy, 50–51, 89

quantum justice theory, 3–4, 23, 26, 32–3; as disruption, 8; 10; 16, 33; energy and, 35–36; as feminist, 40

racism, 174–176
Ramsby, Howard, 74–75
Reese (girl), 131–132
religion, 190–194
Remy Ma, 195
respectability, 191–194
Rhama (girl), 69–70
Rich, Adrienne, 92
Richardson, Elaine, 10, 15, 180
Rifkin, Mark, 50
Roge, Miseret, 162
Roza (girl), 148

Sarah (girl), 106
settler colonialism, 53–54
Shamika (girl), 215–218
Sharifa (girl), 218
Showcase and Remix, 2, 24, 132–133, 229, 240
Sierra (girl), 27, 31, 95, 201
Simmons, LaKisha Michelle, 13, 115, 169–170, 173, 175, 184, 191
Skalli, Helen, 81
Smith, Linda Tuhiwai, 20–21
Sophia (girl), 43–9, 50, 52–3, 147, 197–198
Spoken Word Poetry (SWP): 9; audience for, 90–91, 222; Hip-hop and, 9–10, 211, 218; live performance of, 5, 198; and relationship-building, x, 10, 17, 41; as research method, 2–3, 7, 18, 24
successful girl discourse, 6, 188, 199
Super-Girl phenomenon, 125–127

INDEX

Swai, Elinami, 37, 75, 113, 115, 117–119, 163, 167–168, 223
Swauger, Melissa, 187–188
"Sweet Dream or Beautiful Nightmare" (poem), 136–137
Synthia (girl), 131–132

Taborda, Caty, 4
Tal, Mary, 152
Tasha (girl), 86
Tegnane (girl), 148–157, 160, 167, 173, 198
Thandolwethu (Thando, girl), 55–58, 61
Truth, Sojourner, 89
Tshelofelo (girl), 83, 109
Tshinolog (girl), 96–100

United Nations, xi, 35, 43, 85, 161; definition of childhood, 116–117; International Day of the Girl, 6, 44–5, 50–51, 90

Vanessa (girl), 106
Vanner, Catherine, 77, 129
violence, 158–163, 195, 197

White supremacy, 176, 180
Williams, Brit, 1
Working Group on Girls, 6, 26, 44

Zanzibar, 72
Zanzibar Outreach Program (ZOP), 67
Zola, 66–67